HOSTAGE

HOSTAGE

ERIC JACOBSEN

KINGSWAY PUBLICATIONS
EASTBOURNE

Unless otherwise specified biblical quotations are from the
New American Standard Bible
©The Lockman Foundation 1960, 1962, 1963, 1968, 1971,
1972,1973

Front cover photo (Beirut) – Topham

British Library Cataloguing in Publication Data

Jacobsen, Eric
    Hostage.
    1. Lebanon. American hostages. Jacobsen, David
    I. Title
    956.92044092

ISBN 0–86065–873–2

Printed in Great Britain for
KINGSWAY PUBLICATIONS LTD
1 St Anne's Rd, Eastbourne, E Sussex BN21 3UN by
Courier International Ltd, Tiptree, Essex
Typeset by J&L Composition Ltd, Filey, North Yorkshire

Contents

Acknowledgements

Permission to print Eric Jacobsen's guest column 23rd April, 1986 from *USA Today* has been granted by *USA Today* Reprint, © 1986, PO Box 500, Washington, DC, 20044, USA.

'When the Word Comes (Bring Them Home)' written by Paul Jacobsen and Eric Jacobsen © 1986, Mike Curb Music (BMI). All rights reserved. Used by permission.

Foreword
by
David Jacobsen

'I believe that I shall see the goodness of the Lord in the land of the living.' These words of the twenty-seventh Psalm were my anchor of survival, faith and deliverance. While I was calling upon every inner resource to survive physically, spiritually and emotionally, others were working tirelessly for my freedom, often at grave personal risk.

I had been living in Lebanon only six months when, on the morning of 28th May, 1985, I was abducted as I walked, accompanied by a doctor friend, to work at the American University of Beirut Medical Center. Then several young Lebanese brandishing automatic weapons stopped us just a few yards from the entrance to the building. After a brief struggle in which shots were fired and my friend's life was threatened, I surrendered and was forced into the back of a blue van.

A year and a half would pass before I would finally be set free again on the streets of West Beirut.

I am thankful to be alive and free today. Thankful to have had many remarkable men and women, some total strangers, some friends and family members, working independently and fervently for my release. Of these, three Christian men deserve special mention. The Revd Ray Barnett, Terry Waite, and my son Eric Jacobsen are miracle workers. They carry with them the grace of God, for they have been truly anointed with his Spirit.

7

The life of Ray Barnett is a miraculous story of an Irish orphan who overcame physical disabilities to set captives free throughout the world. Ray's evangelical mission, based in Canada, serves the cause of human rights throughout the world. Ray has risked his life in humanitarian missions to Lebanon from 1982 until now. He shares with Terry Waite the goal to ease the pain and suffering of the innocent victims of the Lebanese civil war, regardless of sectarian affiliation. Unknown to the world at the time, he travelled to Lebanon seeking a spiritual solution to my captivity and that of the other men held hostage.

Six months into my captivity, I learned of another who risked his life for me. I tell people that the Lord has not put many angels here on earth, but when he does, it is done in a spectacular fashion. Terry Waite—Englishman, six foot six inches tall, seventeen stone, charming, erudite, sophisticated, witty, intelligent, compassionate and honourable—these phrases list all the adjectives describing decency, and they would apply to Terry Waite. A giant of a man in more ways than his physical stature, he is truly an independent envoy who works only for a higher mission in life. Like any human rights mediator, he was willing to talk with anyone, any time and anywhere about the oppressed and the captive. Not only did Terry Waite risk his life for me and the other hostages, he gave up his own freedom because he cared for all of the victims of injustice in the Middle East, whether they be Christian, Shia, Sunni, Druze, Palestinian, or Jew.

The third man in the trio of my angels is the author of this book, my son Eric.

There are many possible reasons for my release by Islamic Jihad. One can speculate on the forces that resulted in my freedom: President Ronald Reagan, Lt Colonel Oliver North, Terry Waite, Ray Barnett, the efforts of many Americans and those of my Lebanese Christian and Muslim friends, as well as the prayers of people of good conscience throughout the world. Perhaps no one single factor resulted in my actual freedom, but, as Eric's account shows, it was a combination or series of actions, each reinforcing the other.

One thing is certain. Eric served as the catalyst for action. There is no doubt that without his efforts I could be dead or now dying slowly in some dark, airless basement in West Beirut. He had the sense of urgency that the US government lacked. How fortunate I am to have a son who could convert emotions into positive action.

In our common agony, Eric learned quickly to cope with the frustrations of politics and public attention. Twenty-seven years old at the beginning of this tragedy, he became a strong voice of reason on television, radio, print media and in the public pulpit. He addressed the conscience of politicians, bureaucrats and the public alike with intelligence and perseverance. Throughout the ordeal, Eric conducted himself with dignity, wisdom, grace, and (a trait almost extinct in public life) intellectual honesty.

When my ordeal began, Eric took responsibility for the family. He was the rock of strength for everyone, strength that came from his faith in our Lord. In the pain of my experience as a hostage, I had faith that Eric would step forward and that my family would be in good hands.

This book is not just a hostage story, but more importantly the story of a family in crisis, a family alone and discouraged, a family battered by the unknown and unprepared for international attention. They were as much victims of terrorism as I was. As a hostage, I knew my conditions, locations, captors and minute details of captivity. My family knew nothing. Subject to cruel rumours, media attention and a patronising bureaucracy, they suffered through the symptoms of the three 'hs': haplessness, hopelessness and helplessness.

Having experienced both the hell of being a hostage, and—after my release—a free man's frustration of dealing with politicians, bureaucrats, and journalists, I truly appreciate what Eric accomplished in an impersonal world. I trust that those in government, opinion-makers, secular and sacred, will pause to reflect on the power of a single decent human being acting under God. Perhaps they will realise that their role is to serve, not to be served; to understand, not to be understood; to act, not to procrastinate.

This foreword cannot end without praise for Cathy, my daughter-in-law. For seventeen months her young marriage was disrupted by my kidnapping. She never once wavered in her support for Eric's quest for my release. Yes, I am truly thankful that my son married such a wonderful lady.

PART 1
Spotlights, Long Nights

One day a farmer went out sowing. Part of what he sowed landed on the footpath, where birds came and ate it up. ...
Matthew 13:4

1
28th May, 1985

It was the sound of my wife's voice, not the ringing, that finally awakened me.

'Eric, answer the phone.'

Before I reached for the receiver, I looked for the illuminated face of the clock on the table near Cathy's side of the bed. Twelve-thirty. Who would be calling at this hour?

By then, the ringing had stopped. Before Cathy had been able to awaken me completely, the answering machine downstairs had clicked on and was playing my prerecorded message. In the time it took to orientate myself, determine that this was not a dream, and to locate the upstairs extension, the caller was well into his response. I lifted the receiver to my ear only to catch the last sentence.

'... Your father has been kidnapped in Beirut, Lebanon this morning at 8:12 am. For further information, call the State Department number I've given you after 6:00 am Pacific Standard Time.'

I was too stunned to respond—so I didn't. This unidentified, official-sounding voice hung up without any exchange of words between us. I may have gasped a four-letter word upon hearing the news, but he made no indication of hearing me. I've wondered many times since if he knew I was on the line listening.

Cathy raised herself up slightly. 'Who was it?'

I stood up and began to pace slowly near the foot of the bed. My brain went blank as I mumbled, 'Dad's been kidnapped. ...'

'Oh, dear God!'

'It was the State Department saying Dad's been kidnapped this morning.'

I felt myself panic physically, not emotionally—my mind simply went blank. My heart pounded hard in my chest, and I squeezed my eyes shut. My breath became laboured as if I had had the wind knocked out of me by the news.

I knew this was not a dream.

Cathy jumped out of bed. Not knowing if we should flee the house or find a doorway to stand under, we stood there looking at each other. Guidelines to follow to protect one's self from further injury don't exist in this type of disaster.

One of us finally suggested we listen to the tape to verify what I had heard. The house was quiet. We shuffled slowly out of our room and down the stairs, saying nothing as we walked towards the single flashing red light on the answering machine in the kitchen. We rewound the tape and listened. The message said no more than what I had already heard—Dad had been kidnapped. No mention of why, who, or the actual circumstances of his abduction other than that it had occurred while he was on his way to work on Tuesday morning, 28th May, 1985, at 8:12 am.

Thinking it might clarify the situation, we listened to the tape another time. We played it again, hoping some missed word or phrase might lessen our confusion and our feeling of helplessness. We listened to it again, waiting to hear some vocal inflection that would give us confidence. And then again, because we didn't know what else to do.

Instead of waiting until morning as the tape instructed, I tried calling the Citizens' Emergency Center at the State Department to find out more of the details ... anything ... something. The same bureaucratic, monotonous voice that had left the first message answered the phone. I tried to sound calm, following some of my father's advice that I had heard hundreds of times in the past: 'Control the situation. Don't let the situation control you.'

It was what would become the first of many months of frustrating, non-informative phone conversations between myself and a representative of the United States Department of State. Repeating the sparse information regarding my father's abduction, he sounded as if he was reading from a manual probably titled *Informing Relatives of Victims of Kidnapping Overseas*. I tried to think of some intelligent questions that might in some way make sense of this entirely senseless dilemma, but I had difficulty formulating even the most obvious ones.

'Do we know who took him?'

'No.'

'Is there a ransom note?'

'No.'

'Has there been any communication from his kidnappers?'

'No.'

'Isn't there anything more you can tell me?'

'Not at this time.' Then silence, followed by, 'You'll have to call back in the morning. Here's the number. . . .'

Cathy looked at me impatiently when I had hung up. 'What did they say?' she asked.

'Nothing.'

My eyes drifted back to the phone. I had to call my brother and sister, Paul and Diane. How I was going to tell them? I tried to script it out in my mind before I dialled. Should I lead up to it? Should I just get right to the point? Should I sound hysterical? sedated? paternal? like the State Department official?

'Remain calm so they can remain calm,' I told myself. 'We need composure. We can't afford to let emotion shake us so much that it scrambles our thoughts—Dad's life is at stake.'

As his eldest child, I felt it my responsibility to be rational, supportive, and strong. Besides, I was the first one to hear of his kidnapping. For some reason, I was selected to be the dispatcher of bad news. With a unanimous vote of one, I appointed myself the head of our family and picked up the receiver. Cathy sat beside me quietly as I dialled my brother's number.

At the time, he was living with his future brother-in-law and wife. In only three weeks he was due to get married. The phone rang, and my script dissolved. 'Hi, Al. This is Eric. I'm sorry to wake you up, but I need to talk to Paul.'

I waited a few moments until Paul picked up the receiver in his room. 'Are you awake?' I asked when I heard his sleepy voice.

'Yeah ... what time is it?'

'It's about one in the morning. I just got a call from the State Department. They said Dad's been kidnapped.'

Somehow I managed to gag the panic and disbelief in my voice as I told him what I knew. Paul said very little, stunned by the unexpected news. I chose to interpret that as a sign of strength on his part. I needed that kind of anchor. We agreed to talk in the morning after I was briefed further by the State Department representative and said goodnight without much further comment. I imagine it was only after I hung up that he finally reacted to what he had heard.

I then called my sister. My brother-in-law answered the phone. 'Jake, this is Eric. Let me talk to Diane.'

She came on the line. 'What's wrong?'

I went through the story, and when I was finished, there was silence for a moment before I heard her crying.

'It's going to be all right, Diane,' I said as if I had some inside information. 'The State Department is working on it, and you know the people at the American University of Beirut are going to do everything they can. You know Dad—he'll be all right.'

There was silence again. 'Have you told Mom?' she finally asked.

'No, but I'll call her right now.'

'I think you'd better.'

I put down the receiver and closed my eyes. I didn't

know if I wanted to call my mother then or wait until the morning. My indecision wasn't solely because I wanted to make sure she got a good night's sleep but because I just didn't want to talk to her about Dad. They had gone through a long separation and eventual divorce, and I hated having to talk to either one about the other. But I knew that she still cared deeply about him, and although I would have preferred to wait until the morning, I knew she would want to know immediately.

I dialled her number on the phone and told her in the most matter-of-fact manner I could. It was a selfish reaction on my part, but I couldn't help but think this was just going to further complicate an already complicated situation of a broken family. I wasn't sure where her place was in all of this as my father's ex-wife. I don't think she was sure either. I promised to call her in the morning when I had more information. We hung up. As with Paul, few words of comfort were exchanged between us; we were brief and to the point.

I wondered, what's the use of calling everyone when I have so little information? I'm like a hit-and-run calamity. 'Guess what? Are you sitting down? Sorry, gotta go. ...' I decided to wait until after my follow-up call to the State Department before I continued spreading the news.

Cathy and I went back upstairs and got into bed. The room was dark and silent. There was nothing I could do, nowhere I could go to rescue my father, no one I could call on the phone to resolve this. I just wanted to go to sleep. Go to sleep and escape from it. For ever.

Cathy lay still beside me, but I knew she wasn't sleeping. I looked at her silhouette, and I could see she was praying. I decided to pray also, but my prayer was probably different from hers. My prayer was a demand. Not that the words I used were harsh or angry, but in my heart, I was demanding that God release my father immediately, unharmed, and put an end to all of this so I could get a good night's sleep. Patience was always one of my weakest character traits, and if it was God's plan that my father had to be kidnapped, I wouldn't argue with him, but he only had until the morning to see his plan through to its conclusion. I finished and drifted into a restless sleep, believing that my prayer would be answered by a phone call before the first light of day.

Many times in the next three hours I awoke to a sick feeling in my stomach and a restlessness throughout my body and mind. Each time, the first thought I had was 'Did that really happen?' The second thought was a brief, blunt, shouted 'Yes!' It would start a rush of adrenalin that would keep me from falling back to sleep for what seemed like an eternity. Finally at about 5:00 am, I looked to find Cathy wide awake also. We decided to get up—sleep was impossible.

We sat on the sofa downstairs watching an old movie on television, with the sound lowered to an almost inaudible level. Our eyes were really focused on the clock, waiting for the 6:00 am deadline when we could call the State Department, when they would fill us in completely. Then all of this would make more sense. Then, we thought, we could rest assured that very soon Dad would be home; this could all be chalked up as just a bad dream.

Unfortunately, when I finally made that phone call, it didn't have the settling effect I was hoping for. There was no new information at that point. All I received was an assurance that as soon as anything came in, I would be informed of it immediately.

I asked a simple question: 'What's being done to get my father released?'

I received a simple answer: 'We're doing all we can.'

That was good enough for me. With the US government doing all it could, how could it be more than a couple of hours before my father was once again a free man and we would be celebrating our reunion? The US government had the resources to do anything. Even if it just applied a tiny percentage of its available manpower to this case, the problem could be resolved within hours. Or so I thought.

'What can I do to help?' I asked with modest sincerity.

'We suggest to families that they try to maintain their

normal routines,' she answered. 'The US government is doing all it can.'

She offered one final suggestion. 'Although it's a policy not to instruct families as to what they should or should not do, we suggest that you consider not talking to the press. By doing so you will only increase the value of your father as a hostage, and you could complicate all efforts to secure his release. And, it could be a detriment to negotiations, possibly lengthening his captivity and probably further endangering his life.'

Would I want to further endanger my father's life? Of course not. At that early stage, I was in complete agreement with the logic behind this suggestion. By advertising him on TV, we would only drive up the price we had to pay to get him back. In any case, I was scared to death at the thought of being interviewed. I silently mouthed her suggestion of 'no comment' just in case I might need to use it at some point.

The moment I replaced the receiver, the phone rang. The press barrage began. It was only 6:15 am, and the news media had somehow managed to track me down already. With a listed number, it probably didn't take too long to go through the directory and call all the Jacobsens living in Huntington Beach, California. 'Eric' isn't even near the end of the alphabet.

The reporter for Associated Press was very considerate in spite of my comment of 'no comment', but I didn't like having to be so curt and unfriendly, and from that point on I decided to screen my calls through the answering machine. Within fifteen minutes, the phone began to ring again. It rang continually for the next two days. With each initial ring, I felt myself jump as if reacting to the sound of an alarm.

When the answering machine tapes momentarily stilled, I called the other members of my family—my father's sisters and brother. In between those calls, the phone would ring, my answering machine would click on, and another member of the press would add his or her message to the growing number on the tape.

In the midst of this, I called my father's employer, the American University of Beirut. I found a card my dad had left with me before he went overseas with the number for the headquarters in New York City. My conversation with them turned out to be a very close facsimile to that with the State Department. They might have been reading from the same manual. They knew no more than had been reported already.

I did find one optimistic thread from which I could dangle all my hope—the man I talked to at the AUB said that they expected to have my father released 'in a matter of a couple of days'. I was aware of the confidence my father had in the AUB, in the people working there and in Lebanon. I wanted very much to believe that his colleagues would see to it that he would be free as quickly as possible.

Sometime before 7:00 am, there was a knock at the door. I peered through the peep-hole to see a stranger standing on my front porch. I guessed him to be from a newspaper and had no doubt that he wasn't there to offer me a deal on a subscription rate.

Cathy whispered, 'Who is it?'

I whispered back, 'A reporter.'

That morning, and for a long time to come, whenever we heard a knock on the door, our voices would fall to whispers, and we would find ourselves hiding in our own house, pretending we weren't at home, pretending we didn't exist. After a few more tries, he gave up and went away, probably not deceived in the slightest.

Paul managed to penetrate undetected through the 'enemy's' line shortly afterwards and make it into our house. After my brief accounting of the earlier calls, we had little to discuss. We didn't cry. We didn't babble hysterically. I found it ironic that Paul, Cathy, and I sat mainly in silence, not even speaking among ourselves, and yet the knocks on the door and the ringing of the phone continued.

What did we have to say to news reporters or the American TV viewing public? In my confused state, I didn't even know how I was feeling other than shocked, or what I was thinking other than being dazed and wounded. The panic was beginning to wear into numbness.

Cathy and I decided to try the State Department's advice and follow our normal routines—go to work. Paul chose to wait by our phone and screen the calls in case the State Department or the AUB headquarters in New York tried to contact us. I hoped going to the office would be therapeutic. What could I accomplish just sitting at home and waiting? At least I might get some work out of the way so that I wouldn't fall behind.

I quickly showered and dressed. Then the most pressing problem became opening the front door, which felt like the entrance into a hostile dimension from which there was no return. How would I respond to whatever questions might be hurled at me? I didn't want to watch myself on the evening news, dashing to my car with a twisted, painful expression on my face. I had no idea who or what was lurking on the driveway outside.

Slowly, cautiously, I opened the door. I saw no one. I took a single step outside. The best way to handle it, I thought, was to walk as confidently as I could to my car. I just needed to act as though I was one of the neighbours leaving for work as usual. I closed the door behind me. The street was deserted. To my relief, I made it unaccosted.

On the way to my office, I turned on the radio out of curiosity. I couldn't remember where the all-news stations were so I hunted around the AM dial until I found one. The time was 7:30 by then, and headlines were just beginning. The lead story was of course my father's kidnapping. I say 'of course' now, but at the time, I was almost surprised to hear it. It seemed totally implausible that the David Jacobsen they were reporting on was the same man who was my father.

I searched out the other all-news station, which was running the same lead story. The reality of the situation was starting to sink in. It suddenly struck me that by that evening, my father's name would be mentioned on nearly every news broadcast in the nation. That in itself was almost incomprehensible. In some ways, it seemed to distance me from the situation. Could this national news item be the same kidnapping that I got called about this morning? The story ended as the broadcaster said, 'There is no comment from the Jacobsen family at this time.' Was I the Jacobsen family to whom they were referring? It was all too unreal, while at the same time, too painfully real.

Within minutes of arriving at work, I realised that my 'normal routine' no longer existed. When the owner of Cardiac Research & Development walked through the door and asked, 'How's it going?', I could only turn red and say, 'Not too well. My dad was kidnapped this morning.' He immediately told me to go home.

Having received the same message from her employer at the *Los Angeles Times*, Cathy was there already when I arrived. Paul had just left. All the curtains were drawn and the rooms dark, and she gave me a press update. 'They were at the front door again, and then I heard them outside the laundry room. I thought I heard someone in the back, but I didn't want to open the curtain to see because they would know I was in here.' It sounded like a horror movie with the zombies pushing and banging on every door and window.

The red light on the answering machine remained on, and I assumed that the incoming tape was probably filling rapidly. I rewound it and started listening to the messages, scratching the names and numbers on a piece of paper. I hoped that one would be from the State Department or the AUB, but disappointingly, all were from the media.

Three or four had played back when the phone began to ring yet again. Because I had just begun listening, I didn't want the machine to turn on and possibly erase an important message, so I answered the phone instead of screening the call first.

'Is this Eric Jacobsen?'

'Yes it is.'

'Is it your father who was kidnapped in Beirut?'

'Yes it is.'

The caller identified herself as a reporter from a local paper, and I tried to head off her questions with my 'no comment'.

'I just want to ask you a few questions,' she persisted.

I was trying to be polite and patient. 'I'm sorry. We really have no comment at this time.'

I suppose in an effort to solicit some quotable response, she pressed me by saying, 'We're going to run a story about your father whether you comment or not. Don't you have anything nice to say about him?'

It reeked of a threat. If nothing more, it insulted me. She thought I was so simple-minded she could trick me into exposing my feelings. Anger got the best of me, and I swore as I slammed down the phone. I yelled at Cathy, 'I will never do an interview for that paper . . . ever!' She *had* succeeded in eliciting a response from me, though not a quotable one.

We spent the rest of the morning and early afternoon watching TV and hoping for a news flash. Nothing disrupted the regularly scheduled programming. I spent most of that time picking broken tunes on my guitar and sitting in a fog.

Paul returned in the afternoon with his fiancée, Lori. He told me that while I was at work, he had received calls from the brothers of Terry Anderson and Father Martin Jenco, two other men kidnapped in Beirut and still missing—Terry Anderson for over two months, and Father Jenco for nearly five months. It was then that I learned that Dad was the sixth American who had been kidnapped and was now missing somewhere in Lebanon. Two others, the Revd Benjamin Weir and William Buckley, had been held for well over a year.

The possibility of my father's imprisonment lasting for so long was unacceptable to me that first day. Grateful as I was to those families for contacting us to offer their support, I felt somehow separated from them.

Our situation was different, I told myself. Dad was the administrator of the largest hospital in Beirut—the hospital that treated so many victims of the war. The kidnappers would only be hurting themselves and their families by keeping him. They would have to release him immediately. The words of the man at the AUB kept coming back to me, 'We hope to have him back in a matter of days.'

I was as ignorant as the guy next door when it came to events in Lebanon, and because of this, I could never be too critical of people who knew nothing of my father's imprisonment. Up until that morning, I had no idea of the number or names of the Americans who sat in Lebanon chained and helplessly forgotten.

We grew quite restless holed-up in our dark living room after several more hours of an occasional knock on the door and the constant ringing of the phone. We decided to try to go to Huntington Beach's Central Park and get some fresh air. As we walked around the lake, we could only talk about the invasion of our private suffering by the press. I think we all shared a deep sense of resentment and anger towards the individual reporters. I recounted my experience on the phone earlier, and in a funny sense, we found ourselves at war with the news media. We were hurting, angry people. We didn't know who had taken our father, but we could see the faces and hear the voices of those we considered to be callous, pushy and intrusive—people who were just trying to sell advertising space through our grief and suffering. They made the perfect scapegoat for our anger. Why couldn't they respect the fact that we didn't want to share our pain with other Americans? We were convinced that the average American had enough pain in his own life to deal with without turning on the TV or picking up a paper and being confronted with us.

As Paul suggested, we weren't special. We didn't deserve special attention. Maybe our situation was unique, but we surely weren't suffering any more than someone who watches a relative die of cancer, or someone who gets a phone call saying their spouse or child has been killed by a drunk driver. We don't see those people on the evening news.

Towards the end of our walk Paul said, 'It feels like there's been a death in the family—that same kind of feeling.'

I agreed. It shared the same hollowness, the same draining shock that leaves you empty and helpless, even the same sense of finality. I'm sure we were each weighing just that possibility. Although the finality had no basis, it seemed to come with the package of feelings. Still, when I tried to feel that finality, when I tried to reach somewhere unnamed for the answer, I knew that Dad was alive. In spite of the shock that made it feel like a death of a loved one, I knew unquestionably that he was all right.

We returned home in time to watch the local Los Angeles evening news broadcasts. Dad's passport picture, probably released by his employer, opened the programmes. We sat solemnly and listened again to the brief, factual account of his abduction. As I remember, two of the three stations called him Dr Jacobsen, which wasn't his title, and one even used the wrong first name. I found that amusing in an irritating way. Each piece had interviews with people he had worked with at Alhambra Community Hospital three and a half years earlier—they were the only people who would comment on camera. They talked about what a kind, generous man he was. It sounded too much like a eulogy. I became very disturbed and turned off the TV.

Paul and Lori left a short time later, and Cathy and I skipped dinner. We did absolutely nothing until it was time to go to bed, except that I thought briefly about what I needed to do the following day to get Dad's affairs in order. Then I lay in bed, exhausted, numb from the intensity of my emotions. This day was ending without the news we were waiting for. I tried to figure out what time it was in Lebanon and determined it was probably dawn. I tried to imagine where my father was and what he was doing at that moment. Terrible fears began to rush through me, but I refused to dwell on them. I knew Dad would deal with the situation as well as any person could.

I began to pray silently, 'Father, please release him tomorrow. If not tomorrow, by the end of the week.'

2

8th November, 1984–14th May, 1985

'I've decided to accept the job,' Dad had said as we walked from the terminal gate to the baggage claim area at Los Angeles International Airport.

I was pleased to hear it. 'So Beirut isn't as bad as they make it look on the evening news?'

He shook his head. 'Parts of the city are completely destroyed from the fighting, but you wouldn't know it walking around on the grounds of the university. So far, the campus has remained off-limits to the war.'

It was early November 1984, and he had just returned from a three-day visit to Lebanon. Several months before he had learned through a close doctor friend that the American University of Beirut was in search of a director for their medical centre. They specifically wanted an American.

Before accepting the position, my father went to inspect the hospital and meet the staff, as well as to judge whether he thought it was a safe place to work. Beirut was growing more and more notorious in the American press while Lebanon's civil war raged and the political system disintegrated into anarchy.

'Was there a lot of fighting going on?' Cathy asked.

'No, it was quiet. But the signs of the war are everywhere. Some blocks of the city are levelled from heavy artillery. They say conditions are improving. That's why they think it's safe for an American to return to that job.'

'But you've definitely decided to take it?' I asked.

'At first, I wasn't going to. But I changed my mind halfway home. I looked out of the plane window, and all I could see was the ocean. I thought back to what the wife of one of the professors said to me the last day I was there. She said, "The day the first American returns to Beirut, that will be the day that hope for the future will return for my children." I remembered the faces of her two kids, and I knew I had to take the job.'

When Dad said that, I thought it was typical of him. He always had a soft spot for a person in need, especially a helpless child. His sense of responsibility to those 'innocent victims' would prevent him from declining for personal reasons. The decision to accept the offer was based on a commitment to help the children of Lebanon.

Cathy was concerned. 'Are you going to be safe?'

'Yes,' he said with predictable confidence. 'I met with the leaders of the larger militia factions, and they all agreed to do whatever they could to guarantee my safety. They all feel it is extremely important for an American to be there in that capacity. Don't worry—my living quarters will be on campus, and as I said, it's understood that AUB is off-limits to the war. You have to remember it's where many of the leaders of Lebanon and the Middle East in general were educated. It's a very respected institution.'

He informed New York headquarters of the American University of Beirut of his decision, and a little less than a month later, we again put Dad on a plane to Beirut via London.

This wasn't his first adventure overseas to work in the Middle East. He already had one under his belt. In May of 1982, the day after Cathy and I were married, he had left on an eighteen-hour flight to Saudi Arabia. His job was to oversee the opening of the National Security Forces Hospital in Riyadh for an American management company, National Medical Enterprises. He stayed a little over a year as the hospital administrator before returning to work in NME's corporate offices in southern California.

That must have been a truly difficult undertaking for him. It meant leaving his children for at least a year, and, until then, his existence had centred solely on providing for his family. In addition, having been a hospital administrator in southern California for thirty years, he suddenly found himself in a markedly different work environment and in a foreign culture.

I had encouraged him to take that job. My reason was selfish, based on the geography involved. He and my mother had just divorced, and I wanted the two of them separated by the diameter of planet earth. I tried to rationalise my endorsement by believing that it would give Dad an opportunity to make a break from his past and prevent him from living out the remainder of his life under the weight of domestic failure. When the Riyadh job opened up, we were all still reeling from the painful disintegration of our family, and during the year or two that preceded his trip to Saudi, I had had little contact with either of my parents. As a result, I didn't share the apprehension of separation that my father must have felt. My main concern was that the division between my parents be finally completed and put behind us. I was convinced it would at least ease the tensions placed upon my brother, sister, and myself by making contact between our parents virtually non-existent.

Just as I had hoped, the following year was noticeably more peaceful, and my position of neutrality went unchallenged. When his contract expired, and he returned home from Riyadh late the following spring, I noticed that a significant change had occurred. My father seemed a rejuvinated man. It appeared that he had begun to come to terms with his failed marriage. Once his life didn't revolve entirely around that, neither did the relationship between us.

In his year's absence, he had lived and worked in a world totally unknown to me: a world of Islam, a nomadic world that had suddenly found the camel replaced by the

Mercedes, a world where Americans lived in compounds and Western ways were tolerated for the sake of technical and business expertise. A world not as I had envisioned it—straight out of the *Thousand and One Nights* tales.

During his holidays, he had travelled to London, Italy, Africa, and Greece. He told anecdotes that went beyond the street where our family once lived and fell apart. His stories of being an American businessman working and living within an Arab culture were fascinating, at times amusing, yet always educational. I found we could have conversations that sparked my interest instead of making me cringe from old wounds, or long for the days when our home seemed perfect, peaceful, and secure.

I sensed a peace about him that I attributed to the widening of his horizons. However, the most important factor responsible for the change in Dad had completely escaped me. In my ignorance, I had dismissed a crucial development in Saudi that my father had recounted in one of his letters to us. He had developed a close friendship with an Australian woman who also worked at the hospital—Kerrie—and through her, he had come to know the Lord Jesus. When Kerrie's contract expired, she had come to the US to further her education and was now living in Dallas, Texas.

This new dimension in his life was as foreign to me as were the streets of Riyadh. We had never belonged to a church. Although we considered ourselves Christians, I did not have any relationship with Jesus, and my thoughts of God were basically limited to Christmas and Easter holidays. I was relieved when my father didn't try the 'hard sell' on me as others had in the past.

And it was because of his new-found faith, shown through his concern for the children of that Lebanese professor, that he had ultimately made the decision to go to Beirut. During the drive to the airport, Dad said simply, 'Maybe God has a plan that requires I go to Lebanon.'

So we put him on a plane. My wife objected for his safety, but I didn't. It was just a new adventure to another exotic destination—this time Beirut, Lebanon, the 'Paris of the Middle East' as it had been called.

I felt some apprehension, but not much. I knew my father was not one to make hasty decisions. On the contrary, he had always lived a very conservative life and took no unnecessary risks. With complete confidence in his judgement, and with assurances that he would be protected, I watched him board a plane for London on his way to Beirut on 30th November, 1984. He left with the stipulation that he would be home for my brother Paul's wedding in June, if not sooner.

A month later, his first letter arrived, and it only reinforced my confidence that he had made the right decision.

Dear Family,

I'm writing one letter to all of you because it is difficult to get letters out of the country just because of lack of space in the courier's luggage. So please pass it around.

I arrived in Lebanon on Sunday, 2nd December about 6:00 pm. The people who were to meet me were delayed because of traffic jams. I got through customs without any problem. As I was leaving the airport building to find a taxi, my reception party arrived.

My apartment lacks all the comforts except a beautiful view of the Mediterranean and Beirut's harbour. The apartment will be painted beginning tomorrow, and perhaps by the end of the week additional furniture will be delivered. ... [It] has three bedrooms, two baths, a small kitchen and a combination living room and dining room, plus a balcony on both sides. It can be fixed up but will require a lot of interior decorating.

Yesterday, Joe Cicippio, the hospital's American comptroller, took me on a shopping tour of Beirut. I bought dishes, cutlery, pots and pans, hangers, kitchen supplies, etc. ... One can buy anything in Beirut. Shopping involves going to several stores. Meat and canned goods in the 'supermarket', fresh fruits and veggies from street vendors. It's all very good. The temptation to buy their pastries is strong, but so far I have resisted.

My office staff is excellent and very supportive. The job is going to be tough due to the absolute lack of discipline resulting from ten years of fighting. The university's policy is not to terminate or discipline employees. The fear of retaliation is *real*.

I feel safe, but the university officials want me to be extra cautious. The problem of kidnapping is ever present. Hostages are held by terrorists in Lebanon as pawns for the release of their friends in other countries. The moment I think I need a bodyguard, I will get one. I don't intend to be brave.

The other Americans are really very nice and protective. They have had me to their apartments for supper. ...

I have started to run at the track in the morning, so I'm quickly getting back in shape. Even do sit-ups. Time passes very, very quickly. In the evening I have been reading background documents. The jet lag is horrible. I sleep two to three hours a night—still on California time.

I'm glad that I have come to Lebanon. It's great to be busy with a purpose. The people are friendly, and there is no obvious hostility towards Americans. Ahmed Nasrallah, my assistant administrator, serves as my shadow. He is a graduate of Duke University and is highly placed in the Shi'ite Muslim organisation. I might not see him, but he or one of his friends is never far away.

When you hear things about the situation here, please wait to worry. ...

The days are calm, but the evenings are like the 4th of July. Machine-gun fire with tracer bullets occurs a couple of times between sunset at 5:00 pm and 8:00 pm. Sometimes it is young men 'celebrating', and occasionally the intent is a fire fight with their enemies. It's something you look at out of the windows until boredom takes over, and then it's back to the radio for the BBC. ...

I just want you all—Eric, Cathy, Paul, Diane, and Lori—to know that I think of you often. I'm enjoying my stay so far so please don't worry. I'm not going to do anything foolish.

Take care of yourselves and be good to one another.

All my love,

Dad

I read that letter only once. It and the subsequent letters Dad sent further dispelled any fears I might have had. None of us could have recognised the true threat of danger although he himself had written prophetically of the very reason for his own kidnapping, as well as that of Joe Cicippio (the AUB's comptroller), and more than a dozen other kidnappings. Lebanon appeared to offer no more cause for concern than Saudi Arabia, and Dad had said the greatest problem in Saudi was simple boredom.

The first five months of his three-year contract quickly passed. My own life was at a fever pitch during this time. Earlier in the year, I had been laid off as a result of a staff reduction at a local hospital where I worked as a cardiac technician. I was upset at finding myself unemployed, but, honestly, I was suffering from burn-out and found it something of a blessing. I still had a decent paying part-time job at night with another medical services company, and I hoped eventually to leave hospital work with doctors and patients for ever.

Much to my father's satisfaction, I decided to return to college and finally attain a degree. I was only a year away from it. To my own surprise, I didn't drop out for the umpteenth time after a few weeks. In contrast to my previous attempts, I finished that first semester and found myself on the dean's list of top students.

As the second semester began, something even more astonishing had happened to me. My brother was due to get married the following June, and because his fiancée was Catholic and they were to have a Mass wedding ceremony, he had decided to become a Catholic himself. It required that he attend eight months of weekly classes beginning in September that would culminate in baptism, confirmation, and First Communion the following Easter.

Providentially, my wife was also Catholic. We had been married in the Catholic Church as well, but had only a brief ceremony. Cathy's faith had always intrigued me, but I had no intention of joining the church. I tagged along with Paul because I thought it would give me an opportunity to understand my spouse better. As an intellectual diversion, I had attended Sunday Mass with her once in a while, and I thought if I mastered the lingo, it would in some way strengthen our marriage.

The classes began, and just as I was in the habit of doing during my day at college, I attended them regularly and took careful notes. However, cautious scepticism would best describe my approach. Even during the first meeting where, typically, we had to introduce ourselves and explain why we had decided to join, I did not hesitate to make it known that I was there primarily as an observer, not necessarily as a participant.

But it was as if God was standing at the front of the class asking for a volunteer to come to the chalkboard. I tried to hide behind the kid in front of me. My ploy backfired and only drew attention to me. I found myself pulled forward. Within only a matter of weeks I discovered a yearning within myself. I knew it was bringing change, but I couldn't determine what or how it was occurring. I fought it with an arsenal of rational thoughts. I confronted it as a challenge to my internal debating skills. I was not going to surrender to it without being presented with unequivocal, insurmountable evidence of his existence.

Then, one afternoon in the autumn of 1984, I was sitting in my car at a red light when through the grace of God I suddenly understood with a distinct clarity. It was so simple. The choice was entirely mine. I could choose to believe, or I could choose not to believe. I could rationalise either view depending on which conclusion I wished to reach. To my knowledge, neither believers nor nonbelievers had ever been able to prove or convince the other of their convictions. Science had not been able to demonstrate that God did not exist; Scripture alone was not proof enough to those who didn't believe that he did.

The choice was mine. Did I want to believe that there was a loving, caring God who was offering me the opportunity to share eternal life with him? Or would I rather believe that I was alone in the world fighting against inconquerable adversaries—time, the universe, and death? As I continued to reflect on this, the scope of my choice broadened. Had I come across anything in Scripture that struck me as wrong, inappropriate, or contrary to happiness? No. In my search for satisfaction, peace and fulfilment through conventional worldly means had I found happiness and security? Not yet.

My security had already been shaken when I lost my job earlier in the year. There was no guarantee that couldn't happen again. Besides, I had never had enough money to keep me from wanting more. What if, like my parents, my marriage collapsed after twenty-five years? Could I start over again at fifty? How hard would it be to find another person to replace the love of my wife? Several years earlier, I had watched my best friend die while we were jogging on the beach. How could I cope with the death of someone else I loved when I still hadn't even come to terms with his? Did I want to view my own death as nothing more than an additional source of nutrients for the soil?

The choice was obviously mine, and for me, the choice was obvious. Blind faith in Jesus offered me a shield, a refuge, and a promising future in spite of whatever might occur. It would mean that I could no longer worship my own ego. And if I was successful in that, would I be as vulnerable to the trials of the world?

Once I made that choice to believe, I couldn't choose otherwise. The light turned green, and I drove away a believer.

By January 1985, economics were dictating that I trade school and my part-time job for evening classes and full-time employment. The owner of Cardiac Research & Development where I was working offered me a position as operations manager, and I accepted. Cathy and I wanted to buy a house and start a family. I know I would once again add to my parents' disappointment, but I did intend to continue my education again one day.

The next few months were a period of intense spiritual

growth and awareness. As I learned more about God through the church, I found I was developing a vocabulary for feelings I sensed I had always known. Yet, a host of new feelings seemed to evolve. Somewhere I had heard that we do not choose God; God chooses us. My growing faith was a discovery of that. I was beginning to recognise that Jesus was more than just a character in an often-told story. The church community slowly began to fill the void left by the scattering of my family.

The Easter vigil of 1985 arrived—6th April. The night had come for Paul and me to be baptised and welcomed as members into the Catholic Church. Along with forty other catechumens, we sat patiently in the oak pews and waited to celebrate Mass. My mother and other family and friends had joined us. As the lights went down and the candlelight procession began, I wondered where Dad was at that moment. I remembered how thrilled he was at my high school graduation. In comparison with this night, I considered that not much more important than a Cub Scout meeting.

The Mass lasted well past midnight, and as we drove home, I felt my life was finally on track. Could I be any happier? If so, I couldn't imagine it. I was confident that nothing could ever happen to disrupt my new-found peace. I would have to write to Dad the next day and tell him all about it. One thought kept crossing my mind: *First Dad, then Paul and I.* There was no doubt that God was at work in our family.

Late one evening near the end of April, the phone rang. The connection was thick with static, and when I heard a heavily accented operator say, 'I have an overseas call for Eric Jacobsen,' I knew it was Dad.

'Greetings from Beirut!'

The connection was poor so I yelled into the receiver, 'How's it going? Everything OK?'

'Just fine. How's everything there?'

'Fine.'

'I called to let you know that I'll be flying to California

the second week in May. They're sending me to a medical convention in San Francisco.'

'Great. How long are you coming for?'

'Ten days total. I'll only have two or three days with you all, but they offered to send me so I thought I'd take advantage of it.'

I turned to Cathy and told her.

'Tell him the second bedroom is ready, but he'll have to clean it first,' she teased.

I relayed the message, and we all laughed.

His voice grew a little more serious. 'Actually, my boss felt I needed to get away from here for a break. The fighting has intensified in the last month. The war's been escalating, and the hospital has been very busy. He's sending me home as a kind of a bonus.'

Two weeks later we found ourselves again at the terminal of Los Angeles International. Dad looked healthy and unstressed as he came off the plane. We were all expecting to see some kind of evidence that he was living in a war zone, but he looked just as he did when he left for Beirut the previous November. Had we picked up a hitchhiker on the drive home, he might have thought from the conversation that Dad had just returned home from a Mediterranean holiday.

His storytelling over the next few days tended to avoid the civil war, with the exception of one account of a huge battle he had witnessed from his top-floor apartment window. Intrigued as if a spectator at a sporting event, he had casually viewed the ebb and flow of the opposing militias through the streets of West Beirut until the mortar fire suddenly began to fall near his apartment. Afraid that a projectile would come crashing through his bedroom ceiling in the middle of the night, he pulled his blankets from the bed, went down a couple of flights and slept in the hallway with the other residents.

We were assured that this had been an exception and we had nothing to fear. The majority of fighting was generally some distance from the AUB. He told us again that to walk around the campus it was hard to envision the destruction taking place just blocks away. The AUB had continued to escape the ravages of war.

On one of those May mornings, he and I went to the beach where we used to run along the bike path. I was telling him of my recent baptism and expressing remorse that he hadn't been able to share it with me. For the first time I could remember, we spoke of God and his place in our lives.

'I know he put me in Lebanon to help the victims of that terrible war,' he said in what impressed me as a very humble manner. 'This is by far the most satisfying job I've ever had. For the first time in my career in medicine, I'm not just concerned with turning a profit. I can actually see my work paying off in human lives. Do you know that when I was leaving on this trip, there were employees crying and begging me not to go because they thought I wasn't going to return? I had to promise them I would be back.'

'What about kidnapping?' I asked for the first time. 'A few weeks ago wasn't an Associated Press journalist taken?'

Dad explained. 'He was playing tennis on a public tennis court. A group of young militia was driving by, saw an opportunity to grab an American, stopped, and took him with the intention of working out later what to do with him. I won't take a chance like that.'

I was comforted to know Dad was so circumspect and cautious.

The night before he was to fly back, Cathy sat alone with him at the dining-room table. 'Dad, I don't want you to go.'

'I have to. I'm needed there. Don't worry, I'll be safe. I don't take unnecessary risks. I don't ever wander alone into the streets of Beirut. I basically work seven days a week, and all my time is spent on campus or at the medical centre. There's only one place where I'm exposed to even the slightest danger, and that's when I have to cross the street between the campus and the medical centre garage. And even then I have a bodyguard who meets me there every morning and evening.'

This argument did little to ease Cathy's fears. Myself, I had complete confidence in his commitment to return.

Next morning, Dad insisted on taking the shuttle bus to the airport instead of allowing me to drive him. With a busy day ahead of me, I didn't disagree too adamantly. Cathy had left for work earlier in the morning still concerned about his return, but it was a very casual parting between my father and me at the front door when it was time for me to leave for the office.

'Are you sure you don't want me to drive you?' I asked a final time.

'It's a lot more convenient for everyone if I just take the airport shuttle bus,' he insisted. 'I don't mind at all.'

'OK then. I'll see you in a month.' We shook hands.

'I'll try to be back for Paul and Lori's wedding, even though it will probably just be an overnight trip. If for some reason I can't make it, I've already given them their wedding present.'

'You think there's a chance you might miss their wedding?' I asked, surprised even at the suggestion of his absence.

'I have every intention of coming, but I am working in a war zone—you can't predict the circumstances. I'll make every effort to be here.'

'Have a safe trip,' I said as I turned to walk to the car, and the front door closed between us.

A little concerned by this last conversation, I nevertheless quickly dismissed it. It would take an unforeseen complication for Dad to miss one of his children's weddings. Surely there was no way he wouldn't be at St Bonaventure Catholic Church on 21st June?

I came home at lunch that day thinking I might catch him before his bus left, but he was already gone. On the dining-room table, I found an envelope. It was sealed, and a bald instruction was written on the face of it: 'To be opened in the event of my death or kidnapping.'

Two weeks later, I found it necessary to open that envelope.

3
29th May–30th June, 1985

The morning following my father's kidnapping, I was already wide awake when the phone rang.

With Cathy on my heels, I raced down the stairs two or three at a time to the answering machine. I was sure it was the call that would inform us Dad was once again a free man. Dawn was breaking. The outgoing message ended. We waited patiently to hear the voice of our State Department contact.

'Mr Jacobsen, this is United Press International. I would like the opportunity to ask you a few questions about the anonymous phone call in Beirut this morning regarding your father. I would appreciate you calling me back as soon as. . . .'

'What anonymous call?' Cathy asked.

I began to reach for the phone to echo that question, but something stopped me. It would be better to call the State Department. If I asked this guy, he'd surely want to probe me with more questions. I still had no intention of talking to the press. Besides, the State Department would probably have more detailed information to relay to me.

As his message ended, I opened the notebook in which I had written the number of my contact person in Washington, DC. Before I could lift the receiver and dial, the phone began to ring again. The answering machine kicked in and laboriously repeated its script.

'Yes, this is NBC Network News. I don't know if

you've heard yet, but an anonymous call was received in Beirut this morning claiming responsibility for your father's kidnapping. The caller also took responsibility for the killing of a British professor from the American University whose body was found earlier today. We would like to get your comments in an interview this morning if possible. . . .'

I stood in stunned silence. They also 'took responsibility for the killing of a British professor?' Who was this professor? When was he taken? Why was he killed? Suddenly, the threat to Dad's life seemed imminent. I hurriedly dialled the State Department.

'At this point, the information is still sketchy,' Jackie, my contact person, stated calmly. 'Nothing has been confirmed, and it is our policy not to pass on rumours. As soon as we have something more definitive, we'll call— probably later today.'

My sense of urgency was smothered under a blanket of bureaucratic protocol, but I didn't want to be argumentative. They were the professionals. I was the amateur. The conversation ended. I was left even more confused and frustrated. If the State Department wouldn't comment on the report, did that mean there was a good chance it was false? Was my initial panic unfounded? Had a man really died? Was an anonymous call ever received?

'What did she say?' Cathy asked.

Before I could answer her, the phone rang again. 'Hi, Associated Press, calling to get your comment on the latest development in Beirut. . . .'

This time, I couldn't stop myself. I ripped the receiver off the top of the phone. 'This is Eric Jacobsen.'

'Mr Jacobsen. I'm glad I caught you at home. Have you heard about the phone call regarding your father this morning?'

'Just bits and pieces.'

'Well, it seems that an anonymous caller claiming to be a member of Islamic Jihad has taken responsibility for his kidnapping and that of two Frenchmen abducted last weekend. Also, I'm sorry to say, he claimed responsibility for the execution of a British professor who disappeared over the weekend. They found his body this morning. He had been shot in the head several times.'

'Who was he?'

'His name was Dennis Hill. I believe he worked at the American University with your father.'

I digested this, feeling the panic mount. 'Was there any other news regarding my father? Any threats against him? How about ransom demands?'

'As far as I know, the caller demanded the release of seventeen prisoners jailed in Kuwait for terrorist bombings. ... Do you mind if I ask you a few questions?'

'Sorry, I've really got no comment until I get some confirmation from the State Department. Thank you very much for the information. I really appreciate—'

He interrupted. 'Has the State Department contacted you about this development?'

'I talked to them this morning. Sorry, I've got to go.'

'What did they tell you?' he persisted.

'Thanks again. Gotta go.' I hung up.

'What did they say?' Cathy asked as I sat down at the dining-room table to try to piece together what I'd heard.

'That guy who just called said somebody from a group called "Islamic ... something", I couldn't understand what he said—has claimed responsibility for Dad's kidnapping.'

'Is he all right?'

'I don't know. They killed an English professor from the AUB and kidnapped two Frenchmen. They're demanding the release of some prisoners held in Kuwait.'

'They've killed somebody? Oh, *Eric*. What did the State Department say?'

'She really didn't say anything.' I tried to hide my disappointment at her inability to comment on the report. 'It's not their policy to tell us anything but confirmable facts. But nothing's been confirmed yet.' I could see Cathy fighting to hold back tears. 'Don't worry,' I tried to comfort her, 'they're going to call back later with more information. I'm sure Dad's OK. At least we know he's still alive.'

My words did little to calm her fears. They did little to calm my own. One poor man was probably dead already. Brutally shot in the head. The same gun could easily be turned on Dad. I wondered if Dad had heard the shots fired into the brain of his colleague. The thought crossed my mind that every call I received from then on could represent the pull of a trigger in a terrorist's game of Russian roulette.

I put my head in my hands and rested my elbows on the table, praying silently. 'Father, is he still alive? Is he being tortured? In your plan, does Dad have to die? What can I do to save him? I'll do anything. Just tell me what to do.'

I could not hear his voice. In desperation, I strained my ears, begging for the simple solution. 'Give me a list of three steps to win his freedom, and I'll follow them to the letter. Please, Lord, tell me what to do.'

Still I could not hear his response.

I grew impatient and began to draw up my own strategy. I needed an immediate course of action—something to occupy my mind; otherwise, my undivided attention would have nothing to focus on but my fear of the unknown. Subconsciously, a danger signal was wailing. I knew I needed to move.

First I had to put my father's financial affairs in order. When he had gone overseas, he had entrusted me to pay for a few credit cards, his life insurance premiums, and a few other miscellaneous bills. It struck me that the AUB might stop his salary cheques now that he was a hostage. I thought of my mother, too, who depended on her alimony to make ends meet. It would be a serious complication if that money was held up. I suddenly became concerned that Dad's credit could be ruined by this, and on his return, might cause him almost as much trouble as the kidnap.

I went to our bedroom and opened my cupboard door, where a brown accordian-fold letter file lay on the shelf, then I carried it back downstairs. Cathy left me to get ready for work, while I searched through the folder until I found the two things I needed. One was a generic legal form entitled 'Power of Attorney' that my father had signed and left with me before his initial trip to Lebanon. The other was the six-by-nine brown envelope that bore my father's handwriting: 'To be opened upon my death or kidnapping.' I scanned over the Power of Attorney document and signed my name. Then I tore open the other envelope and inspected the contents. There were two handwritten letters; the first, a Last Will and Testament; the second, instructions regarding the handling of his money should he be kidnapped, including specific instructions dealing with his AUB contract.

Disregarding the Last Will and Testament, I went on to the instructions in case of kidnapping. The final point asked that his cheque be automatically deposited into the local Huntington Beach bank that held his accounts. I called the AUB headquarters in New York to request this. They had no objections, but only required a copy of the 'Power of Attorney' and a letter from the bank verifying that my signature was on his bank account. I didn't mind having to run a few errands. It would make me feel I was doing something constructive.

As we spoke, it occurred to me that I should ask the university to translate into Arabic a statement from Paul, Diane and me and place it in the Lebanese newspapers. It was possible that the men holding Dad might read it. Maybe an appeal from the children of their kidnapped victim might be enough to touch their hearts; it might at least prevent them from shooting him in the head.

Under the guidance of an AUB official, I drafted a brief and simple statement:

> We ..., the children of David Jacobsen, Director of the American University of Beirut Medical Center, are very worried about our father. We request that the people responsible for his kidnapping on May 28, 1985, please release him to the university so that he may continue his humanitarian work.

I put down the receiver and hoped it would somehow gain something in the translation.

Cathy left for work, and reporters continued to call. Since I had to wait until the banks opened at ten, I cooked myself breakfast and took my time getting ready. Just before I was about to leave, I recognised the voice of Jackie from the State Department coming out of the answering machine.

'Have you heard anything?' I immediately asked.

'Nothing confirmable yet, but we're still working on it. We'll let you know as soon as we know something definite.' Then there was a pause in her voice, and you could almost hear the shift in the conversation. 'There are two reasons I'm calling. One is to let you know that we express-mailed the information and suggestions that I promised you. And the other is to schedule a time for someone from our office in Los Angeles to come to your home and interview you. When would be a good time?'

'Any time is fine with me.'

'How about tomorrow at ten?'

'Fine.'

'If you could put together some pictures and handwriting samples of your father, it would be helpful. You should get the letter tomorrow.'

The express-mail package arrived early the next morning. I expected to receive a volume of information and suggestions the size of a phone book. Instead, it consisted of a cover letter, and two pages of information already read to me over the phone. The letter said in part:

Dear Mr Jacobsen,

The Department of State deeply regrets the kidnapping in Lebanon of your father, Mr David Jacobsen, on May 28, 1985. I want you to know that we will assist in every way we can to bring about his safe return.

We are acutely aware of the enormous distress such tragic events cause. For this reason I am enclosing some suggestions intended to help you and your family as you go through this difficult period. The suggestions provided are not definitive and of course should be used at your discretion. We do recommend that you contact us if you need any further

information or assistance. We will certainly call you whenever
we have any new information or guidance we think you
would want to have. ...

We fully share your concerns for your father's safety and
will immediately apprise you of all developments.

Sincerely

... Director, Citizens' Emergency Center

I couldn't help but wonder why the report of the
anonymous call the previous morning did not constitute
a 'development'. Also, why was I still waiting to be
'apprised' of it? To avoid harbouring any negative feelings, I told myself that it was their job to locate and rescue
my father, not to soothe the fears of his family.

At ten o'clock, the State Department agent knocked on
the door. Paul, Cathy, and I found ourselves sitting
around my dining-room table answering questions about
my father's physical features, his character, and his
history. The agent was considerate and friendly, but he
also struck me more as a law enforcement type than as a
career bureaucrat. There was a no-nonsense, fact-finding
impatience about his manner that made me feel we were
truly dealing with a government official. I was confident
we were making progress.

He briefly explained his duties and reiterated the
suggestions contained in the letter from the Citizens'
Emergency Center. 'In the past, we have received some
communication from men who were also kidnapped.
Should you ever receive a letter in the mail, and this has
happened to other families, it's very important you
handle it as little as possible. Try to hold it only by the
corners.'

We nodded in complete understanding.

'Should you receive a letter or a package,' he continued,
'I want you to call me immediately. Here's my card.'

He impressed me as someone who would be able to
answer some of the basic questions regarding my father's
predicament, so I began by asking, 'Can you tell me
what's being done to secure my father's release?'

'Every conceivable effort is being made. I can't reveal specifically what those efforts are because of the delicate nature of this situation. However, we are pursuing many different channels.'

Paul wasn't entirely satisfied with his answer. 'Can't you tell us anything at all? We'll give our word we won't tell anyone.'

He smiled at each one of us. 'We're doing all we can.'

I gave up and handed over several of the recent letters Dad had written from Beirut for handwriting analysis. On his last trip he had brought home several packs of photographs of the campus and himself in his office. With the exception of one studio portrait Dad had had done a couple of years before, these were all the pictures I had of him. I passed them reluctantly across the table.

I didn't want to part with the studio portrait, but he deemed it to be necessary, so it too was surrendered. When the agent left a few minutes later, he had in his hands all my photos and letters from Dad. I couldn't help but think that we were left with nothing. Dad was lost somewhere in a land I could not even visualise, and now all evidence of Dad's existence that I possessed might accidentally be destroyed in some laboratory hidden in the bowels of the State Department building.

Although he said that he would mail everything back in a couple of weeks, I wished I had kept at least one picture of Dad. Just one. Only four days later, my wish was to come true, but hardly in the way I had envisioned.

The weekend passed without any further developments, and by now, the press interest had died completely. No word came from the State Department. No word came from the AUB. Absolute silence reigned. It was almost just another Monday morning at work. But while I was talking on the phone, the second line lit up, and I unexpectedly found myself talking to Jackie from the State Department.

'Eric, a photograph has been released by Islamic Jihad which we believe to be your father. It's been confirmed by several people at the American University.'

He's still alive! 'How does he look?' I asked excitedly.

'I haven't seen the picture myself. It was accompanied by a typewritten message which denied the responsibility for the death of Dennis Hill, the British professor, killed last week. There is no mention about your father other than the picture.'

I was a little confused by the kidnappers' denial of the previous message. 'So the caller last week probably wasn't legitimate?'

'Apparently not. This is why we hesitate to pass on rumours to the families—so many turn out to be false, and it just confuses things.'

'Are there different demands?' I asked.

'I don't believe that any demands are stated in this message. In fact, aside from his picture, your father is not mentioned.'

I began to feel myself swallowed up in confusion. 'Have we discovered anything at all?'

'There's really no new information at this point.'

'What specifically is being done?'

'We really can't say. Many initiatives are being taken, but they must remain confidential because of the delicacy of the situation.'

Her answer was beginning to sound all too familiar. I knew I wouldn't get anywhere pursuing that line of questioning.

For the remainder of the day and during my drive home, I tried to piece together the little information that I had. *We know Dad has been kidnapped, but we don't know why. We know that he was taken by Islamic Jihad, but we don't know who they are. Last week, we thought the demand was for the release of prisoners in Kuwait, but today, last week's message was denied and contradicted. Now we don't know what the demands are. We know that many initiatives are being pursued, but we don't know one single thing being done.*

When I walked through the front door, I was confronted with an answering machine once again full of inquiries from reporters. I listened to them all, hoping for more information, but they added nothing to what I had already heard.

Cathy came home a short while later, obviously upset. Because she worked for the *Los Angeles Times*, it was obvious that she had already heard of the day's developments. 'Did the State Department call you?' she asked.

'Yes.'

I turned on the TV to catch the news headlines. There it was—the photograph. Nothing could have prepared us for it. His face was drawn. He probably hadn't slept for days. His hair was unwashed and combed flat. Behind him, they had hung a blanket or a table-cloth. I tried to search his face for some kind of clue. The picture disappeared from the screen. It was time for the next news story. I turned off the set, and Cathy's brown eyes filled with tears.

We've got to do something, I told myself over and over again. *I cannot just sit here like a helpless slug. Dad would be doing something. If I were held hostage in Lebanon, Dad would have brought me home by now.*

I called Paul to find out if he'd seen the news. He had. We both took turns asking the same question: 'What can we do?'

'I think we should consider doing an interview,' I suggested.

'What are we going to say?'

'I don't know. But it just seems that because Dad is getting national news coverage, we ought to at least try to give the proper picture of who he is and why he was there.'

'Maybe his captors will read it,' Paul added.

'Let's do it.'

The next day Cathy stepped into the *LA Times* editorial department and announced that the children of David Jacobsen would be willing to grant an exclusive interview to the newspaper. They jumped on it. It was set up for the following evening at our home. Paul and Diane both agreed to come over.

The night before our entrance into the spotlight, Paul

and I spoke on the phone and tried to anticipate the questions we would be asked. We drew up a list of points we wanted clearly to state. We talked about things like family 'image'.

More than anything else, our preparation consisted of intense worry. What if we said the wrong thing? What if we were misquoted? What if we came across as babbling idiots? The suggestions of the State Department kept coming back. What if we said something that complicated efforts to win Dad's release? What if we unnecessarily endangered our father's life further? Would it make him a more valuable hostage? Was this the proper thing to do? Was it too late to back out?

The next day, Cathy beat the reporter home to our apartment. She had in her hand the picture of Dad that had come across the wire. Every time she looked at it she cried. I stared intently at every detail. In spite of his grim appearance, something in his eyes comforted me. It was as if he knew we would be seeing this picture, and being the kind of father he was, he was making every effort to tell us he was all right, and there was no need to worry.

Within the hour the participants in our small press conference arrived. Paul and I sat on the sofa with the reporter. Diane sat opposite us in a chair. A tape recorder slowly turned on the coffee table recording every word we uttered. His questions were straightforward: 'What kind of man was your father?' 'Why did he go to Lebanon?' 'What do you hear from the State Department?'

We hesitated each time to consider our answers carefully. When a question was posed to Paul or Diane, I sat reviewing my previous answer. *Did I explain that correctly? Should I have said more? Did I say anything inappropriate that I should ask him not to print?* Never before in my life had I felt that my words carried such weight.

I may have exaggerated the gravity of the first interview, but I wanted to maintain as much control over it as possible. We had several points to make. When we were asked how we felt, we tried to downplay our feelings and focus on the turmoil Dad must have been experiencing.

When quizzed about Dad's position at the AUB, we stressed the humanitarian nature of his work in hopes that his captors might be swayed to release him should they read the *LA Times*. When asked if we would consent to being photographed, we declined and suggested they run a picture of Dad instead.

The interview lasted an hour and a half. When the reporter left, we sat exhausted on the couch, reviewing everything we'd said, trying to predict how the article would turn out. We hoped it would show that Dad was not a mercenary trying to reap the spoils of the civil war in Lebanon. We wondered if we gave an impression of optimism, of dignity in spite of the circumstances, and of a loving commitment to our father.

When I read the article on Saturday morning, I was pleased. There weren't any quotes that made me feel uncomfortable. I felt the reporter had portrayed us reasonably. I was confident that when Dad was released and read it, he would approve. In a sense, I felt we had done our duty and no more interviews would be necessary. Besides, I was still confident it was only a matter of days before Dad was released.

Only a matter of days. . . .

The events of the following week changed my outlook dramatically. Monday's newspaper shook my confidence that a resolution was forthcoming. I read that another American from the AUB, Thomas Sutherland, had been kidnapped on his way from the Beirut airport to the campus. He was returning from the States, where he had attended the graduation of one of his daughters.

A couple of days later, I read news of an airline hijacking in the Middle East. On the tail of that, the headlines told of yet another hijacking that ended with the destruction of the plane on a Beirut runway after all the passengers and crew had been released.

And then, on the following Saturday, another incident occurred which would accelerate the alteration of my attitude towards the State Department, President

Reagan, the news media, and American people generally. TWA 847 was hijacked.

Like the rest of the nation, I sat and watched as the plane was diverted around the Mediterranean, finally settling in Beirut. Hostages were released at intervals. Then it was reported that one hostage, Robert Stethem, had been shot and his body dumped on the airport tarmac. Thirty-nine passengers remained hostage. I watched as it became a hostage crisis equal to that of the Iranian embassy siege several years earlier.

But unlike that of the rest of the nation, my own horror was not contained inside the TV cabinet. I knew these events would drop like boulders in the Mediterranean, and I wondered what would happen when the resulting ripples reached the dark, shallow water where my father was floating helplessly.

In the midst of all this, Paul and Lori were married. Dad's absence was felt, but we all knew he would be extremely upset if they cancelled the date. 'This is something that can never be repeated when he gets out,' I told myself. What else would he miss? What other events would he have to hear of second-hand?

Early in the TWA hostage crisis, while we were watching the evening news, something grabbed my attention. The news broadcast played a radio transmission from the plane in which I thought I heard that in addition to demanding the release of 700 Shi'ite prisoners held in Israel, the hijackers were insisting on the release of seventeen men imprisoned in Kuwait.

Were these same people holding my father?

I suddenly found myself following the ordeal with even more intensified interest. I called the State Department. They told me that there was no evidence that this hijacking and my father's kidnapping were related in any way. I began to watch closely for any contradiction. How many terrorist groups could be interested in those particular seventeen prisoners?

As documented by the intense news coverage, Nabih Berri's Amal militia took control of TWA 847 away from the original hijackers, who were reported to belong to a more radical fundamentalist group with ties to Iran, Hizb'allah. The passengers and crew were spirited off the plane in the middle of the night and were suddenly hidden in the streets of West Beirut. Reports came out that they had been divided into several groups under the protection of Amal soldiers, with the exception of four navy divers who were still held separately by Hizb'allah.

I had read repeatedly that the Islamic Jihad—who had taken responsibility for my father's abduction—was merely a splinter group of Hizb'allah. I did not think it was entirely unreasonable to suspect we were dealing with the same people, and I couldn't help wondering if those four navy divers were at that moment sharing a room with my father.

Nabih Berri's negotiations continued for the release of the remaining hostages from the plane, and the United States demanded the immediate release of those thirty-nine. Our contact with the families of the other men who had already been held hostage in Lebanon began to increase as we all noticed that President Reagan's administration was avoiding any public mention of the seven other American hostages.

The State Department was insistent that those seven, my father included, had to be treated as an entirely different problem. Quite simply, they would not be part of the negotiations taking place for the release of the thirty-nine. I did try to understand the reasoning. I wanted to believe that they knew better than I, but one thing continued to gnaw at me, just as it disturbed the six families of the other previously held hostages—why was there a refusal by US government officials to acknowledge publicly that other Americans were also being held by terrorists in Lebanon? Why didn't my father and the others warrant the same public outcry that the TWA hostages were evincing?

Through the persistence of some of the other families, the press soon picked up on the 'forgotten seven', as they came to be called. My phone began to ring off the hook again. So trusting in the US government was I still at that time that I refused to grant any interviews. The days dragged on, and the media interest and coverage of events in Beirut only intensified. News media inquiries as to the 'forgotten seven' were still treated separately by the President's staff and the State Department. It was as if the file on those six—now seven—American hostages had the word 'classified' stamped across it, and public comment was prohibited.

I began to wonder why in the negotiations my father and the others couldn't be added. Why did they have to be isolated? As the original hijackers had added to their demands, why couldn't we add to ours? Why couldn't we say that no prisoners in Israel would be released until all Americans were freed?

It suddenly became unacceptable to me for the administration publicly to ignore my father and the other six. Out of loyalty to my father, I felt it imperative I take some action. When I found out that other family members of the 'forgotten seven' were appearing on *Good Morning America*, I agreed to join them. If for no other reason, I felt it necessary to try to pressure the government into giving the same attention to my father as it was obviously willing to give to thirty-nine other innocent victims.

For the first time, I returned an interview inquiry that had been left on my answering machine. But as soon as I had agreed to appear, the reality of putting myself in front of millions of pairs of eyes hit me. I felt sick to my stomach. My hands shook. My thoughts phased in and out like poor radio reception. What if, at the sound of David Hartman's first question, I froze and couldn't speak? I tried to dream up some excuse to cancel, but I couldn't.

At 4:00 am the next morning, Cathy and I sat in the back of a limousine and drove along the empty freeways into LA. I prayed silently for God's help. 'Lord, this is the big time. I don't see any room for error. Please don't let me say the wrong thing. Give me the strength to pull this off.'

We rolled into the studio carpark, and I tried to walk confidently into the building. I was handed a cup of coffee and taken into a room for make-up. From there, I was led on to a small riser and put in a chair with a fake bookcase behind it. A microphone was clipped to my tie, and an earphone was pushed in my ear. The TV camera stood in front of me like a huge, menacing eye.

'You'll be on in a couple of minutes,' the director said. He followed with a few brief instructions. I took a deep breath, trying not to think about the fact that this was 'live TV'. Cathy sat off to the side and offered me a comforting smile. She mouthed the words 'You look handsome.' I wondered how handsome I would look if I threw up, but then the director gave a countdown, the red light on the camera came on, and we were on the air. I was joined by Sue Franceschini, the sister of Father Jenco, and I broke from my instructions and glanced at the monitor when she was introduced so I could put a face to someone that I had only talked to over the phone.

David Hartman directed the first question to me. Although I listened attentively until he was finished, the question went in one ear and out of the other. Only a fraction of a second passed, but I couldn't remember the question! Even so, my responses were so well rehearsed that I launched into my concern that the hostages taken before the TWA incident should receive at least equal status as the thirty-nine that dominated the headlines.

Mr Hartman then went with a question to Sue, who seemed quite at home in front of the camera, before he came back to me. This time, I had a better grasp of his question, but I gave an answer to a question that I thought was more relevant; Hartman had just failed to ask it.

At last the segment ended. As we drove home Cathy remarked, 'You did real well.' I was just so relieved that it was over that I nodded and sat numb all the way home.

In the next few days, the press got behind the 'forgotten seven' in full force and began prodding the administration.

The following Wednesday, 26th June, Secretary of State George Schultz publicly mentioned the seven other hostages for the first time when he said, 'We are working intensely on this matter, and we insist on release of our hostages, all forty-six of them, immediately—unharmed and unconditionally.'

Finally, the Reagan administration had spoken of forty-six hostages, not only of thirty-nine. The other seven were part of the package. The State Department now stated in our conversations that efforts were directed at the release of all Americans held hostage. Having felt a little guilty for going on TV and contradicting the administration, I did another interview with the *LA Times*. I spoke of my optimism at the possibility of Dad's release. I tried to sound supportive of the State Department's efforts.

As I read the news reports from Beirut, it became apparent that Nabih Berri's group was making progress. In one article I read, Berri had indicated that the two Frenchmen kidnapped the weekend before my father was taken—the ones claimed to be held by the same group that had my father—would also be freed. Berri continued that he had no control over the fate of my father and the others but promised to sustain his efforts on their behalf. In turn, the State Department suddenly began to speak 'optimistically' of the possibility of a simultaneous release. I was told by Jackie that things looked 'promising'. I found myself extremely confident that Dad would soon be released, roughly a month after he was taken.

On Friday evening, 28th June, the news broke that the hostages would be released in Damascus the following day. We were all so excited that we spent Saturday just waiting for the phone to ring. I called my relatives to tell them of Dad's probable release that day. However, that call never came, and reports started coming out of Lebanon saying that Hizb'allah had refused to turn over the four navy divers they were holding separately. I grew somewhat anxious because I knew that if they didn't release those four, the chances that they would release my father were nil.

Sunday morning came. The State Department called early to say that it looked like today might be the day. There were reports that the TWA hostages were being put on a bus in Beirut and would soon be on their way to Damascus. There was still no word regarding the others, but the State Department remained optimistic.

A couple of hours later, I received another call from Jackie. 'The bus is due to arrive in Damascus shortly,' she said. 'A televised press conference will be scheduled for twelve noon your time.'

I interrupted. 'Is my father on the bus?'

'We don't know yet. We believe that they will be picked up somewhere in the Bekaa Valley on the bus's route to Damascus. But we won't be able to take a head count until just before the press conference. We still remain hopeful. I'll call you as soon as we know for sure.'

I sat on the couch trying to wait patiently for that call. The clock approached twelve. The network news announced that the hostages had been released. The time of the press conference was drawing near, and I prayed feverishly, 'Lord, make sure he's on that bus. Please.'

At ten minutes to noon the phone rang. I would have knocked over anything in my way to get to it. I heard Jackie's voice. 'We've just confirmed the head count,' she said. 'There's only thirty-nine. Your father is not among those released.'

4
1st–29th July, 1985

'The crisis is over!' the headlines proclaimed.

I watched through the eyes of the network cameras the joyful reunion of thirty-nine hostages and their families in Wiesbaden, West Germany. I continued vainly to look for my father's face in the crowd. I waited hopefully for a break in the coverage that would report the remaining seven American hostages had been released just moments before, but the transmission remained uninterrupted.

I heard the nation breathe a sigh of relief. The country began to celebrate the return of its terrorised citizens. Yellow ribbons hung everywhere in the makings of a national holiday. I wanted to join the celebration, but couldn't. I felt like the only person without an invitation. It was as if I could hear the party raging next door, but I had to be satisfied with placing my ear against a wall.

'The crisis is over!' the anchor-man informed us. The country rejoiced. I looked across the room at the solemn expression on my wife's face. I knew there were six other families like mine, sitting in front of their own televisions, in no mood to celebrate.

I watched Vice-President Bush and several Senators greet the former hostages as they filed off the plane. When he stepped to the microphone, the Vice-President said, 'You are back, and America did not compromise its principles to get you back.'

Before I could stop it, a thought flashed through my

mind. Did they compromise the life of my father and the others? If they had taken a harder line and held out a few days longer, would my father also be on that plane?

Bush continued, 'Friends and neighbours joined to help your families in their terrible ordeal of waiting, showing the best of America.' I looked around my living room. Cathy was the only other person there.

Another negative thought struck me. The government wouldn't have even publicly acknowledged my father's plight if it weren't for the other remaining hostage families' assertiveness in the press. Is that 'the best of America'? Would saving the lives of my father and the other six 'compromise its principles'?

I kept telling myself, 'They tried as hard as they could. They're still trying ... harder than ever.' I had to believe it. All the hope I had of ever seeing my father again rested with the US government.

Early Monday morning on 1st July, I called the State Department again. They continued to give me the impression that there was still some basis for optimism. 'We are pursuing through similar channels intense efforts to gain your father's release. We're doing all we can.'

The press probed the TWA hostages for every detail of their horrendous captivity. How were they treated? What were they fed? Were they ever tortured? Did they think we should bomb Lebanon in retaliation? Could they hear the shot that killed Robert Stethem?

I waited patiently for someone—anyone—to inquire about my father and the others, but I guess in all the excitement and distraction of yellow ribbons and American flags, they had slipped the minds of the media. The vacuum of information about my father remained tightly sealed.

I became desperate and overwhelmed with disappointment. 'Why can't they ask even one question about my father?' I yelled repeatedly at the TV screen.

In the course of the interviews with ex-hostages, one response finally hinted at Dad. Robert Brown, one of the four Americans held separately by Hizb'allah gave a brief description of the place where he had been imprisoned. 'We moved to what we called "the bunker". .... It was a prison. There were actually other prisoners there. We don't know who they were because they kept us blindfolded most of the time.' He suggested they were merely 'petty thieves'. I had a sinking feeling I might have been able to identify one of those other prisoners.

Once the TWA passengers were safely back in America, the news media suddenly remembered the 'forgotten seven'. Ironically, it was the Reagan administration who drew press attention back to us by their talk of possible military retaliation. I was completely dumbfounded. Government retaliation was never mentioned while the thirty-nine were held, but apparently seven hostages could now be acceptably sacrificed to set a new precedent in our war against terrorism.

As a result of American threats, Islamic Jihad delivered a typewritten communiqué countering with a threat of its own. Tit for tat. Should the US retaliate, the seven remaining American hostages would then be executed.

Secretary of State George Schultz showed that he couldn't be bullied. 'We don't respond to threats,' he said. 'We don't deal with terrorists.' I watched helplessly as my father's life was tossed across the table like a worthless plastic poker chip. Then Schultz went on in a campaign-promise style, 'We must think not only of the present, but ... about the future.'

Those words sent chills through me. As far as I could see, the present (the fate of my father and the others) was not even under consideration. When the bombs dropped on Lebanon, how could they differentiate between hostages and captors?

I began to talk with the other hostage families more regularly. Our stiff, frightened faces were like granite cliffs from which the same fears echoed interminably. Why did the US government suddenly refuse to negotiate for hostages when they had just successfully done so? Why had the line been drawn to exclude our loved ones? What number of hostages made it a 'hostage crisis'?

We all heaved a sigh of relief when the retaliatory strike did not happen. However, when the volley of threats quieted, the issue ceased. Within two days, the phone calls stopped. The press lost interest. The plight of the remaining hostages failed to warrant coverage any longer. My father once again became one of the un-mentioned, one of the 'forgotten seven'.

The silence of the next two weeks made me feel as if I was sitting underwater in a swimming pool after dark. The press didn't call. The State Department didn't call. I hadn't heard from the American University in Beirut since before the hijacking. I had no indication of progress from any official channel. We were approaching sixty days of captivity for my father with no immediate resolution in sight.

My family racked its collective brain to develop a course of action. We tried to follow the example of the Jenco family, who met every Monday evening, but that lasted only two or three weeks. We had no idea where to begin. We still had trouble comprehending the most basic elements of the situation. Perhaps if we knew who was holding Dad and what their demands were, we could act on them. Maybe if we knew what the State Department was doing, we could confidently rely strictly on their efforts. Maybe if we had a suggestion or two that would have helped occupy our time of waiting, we wouldn't have been facing only helplessness, depression, and pain.

'Lord, I don't know how much longer I can cope,' I found myself beginning each prayer. 'I don't understand why this had to happen. Dad's a good man. Why should he be made to suffer? How long can he survive?'

With each day of silence from the State Department, it became increasingly more difficult to be satisfied with the thought that they were doing 'all they could'. With each doubt that confronted me, my confidence grew weaker and weaker. In my mind, Uncle Sam was starting to look like a feeble old man who was hard of hearing and showing signs of senility.

I talked to Paul of going to Washington, DC for a briefing. I even mentioned to my contact person, Jackie, that we were considering it. She seemed receptive to the idea, which made me think that an in-depth briefing might be what I needed to restore faith in the government's initiatives. Still, I put off the trip hoping that news of Dad's release would make it unnecessary.

On 14th July an unexpected parcel from Washington, DC finally shattered the deafening silence. The return address on the envelope wasn't however the C street number of the Department of State. Instead, it had originated from the Longworth Building at the other end of the Mall, near the Capitol.

When I inspected the contents I found a copy of the Congressional Record dated 10th July, 1985 and a cover letter from the office of Mervyn Dymally, representative of the Thirty-First District of California. Several days before, I had had a brief conversation with a member of his staff who told me Mr Dymally was interested in generating congressional action on behalf of the hostages. I had not expected such expedient action.

After reading Mr Dymally's letter and the words of those twenty Congressmen transcribed in the Congressional Record of the House, I felt renewed confidence that there were after all people—concerned people, powerful people—dedicated to bringing my father home as quickly as possible.

If the State Department failed to secure my father's release, surely Congress would. If the administration was dragging its feet, I could expect our elected officials to set loose the dogs that would snap at their heels and send them running towards the gate that imprisoned my father and the others.

Soon another unanticipated ally joined the ranks. Jim Quackenbush, a southern California hospital administrator who had known my father for years, felt compelled to make an organised effort on my father's behalf. Suggesting that the American Hospital Association might initiate a humanitarian effort aimed at freeing my father, he had called for my approval. Of course, I had no objection. I appreciated his offer.

Perhaps, I thought, it was possible after all to regain some of the momentum lost after the release of the TWA hostages. For the first time, I saw the value of public support in maintaining Dad's captivity as a US government priority. Without the American public yelling and stamping its feet like wild spectators at a major league ball game, the urgency would evaporate.

When a phone call from Washington several days later invited me to join the other hostage families in the nation's capital, I readily accepted. The time had come to make some noise. I couldn't stand the silence a moment longer.

A group of volunteers from several congressional offices was organising 'Awareness Day' in the United States Congress. I viewed it as a threefold opportunity. One, to continue raising congressional awareness and support; two, to meet personally the other hostage family members; and three, to receive a full briefing by the State Department.

My brother Paul agreed to join me, and we planned to arrive two days before the scheduled events on Capitol Hill to allow a day to meet with State Department officials. I had never spoken to anyone but Jackie Ratner, and I knew she was from the lower ranks of State, so I wanted to meet with the policy makers. Coincidentally, our mother had been planning to spend a couple of weeks in Washington, and she would be there simultaneously.

As we boarded the aircraft, I was filled with apprehension about the entire trip. In the two or three days before we left, I grew more and more irritable, often venting some of my anxiety on Cathy. She managed to suppress retaliatory remarks and remained understanding and supportive.

During our approach for landing, the plane banked up the Potomac River and presented me with a clear view of the Mall from the Lincoln Memorial to the Capitol with the Washington Memorial in between. The nationalistic pride groomed in childhood hit me like an explosion of fireworks, and once we departed the plane at National airport, it was like stepping into a world of red, white, and blue.

Karen White, one of the volunteer organisers that I had spoken to over the phone, was waiting for us. We tossed our luggage in the boot of her car and began our final approach into the capital city. We finally entered a residential district near Rock Creek Park in northwest Washington. Lush foliage, well maintained gardens, and quiet, tree-lined streets were a welcome relief. Paul and I followed Karen up the path to the home of Jerry and Sis Levin. From the pavement it looked as if no one was at home.

Jerry had been a hostage in Lebanon for eleven months until his escape the previous February. Sis had worked hard for his release, once even travelling to Syria to meet government officials. Because of her reception there, both she and Jerry felt that maybe his 'escape' had been allowed to take place by his captors.

Although I had yet to speak to either Jerry or Sis, Paul and I were going to be their guests during our stay. I felt uncomfortable imposing on the hospitality of strangers, and compounding that uneasiness was the news that the Levins would be out of town on the night of our arrival. Two other strangers, as yet unknown and un-named, were house-sitting for them. We discovered a note pinned to the front door signed by the house-sitters. They too were out, but we were invited to enter and make ourselves comfortable. Ben, the Levins' four-month-old sheepdog was our welcoming party. As Karen drove away, I couldn't help but wonder if the Levins had even been informed of the arrival of their new boarders.

The next morning, although the sun was up and the clock read 7:00, it was impossible to convince my West Coast mind that it wasn't really 4:00 am. We showered and prepared for our meeting at the Department of State building on C Street several blocks north of the Lincoln

Memorial. I had been instructed to call that morning to schedule a time for our briefing. Jackie was on holiday that week so I wouldn't have the opportunity to connect a face to her voice; but that was fine—I was there to meet the people above her.

'This is Eric Jacobsen,' I informed the woman covering for Jackie when she had answered the phone.

'Are you in Washington?' she asked.

'Yes. I'm calling to see what time our meeting is scheduled.'

'How about 10:00? Call my office from the lobby when you get there, and I'll come down and take you through security clearance.'

We took a cab from the Levins' and arrived early for our appointment. We used that opportunity to discuss one more time the questions we expected to be answered. I hoped that the only reason they hadn't already been fully discussed over the phone was because of security precautions. Maybe within the protective walls of the State Department we might finally hear of the determined, ceaseless efforts being made by the US government.

Security clearance was easy, but locating the phone in the lobby presented a problem. The security people seemed irritated when I asked; I guess I revealed myself a novice in diplomatic matters. By contrast, our contact person was all smiles as she met us at the metal detectors that marked the gates of the bureaucratic kingdom. Introductions were made, and we followed her under a row of foreign flags to the lift on our way to her office.

'Keeping busy?' I casually remarked.

'Busy? That's not the word for it.' She shook her head. 'We've been working twelve, fourteen hours a day. We don't even take lunch breaks any more.'

Paul and I exchanged glances. *Is she just feeding us a line, or are they really sacrificing their noon meal in an effort to secure Dad's freedom? Was it a directive from above that until all hostages were released lunches would be prohibited?* I had an uneasy feeling in the pit of my stomach, and it wasn't a sympathetic hunger pain.

She introduced us to several secretaries as we made our way into the glass-faced cubicle that was her office. A map of the Middle East and Northern Africa hung on the wall behind her desk. Aside from that, the office was furnished only with four chairs and her desk. She sat behind the desk. Paul and I took the chairs that faced her.

'As it happens,' she began enthusiastically, 'today is the first day for the man who now heads the Lebanese Hostage Operation at State. It's a new position. He'll oversee the entire project. You'll be meeting him shortly. He'll be joined by another gentleman who's also working for the hostages.'

Paul and I nodded in approval. It sounded as if an extremely informative meeting was about to take place.

'Did you have any questions I might. . . .' The phone on her desk interrupted her. 'Citizens' Emergency Center,' she answered. 'Can I help you? Just a second please. . . .' She shuffled through some papers on her desk. 'There is very minute chance of precipitation in Israel at this time of year. . . . You're welcome. Goodbye.'

She put down the receiver and returned her attention to us. 'I'm sorry. Where were we?'

Paul spoke first. 'We were wondering about any new developments in our father's case.'

'It would be best to talk to the other gentlemen about that when. . . .' The phone rang again. 'Citizens' Emergency Center. How can I help you. . . . Yes . . . the average high temperature is 98 and the low 64. . . . Thank you. Goodbye.'

In walked a tall, thin gentleman who was introduced to us as the man heading the Lebanese Hostage Operation. After a quick handshake, he sat in one of the chairs that faced us. He wore glasses of the kind that made it extremely difficult to know where he was looking.

I waited for him to begin with the briefing, but he remained silent. The silence became so uncomfortable that I was forced to ask a question. 'Have we discovered the identity of my father's kidnappers?'

'Specifically?' he asked.

'Yes,' I said.

'No, not specifically.'

'Then do we have *any* idea who they are?'

'It's very difficult to say.'

Our dialogue was interrupted by the entrance of another gentleman who was quickly introduced and joined the briefing. He was a shorter, stockier man. His manner indicated that he may have been closer to the daily operational workings. However, he didn't volunteer any information either, and it was again left to Paul and me to ask the questions.

I began again. 'We were just asking if we have any idea who the people are that are holding my father.' Both men sat silent. I looked from one to the other. 'We were told that we don't know specifically who they are,' I continued. The man who had just joined us nodded in agreement.

'Do we have any idea what the demands are for my father's release?' Paul asked.

The smaller man said, 'No.'

I looked at the head of the Lebanese Hostage Operation for a sign of agreement with that answer.

I turned my attention back to the other man. 'What is the Islamic Jihad?'

'We don't really know for sure. They're a shadowy group with shadowy motives living in a shadowy part of the world. We believe that many small independent groups use the name.'

'So each of the hostages may be held by a separate group?'

'We don't know for sure.'

'There's no one person who's the leader?' Paul asked.

'We just don't know. As I said, they're a shadowy group with shadowy motives living in a shadowy part of the world. They don't seem to want to communicate with us.'

There was another uncomfortable spell of silence before we came up with our next question. 'What steps are being taken by the State Department?'

Again, it was the smaller man who answered. 'We are working through our contacts in the region. I can't tell you details because of the delicate nature of this operation. We wouldn't want to endanger our contacts unnecessarily, nor would we want inadvertently to disrupt any present initiative.'

'We won't tell anyone,' Paul and I said simultaneously.

'I'm sorry, but we can't say anything except that we are doing all we can.'

'Has the State Department drawn up any plans to follow?' Paul asked.

The first man remained unresponsive, but the second fielded the question. 'It's difficult because of the nature of this group and the lack of any solid information.'

I was beginning to understand why this was called a 'briefing'. I sensed our meeting coming to an end, and my next question attempted to encapsulate our discussion. 'So we don't know who's holding my father?'

'No.'

'And we don't know why they're holding him?'

'No.'

'Is there *any* information you can give us?'

'I don't know what there is to tell you. As I've said, they're a shadowy group, with shadowy motives, living in a shadowy part of the world.'

It was like beating a dead horse. We tried to be pleasant as we shook hands and thanked them. It would be lunchtime in an hour. I was pleased to know they would all go hungry.

We stood outside wondering what to do next, then stumbled down 22nd Street towards the Mall in silence. Paul finally mumbled, 'If Dad knew that those were the people in charge of getting him home, he'd cry.'

Involuntarily, we found ourselves at the entrance of the walkway for the Vietnam Veterans' Memorial. We followed the pathway down alongside the black marble wall. I looked at the 59,000 names of those innocent men who had lost their lives. I thought of my dad. I thought of that horrible meeting we had just gone through. For the first time since my father's kidnapping, I cried behind my sunglasses.

5
29th–31st July, 1985

Looking down the Mall, I could see the dome of the Capitol in the distance beyond the Washington Memorial. Heat and humidity rose and stifled us. With no particular destination in mind, we began to walk towards Capitol Hill searching for trees to escape the scorching sunlight.

'Maybe we should find our Congressmen,' Paul suggested.

'Do we know their names?'

'Wilson and Cranston. I don't know who our representative is.'

'I think it's Lungren.'

We found Congressman Dan Lungren's office first, walked in and announced ourselves. It was enough to shake up the receptionist noticeably. A member of his staff met with us, asking a few questions for background information regarding my father and his abduction. Still upset from our morning meeting, we gave a brief, angry account of the 'briefing' we had endured earlier in the day.

I found myself unprepared for the staff member's first question: 'What specifically do you want us to do?' We didn't know 'specifically'. *They* were the professionals. 'Get our father home!' came to mind several times, but all we could do was shrug our shoulders.

We left the office having received a large dose of

sympathy, their commitment to help in any way we might suggest, and a promise to 'personally bring this matter to the attention of the Congressman'.

A dinner was scheduled for that evening at a restaurant in town where all family members could meet and discuss the events of the following day. I called the hotel where my mother was staying to invite her to join us. Paul and I took a cab to pick her up, and the three of us headed back across town to the restaurant.

Most of the family members were already present. I already knew some of the names and voices but very few of the faces. An empathetic attachment and dependence made it feel like a family reunion. Over dinner, the agenda for the next morning was distributed and discussed. I learned a request had been made to meet with President Reagan in two days. I also heard that other families had been requesting a meeting for months, but it had always been refused. The State Department told us we could expect a confirmation or denial some time early the next morning. Under the table, my knees shook at the thought of meeting the President.

I sensed a deep frustration and bitterness among some of the families, especially those whose loved ones had been held for a year or more. The stories of stonewalling by the US government were appalling, and to a new member to this group, quite frightening. Here were people whose trust had been slowly eroded by a wash of silence, apparent inaction and indifference to their needs. Only a brief flash of our State Department 'briefing' earlier that day was required to confirm the validity of their stories in my mind.

Just before our plates were brought to the table, I finally met Jerry and Sis Levin. 'How did your meeting with the State Department go?' Jerry asked.

'It was frustrating. They had nothing to say.'

'Did they tell you why your father is being held?'

'No. They said they didn't know.'

'That's a lie!' Jerry exclaimed in obvious frustration. 'No matter what the State Department tells you, they know the demand for his release. It's the exchange for seventeen prisoners jailed in Kuwait.'

'I've heard that that was the demand before,' I interjected.

'During the time I was held, I had to read a script on video for my captors and state their demand—the release of the seventeen Dawa prisoners. That was the only demand.'

Jerry's wife Sis added, 'Did you know that Ben Weir and William Buckley also made video tapes at the same time? They also had to state the same demand.'

I nodded in understanding, though I had known none of this. It was the first I had heard of any videos. The State Department had never once mentioned the seventeen prisoners in Kuwait. I began to become incensed at the thought of their withholding this information from us, especially today, when I was supposed to have been 'briefed' on all aspects of the situation.

'This morning they told us that they had no idea what the demands were. All they said was that we were dealing with a "shadowy group with shadowy motives living in a shadowy part of the world".'

'They're not being straight with you,' Jerry insisted. He told me of how he was held in isolation for eleven months before his escape, but he was convinced that there were four, maybe five, other men being held in the same house. 'Your father was taken to increase the ransom for a prisoner exchange.'

From each family member that evening, I heard the same thing—the State Department was not forthcoming with even the most basic information. It almost smacked of a 'cover-up'. As long as the US government presented a picture of the hostage captors' unwillingness to communicate their demands and their inaccessibility for negotiations, action was impossible. The State Department could keep the pressure off itself by promoting the idea that these men were kidnapped without reason, that their abductors had then disappeared without a trace.

It turns out I wasn't the only one ignorant of the inarguable demand for the Kuwaiti prisoners. The next morning, our 'Awareness Day' for the United States Congress revealed that Congress too was ignorant. I was shocked to find that not one of the elected officials who attended knew of the demand. It was even more disturbing to discover that several didn't even know that hostages were still being held in Lebanon!

Also in attendance at the congressional meeting was Ambassador Robert Oakley, chief of counter-terrorism at the State Department. It was only through Jerry's persistence that Oakley finally admitted before these Congressmen and the press that the release of those seventeen prisoners was indeed the demand made by the kidnappers.

The whole day proved a rude awakening for Paul and me. When we first arrived at the door of room 2105 of the Rayburn House office building, I was floored by the number of news cameras and reporters. I tried to act nonchalantly in spite of the presence of every major network, local TV, and printed media imaginable. Paul and I were still unknown to the reporters, so it was simple to pass between them inconspicuously. We made our way to the chairs at the front of the room marked with our names.

One of the volunteers who organised the meeting whispered in my ear that the State Department had hinted that we were going to meet the Vice-President the following morning. We would receive a conformation after the round-table discussion had ended at 1:00 pm. I settled into my chair as Mr Dymally opened with a statement.

While the scheduled speakers addressed the audience, I wondered if I should contribute my opinion. When an opportunity arose, I stood up and walked to the podium. I heard myself give a brief but emotional, sometimes rambling plea for the proper sense of urgency. Looking directly into the eyes of the Congressman, I spoke entreatingly. Throughout, my voice quavered and my hands clutched the podium. I knew that much more was at stake than at some speech communications course at the local junior college.

When I sat down, I asked myself, 'What was that all about?' I was convinced it would have been better to have remained silent. Expressing emotion publicly made me extremely uncomfortable. I feared it exposed a weakness that would only hinder attempts to secure assistance.

As the press conference was breaking up, I noticed Paul speaking to a man in a uniform. A few moments later this man approached me. Unlike the others in the room—politicians, staff, press—he moved about as if he was trying to remain inconspicuous. 'He sure acted like he was in a James Bond movie,' Paul would say at a later date. We shook hands, and he introduced himself. 'My name is Oliver North. I work from the White House.'

That was the extent of our conversation, and as soon as he was gone, he was forgotten. He gave no hint of the role he played in efforts to seek my father's release. And if it weren't for the fact that he was one of the few people who sought me out to introduce himself, I doubt I would have even noticed his presence.

After the press conference, Paul and I elected to spend the afternoon at the Syrian embassy. I don't know if we had any substantial reason for doing so, but we knew that the other families had gone there on many occasions, and it appeared appropriate. Syria had played a key role in the negotiations for the TWA hostages and was still the most influential foreign power in Lebanon.

Someone arranged an appointment for us with the ambassador, Dr Jouejati, for early that afternoon. Once again, I found myself walking into a situation I considered way beyond my realm of experience and ability. Who were we to sit and drink Arabic coffee with the ambassador of Syria? What training had we ever undergone in international diplomacy? What could we possibly say to him that would result in my father's release?

My fears were immediately put to rest by his unpretentious and gentle manner. We sat in the embassy's reception room on the couch across from Dr Jouejati and sipped our coffee. He impressed me as being genuinely sympathetic to our dilemma and reassured us that his country was working very hard to secure my father's freedom. However, he suggested that we talk to the ambassador of Kuwait because, he said, the Kuwaitis had the solution in those seventeen prisoners.

As we were leaving, Dr Jouejati brought up the subject of the United States' foreign policy in the region. 'We Syrians respect the United States,' he said. 'We admire America. We send our children here to be educated. We wish to be friends with America, but we are confused by the inequity of your foreign policy. As long as the US unconditionally supports Israel at the expense of other Arab states, problems will exist. All we ask for is equal treatment.'

Before this trip, I had never really considered the political dynamics of the Middle East. But that was now changing. Trying to hide behind ignorance was like standing in front of a lighted window after dark—the light made me visible to the outside, but blinded me from seeing anything beyond my own reflection. I knew I had better educate myself as quickly as possible.

I left the embassy assured that I had avoided any diplomatic blunders. As with everything else that had occurred in Washington, it was always a relief when it was over. The ambassador's assurance of Syria's commitment to the hostages was encouraging to a degree. I had felt no indication of deceit or hostility towards us. I chalked it up as a successful visit. It didn't matter if we were really accomplishing anything. The pace was rapid. We were busy. We were ploughing through a series of small challenges that we felt would eventually overcome the larger obstacle. Paul and I discussed every detail—dissecting, interpreting, and second-guessing as our cab speeded us towards our next stop—Senator Wilson's office.

We phoned first to find out about the meeting with the Vice-President. We were told that the State Department still thought it possible, but that the decision had yet to be made. Everyone was becoming increasingly impatient with the delay. Were they just giving us the runaround until our flights departed from National Airport? Or did the possibility for a White House meeting really exist?

'They're messing you around,' Bob White, Senator Wilson's chief of staff, said when we told him of our inability to confirm the meeting. He immediately called a friend who did the scheduling for the Vice-President but who had no knowledge about a meeting with the hostage families. What little respect I had remaining for the State Department vanished completely.

We left Senator Wilson's office for a dinner with the other hostage families at another restaurant. During our meal, the events of the day were discussed over and over again until they numbed us, and I couldn't bear to think about them any longer.

As we were eating, the word came that we would not get a chance to meet the Vice-President; however, we could meet with the President's National Security Advisor, Robert McFarlane. It was a conditional offer, though; only family members of present hostages could attend—this excluded Jerry and Sis Levin.

Our group was torn between accepting and declining. It seemed obvious that the officials were trying to separate us to lessen our strength. We were leaning towards declining the opportunity to meet with Mr McFarlane in protest of Jerry's exclusion, but Jerry insisted we take advantage of the chance. A call was finally placed accepting the invitation to the White House.

The next morning Paul and I had two appointments before we were due at the White House, and they both fell at the same time. We decided to split up and each attend one: Paul went to see the Lebanese ambassador, and I the ambassador from Kuwait.

As I walked to the door of the Kuwaiti embassy, I wondered how I would handle the question of the seventeen prisoners. I was still unsure in my own mind about asking for their release. After all, they were terrorists convicted of several bombings in which innocent people had died. I decided that I would follow the lead of the Kuwaiti ambassador.

Upon entrance to the building, I was informed that the ambassador was out of town, and I would be meeting with the second man in charge. Like the Syrian ambassador, he was hospitable, sympathetic, and willing to do whatever he could within reason. We were not long into our meeting before the subject of the Dawa prisoners came up. He did not consider that releasing those seventeen convicted terrorists was 'within reason'.

'One must understand,' he told me in a friendly tone, 'that the government of Kuwait is a democracy. We have based our system of justice on that of the United States. These men have been tried, convicted and sentenced just as they would have been in your country. For us to give in to the demands of terrorists and release them would make our system of justice a joke.'

How could I argue with him without sounding like a desperate, irrational, emotionally driven son of a hostage? I racked my brain for a logical suggestion. Nothing materialised.

'Why don't you go to see the Syrians?' he advised. 'They are in control of Lebanon. They could have your father released like that,' and he snapped his fingers.

'I've been to see the Syrian ambassador.'

'And what did he say?'

'He told me to come and see you.'

'As I have told you, we are powerless to help. The Syrians on the other hand are not. They are the ones you should be speaking to.'

Our meeting ended just as it had with the Syrian ambassador with talk of US foreign policy in the Middle East. 'The United States claims to be a democracy in which the majority rules, but the rights of the minority are respected. But your foreign policy for the Middle East is just the opposite; the rights of the minority take precedence over the rights of the majority.'

Sis Levin picked me up as I stood outside the iron gates

surrounding the embassy. We had just about enough time to drive to the White House. As we passed through town, we talked about my meeting. Sis was one who felt passionately about peace through understanding, dialogue and equal justice to resolve the Middle East conflict. She was convinced that it was as a result of this belief that her private efforts had contributed to Jerry's freedom. I listened attentively. Nothing she said contradicted my idea of national values. I began to wonder how democratic and fair our national policy truly was.

Several family members were already waiting at the White House gate when we arrived. Paul and I quickly relayed our respective accounts of the morning between us just as the last of our party showed up. We were notified that it was time to enter through the black iron gate, and we fell into line for security clearance.

As we made our way up the driveway on the White House grounds, we were met by someone I recognised but whose name I couldn't remember. Dressed in a dark suit and tie, he introduced himself as Colonel North, and he led us right into the White House. We were guided through a series of rooms, down a staircase, and through some more offices before we finally ended up in the National Security Council chambers deep in the building.

It was a small, windowless, wood-panelled room with one oblong table surrounded by chairs. Col North ushered us to our seats around the table and offered us each a soft drink. I looked around the room, feeling very nervous.

Two clocks hung high on the wall. One showed Eastern daylight time. The other had a sign under it that read 'Beirut'. *They sure went all out for this meeting*, I thought to myself, trying not to feel insulted by what I assumed had been a hastily hung prop.

Robert McFarlane entered the room with a determined stride. A man of smaller stature than myself, he still seemed to loom above the rest of us. He walked around the table and introduced himself to us one by one. Not a trace of levity was on his face. As I shook hands with him, he stared directly and firmly into my eyes, and I tried to meet his eyes in a friendly way. His look told me this was no social gathering. Strength and purpose seemed to characterise him.

When introductions were complete, he sat at the head of the table and listened patiently as John Weir, the son of the Revd Benjamin Weir, listed our concerns. We wanted a better line of communication with the State Department; we wanted the Reagan administration to make a public appeal to the captors; and, most importantly, we wanted them to put some effort into establishing direct communications with the kidnappers.

As I sat and listened to John, I couldn't but admire him greatly. I knew I could not match the poise and clarity of his presentation. I envied the manner in which he could adapt to talking on such a level. Mr McFarlane must have been impressed, also, for he sat quietly and listened attentively while John spoke.

John continued with our suggestion about the seventeen Dawa prisoners. Most of those tried and convicted were Iraqi, but three were Lebanese. Two of those three were relatives of the Mousawi clan in Lebanon. It was rumoured that our relatives had been kidnapped by members of the Mousawi family for a prisoner exchange. Therefore, we suggested that the US government consider asking Kuwait to release only those two, confident that this would be sufficient to gain the freedom of our loved ones.

When John had finished, McFarlane addressed our points of concern one by one, and then proceeded to speak confidentially on several initiatives presently being pursued, all involving third-party nations. Nothing earth-shattering was revealed. But since we had a chance to question him, and because I was still struggling with the antagonistic approach I had found myself pursuing through the media, I asked what course of action he might suggest the families follow.

'I think you should do exactly as you have been doing,' was his response.

I was stunned, to say the least. I had expected a comment similar to the words the State Department had repeated time and again. Instead of admonishment, we received encouragement. His confidential comments exhibited some trust, unlike those of the State Department. I decided that as long as the National Security Council had a hand in the operation, we had reason for optimism.

The meeting ended as McFarlane left and Col North reminded us of the confidentiality of subjects discussed. He then asked which of us would like to address the White House press corps waiting outside. All but a few decided to do so, and we followed Col North out of the National Security Council chambers to meet the press.

The sky was threatening rain as we stepped out in front of the cameras. Paul and I hung back in the crowd as several others were led to the microphones. The noise and energy among that group of reporters made me bewildered. I felt as if we were throwing several of our own to the lions as the rest of us stood safely by the White House door that would serve as our avenue for a speedy escape. I was extremely grateful that I still had some anonymity.

A sudden, heavy cloudburst brought an end to the questions; and after waiting inside for a minute for the rain to cease, we walked undisturbed out into the streets of Washington. I tried to replay the meeting in my head, but the 'tape' was jumbled. I didn't know what to think.

As our plane lifted off from National Airport, I said a quick prayer for a safe flight home. 'Lord,' I added, 'the next time I return here, I'd sure like to come strictly as a tourist.'

6

28th August–19th September, 1985

'Is this Eric Jacobsen?' the caller had asked.

I was sitting behind my desk at work when the phone rang. I could tell it was a long-distance call by the noise on the line. It wasn't the quality of the connection that made my heart start pounding hard from a flood of adrenalin; it was the quality of the caller's voice—he had a strong Arab accent.

'This is Eric,' I said hesitantly.

His voice, edged with nervousness, only increased my concern. 'Is it your father who is a hostage in Lebanon?'

I paused while I considered my answer. 'Yes . . . who is this?'

'I'm sorry. I cannot tell you my name. But I have some information about your father. You must promise to tell no one of this conversation.'

Nothing would have prevented me from promising whatever he wanted. 'I won't tell anybody.'

A thousand thoughts raced through my head. *Was this one of the captors? How did they get my number? Did they have to torture it out of my father? Was I now in danger of being kidnapped? Was he going to threaten my father's life should I fail to deliver the seventeen prisoners in Kuwait?*

'I am calling you from London,' he began after receiving my assurance. 'It is very important that you tell no one of my call.' I promised him again. 'I want to tell you that your father is all right. He is in good mental and physical health.'

I remained silent, although a myriad of questions jumped in my mind like popcorn.

His next words caught me by surprise. 'My father and your father were imprisoned together in Lebanon. My father says that your father saved his life, and he promised your father he would call you when he was released. He memorised your telephone number and gave it to me to call you.'

'Is my father all right?' I burst out desperately.

'Yes. He is fine. My father says he is a very strong man, and if it were not for him, my father would have died.'

'Is your father safe now?'

'Yes. I am sorry I cannot say any more. You see, I am Lebanese, and my family still lives in Lebanon. If anyone found out that I called you, it would mean extreme danger for my family. Again, I ask you, tell no one besides your family of this call.'

'Thank you. And please tell your father thank you also.'

'Maybe when your father is released we can meet.'

'I hope so,' I said, and before I could ask another question, he hung up.

I jotted down the date and time, and then tried to record our conversation as well as I could remember. After I had finished, I just sat and stared at the tiny piece of scrap paper for twenty or thirty minutes.

During that time, doubts began to cross-examine my memory. *Had it only been a cruel prank? Was it just some nut disguising his voice and calling me from a phone booth a couple of blocks from my office? Was there anything in what the caller said that sounded improbable or out of character with Dad?* Nothing appeared so.

These questions suddenly became irrelevant. I slapped myself on the side of the head when I realised the blunder I had made. How could I have let that guy off the phone without getting more information out of him? Assuming he was telling the truth, his father could help locate where Dad was held. If he would agree to co-operate with the State Department, they could determine the building that served as Dad's prison, and a rescue attempt could be mounted. I belittled myself over and over again. How could I have been so stupid not to have somehow obtained at least a name?

To help cover my own ineptness, the possibility of the call's being a hoax at first regained some credibility. I spent the rest of the day wrestling with cautious, protective disbelief on one hand and the desperate desire to accept the verity of the call on the other. Once, I began to dial the State Department to inform them, but the thought of my 'briefing' just days before, and the probability that the report would be lost in the 'hostage' basket on a cluttered desk made me hang up.

I told Cathy about the anonymous caller that night, and then immediately called Paul. I reported the incident with as much objectivity as possible. Cathy found the news reason for optimism; Paul, as his character would dictate, viewed it with some scepticism. I decided then not to mention the news to anyone else unless something developed from it in the days that followed.

Paul and I talked briefly of our recent trip. In the few days since our return, we had both become convinced that we had received little of substance from government officials, certainly not from the State Department. And even our meeting with McFarlane was unsatisfying. All seemed to be avoiding the most immediate means of bringing matters to the fastest resolution—establishing communication directly with the captors.

I knew how a hostage situation was handled in the States. If someone walked into a corner store and took the cashier and a few customers hostage, the local officials would promptly surround the building and begin negotiating with the hostage-taker. This was the proven, effective way to deal with that type of stand-off. Why couldn't they use the same approach to secure my father's freedom? Paul concluded that our purpose should be to ensure that Dad's problem remain one of President Reagan's highest priorities. If the President was demanding results, an all-out effort would be made.

The days that followed were truly an emotional roller-coaster. The call from London was only the beginning of the slow ascent. The 'slope' steepened when the Kuwaiti newspaper *Al-Siyasah* reported that five American and three French hostages would be released by Syria to steal the spotlight from an Arab summit conference to be held in Morocco. Our elevation soared further with the news that Representative George O'Brien from Illinois would be the first Congressman to travel to Syria to discuss the hostages with President Assad. The press was suddenly asking, 'Where will you be in case a release occurs and we need to get in touch with you?' I tried to remain cautious in my optimism, but failed.

As with any roller-coaster, the descent finally began. The Arab summit conference passed without a hostage release, although rumours persisted. The roller-coaster car banked sharply when I received a copy of a letter via Jim Quackenbush in which the American Hospital Association determined it was inappropriate to take any action on my father's behalf.

> I understand well the concern all who know him have for David Jacobsen, [the letter read. Then the escape clause:] Preliminary investigations in Washington indicate there is more going on to release the seven hostages than appears, and since effort is being expended by thoroughly knowledgeable people, some kind of 'bold and humanitarian effort' might be counterproductive. ...

I was quite angry and yet intrigued by the AHA's refusal to help. To whom had they talked in Washington? Obviously not to the same people I had! How was it that they discovered enough of the efforts underway to cause them concern that they might be 'counterproductive'? Did they really know something I didn't, or was involvement in this issue determined to be politically unsound? My thinking leaned towards the latter.

The roller-coaster rose briefly with the news that UN Secretary General Perez De Cuellar had publicly agreed to assist in securing the hostages' freedom. But a sharp descent began again with another report. Congressman O'Brien returned from Syria with only President Assad's assurance of help. He was unable to discover any more information about the condition or whereabouts of the hostages.

The force of the final wide turn on this roller-coaster ride nearly threw me from my seat—I began to realise just how forgotten the 'forgotten seven' had become. I met a woman whose comments typified those of many when she said, 'I thought all the hostages were released a month ago. What was your father's name again?' The barrier we faced seemed almost impenetrable.

All the hostage families met with the same frustrating ignorance. We agreed on the need to travel again to Washington, DC in mid-September. This time we would submit a formal request in advance to meet with the President. We hoped we could fly to the capital with an appointment already confirmed, one that would remind a few Americans that not all the hostages in Lebanon had been released.

While the majority of the nation had suffered a lapse of memory regarding my father and the others, I learned that there were still a few who remembered. The residents of Hy-Lond Convalescent Hospital in Westminster, the next town north of Huntington Beach, had prayed daily at 3:00 pm for them ever since the time of the TWA hostage crisis. It was touching and comforting to picture these senior citizens remembering my father in prayer every afternoon. And it was even more comforting to know that although months had now passed since the TWA hostages returned, they continued their prayers. If the rest of the nation had forgotten my father, at least these wonderful people had not.

Nancy Fontaine, activities director at Hy-Lond, began to organise a community event co-sponsored by the Westminster City Council and chamber of commerce. It was to be called the 'Freedom Day of Prayer for 7 Not Forgotten Hostages'. I readily agreed to attend, and

as the programme was developing, it was decided that
as many as possible of the other hostage families should
also be present. Air fares and accommodations were
donated, and many restaurants and local businesses
contributed.

On the evening of 29th August, all the hostage families
able to attend flew into southern California. I had just
seen some of them in Washington—the Revd Weir's wife
Carol and their son John, Father Jenco's sisters Mae
and Sue and his brother Joe. Others, such as Terry
Anderson's father Glen, his brother Glen, Jr (or Rich
as he was called) I had not met before. (Terry's sister,
Peggy Say couldn't join them on this trip.) Cathy hadn't
met any of them, so she thoroughly enjoyed the chance.
Unfortunately, Tom Sutherland's, William Buckley's,
and Peter Kilburn's families were unable to attend.

There were a million things to discuss, some of them
repetitious, some not. I was beginning to recognise the
character of each family, almost amused at how different
we all were. Only circumstances such as these would have
brought us together. All of them struck me as good,
down-to-earth people; and all of them offered strength
or comfort in some way or another.

Several hundred people from the community attended
the programme. To experience the proof of concern and
prayer for my father and the others by their presence was
uplifting for all the hostage families. The news cameras
were there in force, and I knew that most of southern
California would indirectly participate later in the day
when they turned on the evening news.

In the brief time we had to meet following the afternoon's activities, we finalised the dates for our next trip
to Washington and drafted a letter to the President formally requesting an appointment with him. This allowed
him several weeks to find a small slot in his busy schedule.
We were confident that an appointment would be granted.

Once the other families boarded their respective flights
home, things went quiet again. Press interest was nil

except for one reporter who contacted me the next week. That report, however, added another dimension to the hostage crisis—in my mind, at least, he had increased the number of the forgotten seven hostages by one.

Unknown to me, Alec Collett, a British subject taken hostage while working for the United Nations in Lebanon, had a son from a previous marriage, David, who lived within fifty miles of us. As I learned, the Colletts were lost in what appeared to be an even greater bureaucratic shuffle than ours.

Alec, who had been a legal resident of the United States for twenty years, had an American wife, Elaine, and another son named Kareem. They still lived in New York City. Elaine had little contact with the British government about her husband. As an American citizen, she had turned to the US State Department only to be told it was strictly a concern of the British. Imagine the bureaucratic nightmare one experiences on an international scale!

I began to make arrangements for the next trip East. Still disillusioned by the last adventure, Paul decided not to come this time. This meant I had to go alone, and I wasn't too thrilled. Our church paid my air fare, and I arranged to stay with the Jenco family at a Catholic retreat house near the Catholic University in Washington.

The Sunday before I was to leave, I was surprised to hear the phone ringing once again. According to an anonymous phone call in Beirut, one of the hostages, the Revd Benjamin Weir, had been released. The press could not locate his wife, Carol, and his family would not confirm the story. The State Department denied his release.

The news media was desperately calling the families of other hostages for verification or denial. As usual, this was the first I had heard of it, and I had to concentrate as much on keeping my excitement in check as I did on responding to the media's questions.

I too attempted to reach the Weir family and I finally did talk to one of their daughters, who told me it was a false report. Like all the other false reports, I quickly pushed it out of my mind before it began to fester. I refused to allow myself to react or dwell on false possibilities. By Monday, the rumours had faded, and the press became quiet.

Early on Wednesday morning I was up packing for my noon flight when the phone rang. Six am marked again the beginning of a press barrage trying to confirm the rumour of the Revd Weir's release. They believed he was already back in the United States being carefully guarded by the government. Again I responded, 'I don't know anything about it, but I hope it's true.'

With some difficulty, I reached the State Department. My contact person, Jackie, was unavailable, and I was forced to speak with an unfamiliar co-worker.

'I was going to call you this morning anyway,' she began the conversation. I waited to hear her inform me that Ben Weir was a free man, but she began to talk about something else.

'Wait a minute,' I interrupted. 'What about these rumours of Ben Weir's release? The press has been calling me all morning.'

My words hit her with so much force that they must have knocked her off her chair. Either she knew nothing of it, or she didn't expect me to know anything. 'I'm sorry,' she said after she caught her breath, 'I'll have to check this out with my superiors and get back to you.'

Each minute that passed was filled with more phone calls, more unknown voices whispering hints of the rumour's validity and teasing me to pick up the phone. I finally did when I heard CBS News say that Carol Weir had been located and had confirmed the story. I lifted the receiver and spoke to the woman. I had heard correctly. Carol had confirmed that Ben had been released the previous Saturday night. After sixteen months, he was once again a free man.

After hearing that, I couldn't wait for the State Department to call me, so I called them again. I told the woman I had spoken to earlier what I had learned from CBS.

'I'm sorry, Eric,' she said, after waiting for me to finish. 'The State Department cannot confirm the reports of Ben Weir's release at this time. If we get confirmation, I'll call you immediately.'

I didn't raise my voice, although I wanted to. I didn't shout obscenities over the line, although several appropriate words came to mind. I managed calmly to replace the receiver despite the fury and frustration that overwhelmed me. I tried to call Carol Weir's number again, but there was no answer.

I went to work hoping to put things in order before I flew out. The thought of postponing or cancelling the trip never crossed my mind. When I arrived at the office, the news cameras were waiting. By nine o'clock it was official—the Presbyterian Church had announced that the Revd Weir had been released the previous Saturday night and was now in Norfolk, Virginia, with his family.

The woman from the State Department managed to track me down at my office. She told me that President Reagan was going to make an announcement at noon that would be of interest to me. I expressed no interest. She didn't tell me any of the details. The Revd Weir's name never came up. To this day, I still haven't received confirmation from the State Department that the Revd Benjamin Weir has been freed by his kidnappers!

With the story of Weir's release, the local NBC affiliate decided to send a reporter to Washington with me to cover the fast-breaking news. I wasn't thrilled with the idea. The trip would be difficult enough without being under constant scrutiny of a TV camera. Although I knew the reporter somewhat from a number of interviews, I didn't want to travel with a stranger. It would mean being courteous, friendly, insightful and accessible. I didn't want to worry constantly about what kind of impression I was giving even in my private moments.

I didn't see my travelling companion when I boarded the plane, and for a brief moment thought maybe her producer had changed his mind. But just before the aircraft doors closed, the reporter ran on and took the seat next to mine. I considered telling her that it was occupied, but I stopped myself. I didn't want to be rude. *Besides*, I told myself, *don't just think of your own comfort. This will mean a lot of coverage in LA, and that can only help Dad*.

Five and a half hours in the air is long enough in a tiny economy-class seat, but briefing a reporter on the minute details of life as the son of an American hostage in Lebanon will make you sicker than eating airline food. She was a nice enough person, but it was too much then. It's like being pestered by a gnat that crawls around your ears, nose and mouth trying to get inside.

When we arrived at National Airport, an NBC film crew was there to meet the reporter, and they offered to drive me to the Catholic retreat house. I'm sure their reason was to know where I was staying as much as to show kindness. But I didn't mind; I had my own hidden agenda as well—I didn't want to spend what little money I had on a cab fare, so I accepted.

Along with my room key, I received a fistful of messages from the press requesting interviews and appearances on early morning news shows. I met the Jencos in the lobby and was warmly greeted. No one had yet been successful in contacting the Weirs, so information was extremely sparse. The only news we had was that the Revd Weir was coming to Washington for a press conference in the morning.

My sleep was light and often interrupted by 'false alarms'—was it time to get up?—and persistent questions. Finally only one dominated my thoughts. What would the Revd Weir know about Dad?

The next morning the families gathered before the Revd Weir's press conference at the National Presbyterian Center. Two new families were present: Elaine Collett had flown down from New York; and Jean and Kit Sutherland, the wife and daughter of Tom Sutherland, had come from Colorado. Others in our group with whom I was beginning to feel familiar were Peggy Say, Sis and Jerry Levin, and the Jencos.

I drove with Sis and Jerry to the National Presbyterian Center, all of us nervous and excited about what Ben might reveal. Every pew was full, and what looked like thousands of TV cameras stretched across the front of the church. Someone ushered me down the aisle to a pew reserved for the hostage families.

While I waited, I closed my eyes and began to pray, 'Father, I don't know what to expect, and I promise I'll try not to be disappointed, but please, please, give me some word about Dad. I don't expect to see him suddenly walk out with Ben Weir, but I need to know that he's alive.'

The room grew suddenly silent, and I opened my eyes. In walked John and Carol Weir, and I knew the man with them was Ben. He looked in remarkably good health in spite of being held hostage for sixteen months. He wore a beard which considerably altered his appearance from the picture that I had always seen in the papers. I could see no sign of physical abuse, which relieved some of my fears.

He sat down and read a brief statement which filled in some of the unknowns but made no mention of my father and the others beyond the need to 'focus continuing concern for the immediate release of the remaining six [American] hostages'. Again, I was relieved to discover that he appeared to be mentally sound and especially lucid.

He had been released before midnight the previous Saturday, but because he was told of the possibility of another hostage's release, he went into seclusion. When it was apparent that no others were coming out, they decided to announce and confirm his freedom.

The church was silent except for the hum of television cameras and the scratching of pencils. In what was to remove all doubt about the demands for the release of the hostages, Weir stated, 'The message I have received from my captors is the following. They have one demand, namely, the release of seventeen prisoners being held in Kuwait.'

He continued with his captors' instructions, saying, 'They are prepared to work out the details of the exchange, which can be done without publicity. They have released me as a sign of their good intentions. However, they are not willing to wait much longer. They believe the US government has been unwilling until now to negotiate a settlement even though they believe various options are possible. They ask the US government to put pressure on the government of Kuwait to release their prisoners. . . . They state that if there is not a positive response to their demand in the near future, they are prepared to kidnap other Americans; and that though they do not wish to harm anyone, they will go so far as to execute their hostages if their demand is not met. . . .'

There it was—the word 'execute'. Just its utterance from the mouth of an ex-hostage made me cringe. Although no mention had been made of my father, it was his head in the noose that flashed in my mind. I looked at Peggy Say, Jerry Levin, and the others. We all wore the same expression of terror.

'I personally believe this appeal from my captors should be taken seriously,' Weir continued. 'I am aware that US government officials are concerned for the safety and welfare of the remaining six hostages. I urge that new efforts be made and that new and creative options be explored for negotiating their release.'

His statement ended, and the press conference was turned over to questions and answers. I didn't know if I was allowed to ask anything, so I sat in silence with the other families. It took only three questions from the press before someone asked the one we all I wanted to hear. 'Do you know anything about the whereabouts or the safety of the other six?'

My heart-rate seemed to drop to a single beat per minute as I listened to Ben's answer. 'I have, from time to time, met four of the other hostages, and in recent months been allowed to talk with them, even to worship with them on occasion. And they are all well.'

A silent voice was screaming in my ear, 'Which ones?!'

'And how recently?' the reporter pursued.

'I saw each of the four—I'm speaking now of Terry Anderson, David Jacobsen, Thomas Sutherland, and Father Lawrence Martin Jenco. I saw them on the day of my release.'

If I have ever come close to fainting in my life, it was at the moment that I heard my dad's name. *Thank you, Lord!* I sat rigid and expressionless, silently repeating over and over, 'Thank you, Lord!'

I don't know how much time had passed before I looked at Peggy. She was crying. My eyes moved to the Jenco family. They too were hugging and shedding tears. I didn't know where Jean and Kit Sutherland were, and while I looked for them, my eyes came upon Elaine Collett. My heart sank. Why were only four mentioned? Why couldn't we have had some news about Alec? . . . and Peter Kilburn? . . . and William Buckley?

Fifteen more minutes passed with questions and answers before the press conference was called to an end. Ben and his family were escorted through the door at the side of the altar. The press swarmed upon the hostage families to record our reaction, but we pushed our way forward towards the front of the church, more interested in following Ben.

We gathered near the door through which Ben had gone and milled about impatiently until it opened again, inviting us into the room where he was waiting to meet us. A few members of the Presbyterian Church were present, and I waited as patiently as I could just to shake his hand and introduce myself.

A few minutes, disguised as an eternity, passed before I finally had the chance. I felt as if I had been hit by a tranquiliser dart, and the drug was now taking effect. The unexpected news had left me ready to drop to the floor and convulse into unconsciousness. Although I had prayed for some news of Dad, I was not prepared to receive it.

When I finally stood facing Ben, we embraced warmly. I tried to look into his smiling eyes for some glimpse of my father—some indication for his health and condition. Ben reached into his jacket pulling out a small white envelope that had 'The Jacobsens' written on it and handed it to me. At first, I thought it might be an invitation or a thank-you note; then I realised what it truly contained.

I went to a quiet corner of the room and found a chair. My hand shook noticeably even to myself as I opened the envelope and recognised the handwriting on two six-by-eight-inch pieces of lined paper. I began to read silently:

September 14, 1985

Dear Eric, Cathy, Paul, Lori, and Diane,

Greetings in the Lord's name to everyone and especially Kerrie [his friend in Texas], Dad, and my family. Pastor Ben Weir is being released tonight. If I and the other hostages are to be released, the seventeen men held by the Kuwaiti government must be released. That is the only condition for my release.

Please contact all the politicians—your representative and Senators Wilson and Cranston. Telephone, write to them, pester them. Have others write letters. ... My release is dependent on public pressure on the US government. Believe me, those who believe in quiet diplomacy would change their philosophy after a day of captivity.

I am being well treated. There is no torture or physical abuse.

I am with Tom Sutherland, Father Lawrence and Terry Anderson. We have church services twice a day. Also plenty of time for exercise.

My dearest family, I love you very much. Please love one another. Take care of Kerrie and provide for her needs. She is very special to me and her bringing me to the Lord has made it possible for me to survive.

God bless all of you. Please reassure Dad that I will be home soon. Encourage him to write his book. In regards to money, the AUB should be sending you my monthly salary. The first cheque should have been for May. If they are not doing it, contact them in New York.

Please don't worry about me. My captors are kind to us and want us to go home, but they demand that their friends be released from Kuwait. Please impress this on the US government officials. Again, have faith in God and pray for me and the safe release of my fellow prisoners.

I have only a few minutes to write this letter, so my thoughts are not organised. Remember that I love you very much. Help one another in every way possible. May God bless you and keep you. May his face shine upon you and give you peace. May God hold you in the palm of his hand until we meet again.

Again, it is vital to tell the government of the conditions of my release. Be forceful with them. If the US can exchange prisoners with Russia, we certainly can be exchanged for the seventeen prisoners in Kuwait.

If you have problems with AUB New York, telephone Joe Cicippio of the AUB in Beirut. He is my friend and he will help you.

Oh, time is short to write. I think of all of you constantly. I am in the best spirits possible under the circumstances. My health is good. ...

God bless you,
All my love,

Dad

I was in a state of emotional catatonia when I finished reading. I had come that morning with the simple hope that the Revd Weir might have a tiny bit of information regarding my father. To discover that he had actually seen him, and then delivered a letter from him, was almost too much good news to digest. From the day that my father was kidnapped, I had attempted to prevent my emotions from surfacing, and now they all rushed forward unrestrained with such force that I could not react; I was numb.

It was the first concrete evidence we had that my father was alive. In spite of the obvious haste in which the letter had been written, I could see that Dad was holding up well. It said little about the conditions of his captivity, but the fact that he was not being tortured brought me tremendous relief.

The press was waiting outside the door to record our reactions to our meetings with Ben. It was arranged that we would have some private time with him in the afternoon to speak specifically about our relatives. He would leave by another exit, and we would go out to meet the news media.

I was in too much of a state of shock to answer questions, so I stood to the side as the Jenco family read the letter they had received. The press was pushing in on us like a mudslide. All that prevented us from being suffocated was a small red rope barrier stretched across the corridor where we stood. I stood near Elaine Collett on the edge of that writhing mass of reporters and camera crews. The attention was focused completely on the Jencos, and I turned just in time to see one cameraman hit Elaine on the head with his camera. He offered no apology and pushed his way around to his right, struggling for position. *These people are animals*, I thought to myself.

For the first time that day, I saw the reporter who had travelled with me. She motioned me to walk over to her. As I got just close enough so we could talk, I heard a male voice shout at me, 'Hey!' he yelled. 'Get out of my way!'

I felt something snap inside me. I had already taken two steps towards him and sworn at him before I realised what I was doing. The morning headlines flashed through my mind—'Hostage's Son Goes Berserk and Kills Cameraman'. Just in time, I regained enough control to turn my attention back to the reporter from Los Angeles. She had walked around to the side of the jumble of cameras and microphones. I tried to act perfectly composed, although I knew she must have witnessed my fury.

'Did you get a letter also?' she asked.

'Yes.'

'Can I see it?'

'No.'

She looked puzzled. 'Why not?'

'Because I think my family ought to be able to read it

first and not have bits and pieces of it read to them over the television. This is all we've got of my dad, and I don't want to depersonalise it.'

'When can we see it?'

'I don't know ... after the rest of my family has seen it.'

'Are you going to call them today and read it over the phone?' she persisted.

'Probably ... my wife and my brother maybe.'

'Could we see it after you call?'

I had to work especially hard to control my already aroused temper. Fortunately, I was able to respond with a calm, 'No.'

'Can you tell me basically what it says?'

'I really don't want to talk about it until my family has seen it.'

'You don't have to quote from it. Maybe you could just tell us what it says.'

'Listen,' I struggled to keep my voice from rising, 'I promise that after my family reads it, you will be the first to see it. OK?'

The interview was over, and we were now all shuffled through another exit and into a car on our way to eat lunch before we were to meet with Ben again an hour or so later. Some of us exchanged our letters looking for any references to our loved ones or further details about the conditions of captivity. Others wanted to keep theirs completely private.

Not surprisingly, my private meeting with Ben seemed far too short. I wanted to hear every detail, no matter how insignificant it might seem. Ben told me how, early in July, he and Father Jenco were first brought together, then Tom Sutherland. At the same time, my dad and Terry Anderson were in one of the adjacent rooms. Initially they were brought together to worship once a week or so, and as time passed the frequency increased until it finally reached the point that they were all being kept in the same room.

The leader of the kidnappers now had a name—the Hajj. A week before Ben's release, the Hajj had entered their cell and told them he was going to release one as a good-will gesture; they were to decide who. Ben said the vote came down to Terry Anderson, because he was a journalist, and my father, because he had experience dealing with the public and the press. But when the Hajj returned on the night of Ben's release, he overruled the hostages' vote and selected Ben Weir.

To be truthful, I can remember few details of my conversation with Ben that afternoon. He told a few anecdotes of my father that reflected my father's character in such a way that I knew they had truly been locked up in a room together. He avoided discussing any details of where they were held except that it was hot, and they wore nothing but their underwear. He assured me that the most difficult part of the captivity was boredom. It didn't matter what I was told; everything made me feel elated.

One statement of my father's that Ben did relay to me overshadowed all else I heard from him. While in captivity, Dad had told Ben, 'I have no faith that the US government will get me out of here. It will be up to my sons, Eric and Paul.'

Those words would haunt me for nearly the remainder of his captivity. They produced a sudden metamorphosis of my sense of duty into an obsession that insisted every waking moment be devoted to his freedom. I was ready to rise to the challenge. Dad had put his confidence in me; I could not fail him.

Not anticipating the Revd Weir's release, our volunteers had organised a series of meetings for that afternoon. Obviously my private time with Ben Weir took precedence over meetings with any Congressman. As a result, I completely missed the first appointment, and although I knew I would be slightly late for the second, I raced across the Mall on foot to the congressional office where the meeting was to take place.

When I arrived, I was informed that I was the first and only hostage family member who had showed up. No one had called to explain, and as far as the Congressman was concerned, the meeting was cancelled. I felt horrible. I knew how valuable his time was, and I should have thought enough ahead to have someone call. I asked the receptionist if I could have just enough time with the Congressman to apologise. She called into the inner office, and he agreed to meet me shortly.

Meanwhile, I took a seat that was up against a portable room partition. I could hear clearly the voices of some of the office staff working just out of sight behind me. Their proximity was unfortunate for them, and for me. Apparently, the failure of the hostage families to keep their appointment was the talk of the office, and two young aides found the subject quite amusing.

'Those hostages are getting exactly what they deserve,' one said.

The other laughed, 'What were those idiots doing in Lebanon in the first place?'

I was up out of my chair and around that partition before I knew what was happening. 'One of those men you're calling an idiot happens to be my father.' I could feel rage colour my face, but my tone remained low. 'I've got enough to deal with without having to listen to a couple of stupid jerks like you.'

I turned to the receptionist. 'I'll be waiting outside.' I stormed out into the corridor. I was so angry I considered punching a hole in the corridor wall of the Rayburn House office building.

'You've got to get control of your anger,' I told myself as I leaned over a drinking fountain. 'Twice today, it's got away from you.' I took a deep breath.

I stood up straight after I finished my drink and found the two staff aides standing next to me. 'We're really sorry,' they each apologised. 'It was a stupid thing to say.'

'Don't worry about it,' I heard myself respond. 'Let's not discuss it any more.'

When I walked past the receptionist, she joined in with an apology, 'I'm really sorry. They'll be properly reprimanded.'

'That's not necessary,' I replied. 'To be honest, I don't want to think about it any more.'

Before I could take my seat, the Congressman walked through a door into the outer office. We were introduced, and I tried to offer an explanation for our bad manners and rude behaviour. There seemed to be no hard feelings on his part.

I did, however, encounter plenty of hard feelings when I once again met up with the other hostage families. In spite of several weeks' notice, no decision had yet been made regarding a presidential meeting. We wanted it, especially now that Ben Weir was free. My father's letter flashed in my mind. 'My release is dependent on public pressure on the US government. ... Be forceful with them.'

The meeting with President Reagan was denied. Instead, we were to meet with Vice-President Bush. We had nothing against Bush, but we were all very disappointed. Disappointment grew to anger when we were informed that only family members of remaining hostages would be allowed. Not only did this exclude Jerry Levin as it had the month before, but Ben Weir and his family were not invited to attend either.

We took a vote around the dinner table; it was unanimous—we would boycott the meeting. The White House offered a compromise—Ben Weir was allowed; Jerry Levin was not. Another vote for boycotting followed, but Jerry once again convinced us otherwise. 'It's too important to miss because of my exclusion,' he insisted. We took another ballot and reversed our decision.

I rode with the Jenco family back to the Catholic retreat house. The lobby was crowded with newspeople when we arrived, and I picked up a handful of messages scribbled on pink paper from the front desk. Several associate producers from the morning news shows scrambled after us to convince us to do their particular show first the following morning. When the Jencos agreed, I did too. Anything to get to bed before midnight, even though it meant setting the alarm for 5:00 am.

All I wanted to do was call Cathy. I needed someone to restore my balance. Her voice was enough to soothe my frayed nerves. I read her the letter and asked her to call the rest of the family. She seemed a very long way away that night.

I took the lift up to my room on the men's floor. The room was small with only a bed, a table against the wall, and a basin. The bathroom was across the landing. I looked at my watch; it was approaching midnight. Now the thought of getting up at five made my stomach feel queezy. As I undressed, I longed to be home and in my own bed.

I pulled Dad's letter out of the inside pocket of my jacket but didn't read it for a while; I just stared at it. I couldn't believe the whole situation. Was I really sitting in my underwear in a tiny room in Washington, holding a letter from my father who was also sitting in his underwear somewhere in Lebanon? Was I really going to meet the Vice-President of the United States tomorrow afternoon? How did I ever get tangled up in an international hostage crisis? Was there any reason or logic behind any of this?

'Lord, if this world spins any faster, I won't have the strength to hang on. What's the purpose for all this? This is chaos. This is utter anarchy. Could you possibly have a plan?'

The moment I uttered those words, it was as if I finally discovered the answer to a riddle that had been teasing me for months. A seed was dug up and replanted. My perspective was instantly altered. I read over my father's letter again; '... the Lord has made it possible for me to survive. ...'

I tried to review all the conversation with Ben Weir earlier in the day; '... We were brought together by our captors to worship ...', 'We were given a Bible to read.' I suddenly remembered the story that Jerry Levin told of how he came to know the Lord Jesus while he was a hostage. The clues continued to fall into place.

I was shocked. *Why had it taken me so long to realise this?*

What was the one link in an otherwise chaotic, irrational, unexplainable mess? What was the only imaginable good that I could perceive that would justify my father's captivity? Would the Lord have given me the strength to endure this hardship without a further promise of his grace and protection? God had a plan—I was convinced of that. His presence was easily identified as soon as I began to look for it.

Once I believed that my father's captivity was not simply a random, meaningless act of human violence, but could possibly be an integral part of a divine plan in which the Lord was using us for his good, many of my fears were dispelled. Under God's protection, I knew unquestionably in my heart that Dad would some day walk out of Lebanon. I also understood that I could have no idea how long it would take for his plan to unfold. He was asking me to be patient. He was inviting me to be confident.

I thought back on the past four months. I was shocked with myself. I had not viewed God as an active participant, but rather as a referee in a world-wide wrestling match. I had ignored his real presence. He had been merely a sounding-board for me, not a companion. I could see that now. The Lord was my ally. I was an active participant in his plan. He already knew the outcome. Who better to have on my side?

As I crawled under the sheets and turned out the light, my brain was still lit by the electricity of racing thoughts. I felt I had been issued yet another challenge, another riddle, another test. The question was simple: What *was* God's plan?

PART 2
Headlines and False Signs

*... Part of it fell on rocky ground where it had little soil. It
sprouted at once since the soil had no depth, but when the sun rose
and scorched it, it began to wither for lack of roots ...*
Matthew 13:5–6

7
20th September–2nd November, 1985

'It's through this administration's efforts over the past eighteen months that the Reverend Weir is here with us today,' Vice-President Bush said confidently from a chair in his office.

I looked at Ben Weir and then to the other hostage families present in the room. Did anyone believe that statement any more than I did? I glanced back over my shoulder at Robert McFarlane, Col Oliver North, Ambassador Robert Oakley from the State Department, and half a dozen other members of the White House staff. They sat expressionless, like stone figures draped with dark suits.

'Exactly how was that accomplished?' someone in our group asked.

The Vice-President shifted in his chair. 'I can't say, except that we are responsible for his being here. You'll just have to believe it.'

It would have been easier to believe in Santa Claus at that moment. I glanced once again at the other hostage families. They didn't look any more convinced than I was. Our expressions joined in a resounding chorus of 'Nice try, Mr Vice-President'.

I had walked into the old executive office building adjacent to the White House with my private agenda focused on three points. The comments of the Vice-President now threatened to divert me from them.

I quickly ran down the list in my head. One, it was imperative that the US government attempt to establish direct communication with the captors. Two, steps needed to be taken immediately to correct the lack of communication from the State Department. And three, the US should consider exploring new and creative initiatives, including those involving the seventeen prisoners in Kuwait.

I wanted to avoid any emotional outbursts, petty arguments, or appeals for pity. I wanted to maintain a sense of business-like decorum. It was the only way to ensure we would walk out of our discussion with Vice-President Bush feeling that a truly constructive meeting had taken place.

Unfortunately, it didn't happen as I would have hoped. The meeting deteriorated into the families rehashing the same frustrations, the same gripes of non-communication, and the same accusations of inaction that we had all previously aired in the media. The ninety-minute dialogue could have easily been condensed into fifteen seconds without sacrificing one iota of pertinent information.

I'm sure George Bush didn't hear anything he hadn't already heard or read. I know Bud McFarlane and Ollie North certainly didn't. With one significant exception, I definitely didn't.

The one exception came in response to someone's question: 'Would the US government be willing to talk directly with the captors?'

'Sure,' Bush replied. 'We won't negotiate with them, but we're always willing to talk.'

Upon hearing that, I felt a silent but significant victory for our side. For the first time, the administration did not simply repeat a one-line script that read, 'We don't deal with terrorists.' It could have been a blunder on Bush's part, or a premeditated adjustment in policy. Either way, it sounded to me as if a concession might have been made.

Was the US now willing to take the measures necessary

to end the captivity of our relatives just as they had for the hostages in Iran, TWA 847, and on the Achille Lauro? Had I just witnessed a change in policy that would still protect the government's public image of strength and inflexibility in dealing with terrorists, but would actually allow them to seek the release of my father and the others? Probably not. Still, the Vice-President had said they were now willing to talk, and I was going to quote him on that.

When our meeting ended, we were escorted out to face the White House press corps, and on this occasion, I was one of the reluctant family members to find himself standing in front of the microphones. Bombarded by the sound of a couple of dozen reporters yelling questions simultaneously at the top of their lungs, I felt it crucial to concentrate on Bush's willingness to talk with the captors.

With each question that came my way, I tried to turn the answer into a reiteration of that point. After a couple of minutes, one of the reporters yelled, 'Get somebody else up to the mike!'

In the private interviews that followed as we walked through the White House gate back on to the street, I stressed and stressed again the importance of the Vice-President's statement. If it had been a blunder, I was determined to make it as difficult as possible for the administration to disavow it by 'clarifying' the statement at a later date.

As it turned out, I was correct in my predictions. The next day, the White House denied that there was any change in policy. They were still not willing to negotiate. Talk maybe, but never negotiate. A day later, the comment 'We don't deal with terrorists' was replaced for ever by 'We will talk with anyone, anywhere, at any time regarding the hostages, but we will never negotiate or make concessions.' It was a game of semantics, and we were scoreless.

The meeting was not a total failure. The US did make a concession in their war on terrorism. Not to the terrorists, but to the hostage families. Jackie, our contact person at the State Department, was replaced almost immediately by a man named Doug Jones. I don't mean to imply that communication between hostage families and the State Department improved drastically simply because of the change of our contact person, but this change in personnel did mark a shift in policy; from then on, we were to receive weekly update phone calls, regardless of how sparse new information was. Even rumours, not just 'confirmable facts', would be relayed to us.

Unlike the guidelines within which Jackie had worked the new job required the contact person to befriend us as well as to be a loyal State Department employee; an intermediary *and* a buffer zone between the families and the US government. I can't think of a more thankless job, but Doug Jones, and his replacement a few months later, John Adams, handled it admirably with understanding, compassion, and respect. It's regrettable that this change of policy hadn't occurred earlier— I know I would have had a better relationship with Jackie had she not been so restricted by policies and procedures.

When I flew out of Washington, the day after our meeting with Bush, I was unaware of this adjustment in policy. I just wanted to get home to my wife. I was so emotionally exhausted that I found it difficult to form complete thoughts. I was left staring out of the window at a blanket of cumulus clouds filled with the shadows of a setting sun.

The NBC TV reporter sat doggedly next to me, still trying to pinpoint the exact time and date of the availability of my father's one letter. To settle the question and end the interrogation, I promised again that her station would be the first to have access to it once my family had seen it. That seemed to calm her fears that it would end up in the hands of one of her competitors. The press was, I thought, becoming very predictable. I finally understood what editors deemed to be 'newsworthy'.

Scooping the story topped the criteria. Sensationalism was essential. Straight hard facts made bad copy. The press needed a 'hook', whether it be a letter carried out by an ex-hostage, or a flood of tears by an emotional family member.

Although I honestly wanted my family to read the contents first before making it public, I also knew that we might be able to drag out the coverage a couple of days longer by waving the letter in front of their noses. We might get five days' press interest instead of two. Who knew how long it would be before anything else 'newsworthy' came out of Lebanon?

Back home, it took me several days to recuperate, then I began to think more and more about the nature and particulars of God's plan. I knew a plan existed; it became a challenge to discover the details of it.

The spiralling cycle of violence in the Middle East became a recurring concern. Under the influence of the other hostage family members and the events in Washington, I began to look to that for my solution to the riddle of God's plan. I suppose I wanted to believe that it was of a much larger scope than merely the spiritual growth of six American families.

Statements from the Islamic Jihad fell under a different light. I saw the references to America as the Great Satan. I heard through Ben Weir of the captors' confusion and anger at the United States' military intervention in Lebanon and at our unconditional support of Israel. When Israel bombed Shi'ite communities in Lebanon, the captors saw that the bombs fell from planes made in the USA.

I began to dissect the events of the TWA hijacking, and tried to understand the mindset of my father's captors and that of the rest of the Shi'ites in Lebanon. Altogether, forty-six hostages had been held. Israel held 700 men without formally charging them of any crime. In the minds of the Shi'ites, those 700 men were also hostages. I wondered if perhaps the hijackers weren't the only ones guilty of kidnapping. The United Nations had said Israel was in violation of international law. Prior to the TWA hijacking, even the United States had publicly objected to the illegal detention.

The more I thought on the matter, the more it seemed apparent that there were no completely innocent parties in the Middle East conflict. All sides were victims, and all sides were victimising each other. And of course, all sides were shouting about their own injuries while refusing to acknowledge or discuss the injuries they inflicted upon their enemies.

Was the Lord asking me to speak out on this? Was this a part of God's plan for us? Was the Lord asking me to speak to other Americans about the root causes of Middle East terrorism?

I prayed, 'Lord, I know I'm as ignorant as the next guy when it comes to the problems in the Middle East. But if it's your plan that we speak out about injustice and use our position as hostage family members to bring this to the attention of the American people, I just ask that you give me direction. I'm ready to do whatever you say.'

I decided I would join ranks with the Levins and the Weirs and start publicly addressing the need for peace in the Middle East through understanding and equal justice. I remembered the words I had heard at the Kuwaiti embassy: 'The United States claims to be a democracy in which the majority rules but the rights of the minority are respected. Your foreign policy is just the opposite; the rights of the minority take precedence over the rights of the majority.' Maybe all sides would benefit if we refrained from favouritism.

Piecing together the puzzle of God's plan, and reflecting on the TWA hostage ordeal, led me to another startling conclusion—my father's captors were watching everything that the media reported on the Middle East, especially those things directly related to the hostages. I was convinced that my public comments were being scrutinised by the men who held my father. Everything I said in the press suddenly carried even more weight.

Now that I thought I understood God's plan, my commitment to my father was greater than ever. I knew that the last trip to Washington had changed my style and approach immeasurably. Seeking his release had now become a full-time job.

Cathy understood when I told her I needed to devote more hours to Dad's cause. The only way that would be possible was if the role of wage-earner were reversed. She agreed to increase her hours from twenty to forty a week and allow me to decrease mine. It would mean less money, but we hoped that the additional hours I could put in would resolve the issue in less time.

My boss didn't protest too much when I told him I wanted to cut my hours in half. We both knew that I was spending more and more time on the phone on personal calls, and there were days he was chased out of his own office by camera crews. For the previous month or two he had been paying my full salary while I devoted as much time to my father's business as I did to his. Reducing my hours and hiring someone to assume some of my responsibilities at work seemed the only satisfactory solution.

At the end of September, four more foreign hostages were taken in Lebanon. For the first time, Soviet citizens fell victim to terrorist kidnapping. Their captors demanded a halt to Syrian (and therefore Soviet) backed offensives against Sunni Muslim forces in Tripoli. Two days after those four disappeared, one reappeared, shot dead. Threats of further executions coincided with the discovery of the body.

Suddenly, the message of possible executions that Ben Weir brought back from his captors held new potency. My confidence in Dad's safety was shaken considerably. Even as these alarming events unfolded, yet more violence was erupting. Israel bombed the PLO headquarters in Tunis and sixty Tunisians and Palestinians were killed. The initial response by the Reagan administration was to condone the bombing.

'Please, Lord,' I prayed when I had heard the news,

'don't let this be the reason that Dad's captors begin to follow through on their threats. If it furthers their resentment and hate towards the US, please don't let them retaliate through Dad.'

A couple of days later at 4:00 am, the phone rang and a reporter's voice confirmed my worst fears. 'Has the State Department called you yet about the latest report from Beirut?'

'No.'

'Islamic Jihad has claimed to have executed one of the hostages—' he paused to read the name, and my heart stopped. '—William Buckley.'

'Have they found a body?'

'No. There's only a blurred photograph showing his corpse, and there's no positive ID yet. The message accompanying the photograph says he was executed in retaliation for Israel's bombing of Tunis. Do you think Israel was wrong?'

Why did I feel as though I was being questioned as if I was an expert on Middle East politics? 'I think any act of violence is wrong,' I answered. 'And every act of violence that takes place in the region will at least indirectly have a negative effect on my father's situation. That's all I want to say. Thanks for the information.'

I lay awake the rest of the night wondering how long it would be before the call would come telling me that Dad had, too, been used to even the score. Although it was reported in the press that William Buckley had no known living relatives, while I was in Washington the last time, I thought I'd heard one of the other hostage families say that he had a sister somewhere in New England. I prayed for her and for any other family he might have had that I wasn't aware of. I tried to calm my own fears, the same fears that first appeared when Ben Weir had mentioned executions. This time it didn't work.

'Father,' I prayed desperately, 'please protect Dad. I know you have a purpose in all this, but I can't deal with it if, in your plan, Dad has to die. . . .' Part of me knew I had to accept the possibility. Part of me would not accept it.

I saw the picture the next day. I didn't know if it was William Buckley or not, but one thing was indisputable, the man was dead. He was wrapped in a burial shroud. His eyes were open and lifeless.

Anger began to flood my senses. I realised that if Dad was killed in captivity, it would probably be in retaliation for some other stupid act elsewhere in the Middle East. The cycle of violence would not abate. Whichever party indirectly pulled the trigger would never consider how far the bullet would travel.

Within days after the Tunisian bombing, related violence crossed the Atlantic Ocean and displayed itself within miles of my own home. In Santa Ana, a city only a few miles east of Huntington Beach, a bombing took place at the Arab-American Anti-Discrimination Committee offices. Alex Odeh, an executive in the organisation, was killed in the explosion.

The previous night Odeh, the man who had opened the office door that triggered the bomb, had made pro-Palestinian remarks in a TV interview about the bombing of Tunis. Someone had silenced him for ever. This news sent a chill through me when I realised that Middle East terrorism was no longer separated by oceans; it was closing in all around us.

This, and the threat of execution, prodded us forward. Another meeting of hostage families was planned for the end of the month. This time, we weren't going to settle for anything less than a face-to-face briefing by President Reagan. Hostages were being executed. Our sense of urgency was fired by panic. Either President Reagan should be forced to commit himself publicly to the hostages, or he should admit to the American people his intention to sacrifice them. With this end in mind, I had an idea that I felt sure would benefit us regardless of how the administration responded. It was time for gimmicks.

Yellow ribbons had been a prominent symbol of hope and commitment during the Iranian hostage crisis and the TWA hostage crisis. Why not request a meeting with

President Reagan to present him with a huge yellow ribbon to hang conspicuously on the door of the White House?

Except for the President's remarks on the return home of the TWA passengers, I had never heard him or his staff publicly utter one positive word of support for the forgotten hostages. I couldn't help but wonder if my dad was sitting in some tiny windowless room reading *USA Today*, searching for hope in the words of the President. Day after day would pass without one printed message of concern from the man he was relying on to save his life. I wanted to make sure he would find those words, even if we had to force them from the President's lips.

If the President agreed to meet with us, he would have to accept the yellow ribbon. If it turned up on the door of the White House, it would be a sign to all America that he cared, and that other Americans should follow his leadership and be concerned too. If it was never seen after our meeting, we would whine that he had tossed it in the rubbish in a gesture that symbolised perfectly his abandonment of innocent American citizens.

Should our request for a meeting be denied, we had a contingency plan. We'd stand outside the White House gate, looking as pathetic and injured as possible, holding our rejected yellow ribbon. I knew the press would eat it up. The President would look like a cold-hearted fiend. With the press playing that up, we were sure to generate some public support. The gimmick of the yellow ribbon seemed guaranteed to succeed.

Paul and I decided to mount a petition in the month of October, which would end in time to carry those signatures into the meeting with the President along with the yellow ribbon. We drafted a simple petition and distributed it among our friends and relatives. Signatures started pouring in, proving that, given something to do, people would respond.

As our plans unfolded, several groups arrived with

'supplies and ammunition'. The city of Huntington Beach declared October 'Hostage Awareness Month' and raised a yellow flag over City Hall. The California Hospital Association (not to be confused with the American Hospital Association) invited me to speak at its annual convention in Monterey, California, at the end of the month, while several colleges asked me to speak to the student body. NOVA, the National Organization for Victims Assistance, began a project for the hostage families that included a monthly newsletter and (more important to me at the time) supplied me with a telephone calling card that rescued me from 300-dollar-a-month phone bills.

One of the most unlikely gimmicks for public awareness came from my sister. Paul and I had been writing songs for quite a few years, and Diane suggested we try to write one with the intention of getting daily radio airplay. 'We Are the World' had just been a huge success for raising money, and more importantly, drawing the world's attention to the famine in Africa. She saw the same potential for Dad's situation.

I was hesitant at first, partly because I felt that the idea wouldn't work a second time, but more because of my doubts that we could write an appropriate song. In the end she convinced us we had nothing to lose and every angle needed to be explored, so Paul and I started work. I began several songs, but they all reeked of bitterness and frustration. With the instructions that we needed a hopeful lyric, I turned it over to Paul.

He took a melody I had written ten years before that he said had a plaintive, melodic feel and revised it considerably. He then wrote a lyric and turned it back to me. On my initial reading, I knew the verses were exactly what I had intended but had been unable to accomplish. Only the chorus needed to be rewritten. I asked the Lord to inspire me with the right words. Within a few minutes, the title, the chorus and a few minor changes in the verse were complete. I knew the song was a gift from God.

When the Word Comes

Never let go
Deep in your soul
Hold on to a single prayer
God only knows
Freedom's so close
The innocent can be spared
And the constant fears of days turned to years
Will suddenly disappear.

When the word comes
Their freedom won
They'll already be bound
Home safe and sound.
When the word comes
And we'll be done
Waiting and praying
For the day when we're finally one.

Spotlights, long nights
Headlines and false signs
Strike again like lightning.
Old news and no news
The same lines and the slow times
Are always frightening
But the worries and the fears
Of the days that have turned to years
Will finally disappear.

When the word comes
Their freedom won
They'll already be bound
Home safe and sound
When the word comes
And we'll be done
Waiting and praying
For the day when we're finally one.

Bring them home ...
Bring them safe and sound.

Now that the song was complete, the problem was what
to do with it. I knew that to get it recorded, distributed
and on the radio we would need a well known singer to

perform it. I had no idea where to begin, but I knew I had written it only with God's help, and it would happen somehow. With the help of my friend Ron, I made a simple, quick demo of it on a four-track recorder I had in the back bedroom. Then I began to wait for some opportunity to present itself.

With the expectation that we might finally reach the President, all the hostage families were in a fever. It seemed appropriate that we now expand our group from an informal support network to a formal organisation. This would give us a stronger method for information exchange; it would unify us for our lobbying efforts in Washington; and it would help us in fund-raising activities to defer some of the costs incurred, such as air fare and travel expenses.

The American Hostage Committee was the name selected, and through our volunteers in Washington, steps were taken to begin formal organisation. Over the telephone, a statement of purpose and points of concern were drafted and circulated between the hostage families for input and approval. The statement of purpose was simple; to be a clearing house of information for hostage families; to be a focal point for expressions of support for the families and hostages by the American public and the United States government; to raise public and government awareness of the critical situation of the hostages; and to contribute towards the safe release of the hostages in Lebanon.

The day approached for our next trip to Washington. This time, Paul, Diane and I would all go. Although there was some hesitation on their parts, I was insistent that they do so. First of all, it would give them the opportunity to meet Ben Weir personally; second, in Diane's case, it would familiarise her with the workings of Washington; and third, after the last trip, I didn't want to go alone.

Much to our delighted surprise, our presidential meeting was granted. The yellow ribbon would hang on the White House door after all. I was excited at the prospect of finally meeting President Reagan, and at the same time, frightened at the implications of a face-to-face dialogue with the most politically powerful man on the planet.

Two days before we were scheduled to depart, the employee hired to replace me left without notice. That meant that if I went East, the office would close down. The responsibility I felt towards my employer made me decide to remain at home. He had continued to be supportive in every way I had asked, and I felt it necessary to honour that support. My disappointment was immense, but I knew Paul and Diane could do anything I might be able to do. Longing to be squeezed into one of those uncomfortable seats between my brother and sister, I watched the plane leave the runway at John Wayne Airport in Orange County. Only my confidence in them prevented my driving back to the office and submitting my resignation so that I could catch the next flight to DC. But they knew what I would have said, anyway. Now it was just a matter of waiting for one of them to call me after the presidential meeting had taken place and fill me in on what had transpired.

When the phone call came from Paul, he sounded just as I imagine I always sounded—wanting to be positive and optimistic, but fully aware he was putting up a front. His initial satisfaction from the meeting was begrudgingly surrendering to disappointment. Deep down I could sense that he saw little real progress. When I asked him how things had gone, he offered no details, and his disappointment showed through. The President had impressed him as a person and had said he understood how much we were suffering, but then after only fifteen minutes had excused himself, turned over the meeting to Bud McFarlane, and left. I knew how frustrated Paul must feel.

'What's scheduled for tomorrow?' I asked.

Paul yawned. 'We meet with the House Committee on Foreign Affairs, and go to a few embassies.'

'I guess I'll talk to you when you get back. I'm going up to Monterey to speak to the California Hospital Association. Maybe we can get together this weekend and talk in more detail.'

Diane was supposed to fly home from Washington, and then take a connecting flight with me to San Jose, but not long after I finished talking with Paul, she called from the Levins' house.

'I can't go with you,' she said. 'I'm just too tired. I just want to go home.'

'They're expecting both of us,' I said, disappointed. Besides, the air fare was coming out of our own pockets, and I didn't want to forfeit it.

'I just can't go.'

'What's wrong?'

'I've just had enough. I'm sorry. Maybe Cathy can go instead.'

I knew that once she had made up her mind, she wouldn't change it. I was angry, but I couldn't blame her; unless she flew home from Washington with Dad sitting next to her, it was hard not to view the trip as an utter failure.

Cathy accompanied me for the first time on any trip for my father to the CHA convention. I spoke briefly and accepted the resolution that the association had passed. It gave me a chance to see and meet some of Dad's friends in the profession. It also gave me the opportunity to address the largest audience of my life—hundreds of people. I tried to keep my voice from revealing my nervousness. My hands shook noticeably. I don't know what happened that morning, but after that speech, I was never nervous talking in front of a crowd again.

When we returned to southern California, I was eager to talk to Paul. 'You made it back from Washington, I see,' I said when I reached him that evening.

His response caught me by surprise. 'Just be glad you

weren't there. Things got really out of control the last two days. Have you talked to Jerry or Sis?'

'No,' I replied. 'I've been out of town. What's wrong?'

'I guess the American Hostage Committee has broken up.'

'Broken up?' I echoed. 'From what? It's only been in existence twenty days.'

'It all started at our meeting with the House Committee on Foreign Affairs. Jerry, Peggy Say, and Ben Weir were scheduled to speak. I didn't have to say anything, and I was glad. We had drafted a list of points for discussion—twenty or so. Earlier that morning we heard that Israel had just bombed the Bekaa Valley in Lebanon. Of course with the rumours that Dad and the others were being held in the Bekaa, we were really upset. One of our points asked that the US restrain Israel from bombing there as long as there was a possibility that our loved ones were held in the vicinity.'

I had a sinking feeling I knew what had happened next.

Paul continued. 'When we'd finished talking, one Congressman got really upset. He started telling us he could understand our feelings and agreed with our humanitarian suggestions, but the minute we started to talk contrary to the security of Israel, we were way out of line. He then launched into an emotional speech about how he lost his family in the Holocaust, and when he was finished, he walked out of the room without giving us a chance to respond. The rest of the meeting was spent by Congressmen either defending or criticising his actions. We got nothing accomplished. I wasn't going to say anything, but I was so angry that I did. I said I thought he had done us a great injustice. We were only voicing our concern for the safety of our relatives, and by storming out without offering us a chance for rebuttal, he had completely disrupted the meeting.'

I could tell Paul was deeply upset, so I tried to down-play it by saying, 'Oh, well, we'll know how to handle that the next time.'

'That's only the beginning,' Paul interrupted. 'Sis called me earlier today to ask me to call the Jencos and try to convince them not to quit the American Hostage Committee.'

'Why are the Jencos quitting?'

'I flew out immediately after the Foreign Affairs meeting. I guess the next morning, the *New York Post* ran an editorial saying basically that the American Hostage Committee is a front for the PLO.'

'*What*?' I couldn't believe my ears.

'I guess it claimed the American Hostage Committee was just a front for Palestinian sympathisers, and the hostage families were being used as pawns against Israel.'

I yelled furiously into the receiver, now sharing Paul's anger. 'Yeah, we're pro-Palestinian. ...And we're pro-Israel. Why can't we be for both sides? All we've been saying is that we want a just, non-violent peace in the region so that no other Americans will find themselves in our position. We're supposed to say, "OK, bomb the Bekaa; kill our father"?'

'I guess they had a meeting the morning that the editorial ran,' Paul continued. 'Things really disintegrated. The Jenco family got scared and pulled out of the American Hostage Committee. Then a big fight broke out because someone suggested that we shouldn't have anyone with an Arab name associated with our group. This made other people mad because it was obvious discrimination. ... Anyway, I was just glad that I had flown out the night before.'

'You're right,' I finally said, 'I'm glad I wasn't there.'

I hung up quite depressed. I was sickened at the thought that our media focus might now have to shift to defend ourselves against totally false accusations of being a front for the PLO. I shook my head. It seemed that the editors of the *New York Post*, by calling us pawns, were in essence trying to use us for the same purpose, to promote their own interests. We could not win. And we didn't have a column on the editorial page to stage a defence.

I told Cathy about my conversation with Paul and the

events in Washington. I was angry at the Congressman. I was angry at the *New York Post*. I began to think about radical elements in my own nation fighting the Middle East conflict here on the streets of America. I didn't want to be an unwilling participant. I just wanted Dad home safe and sound.

'I sure don't want to take on the Israeli lobby or any other group,' I mumbled to Cathy. 'It looks like the American Hostage Committee just got caught in the cross-fire between Israeli and Arab sympathisers.'

'Eric, I don't want you to say any more in the press about the conflict in the Middle East,' Cathy pleaded. 'Remember Alex Odeh who died in the bombing right here in Santa Ana? I don't want some nut shooting you.'

I shrugged my shoulders. 'I don't know what I'm going to do or say.' I could see she was really upset. 'Don't worry. Nobody's gonna shoot me.'

As I lay in bed that night, I was forced to re-evaluate my feelings and the direction I had pursued recently. Maybe I had been mistaken. Maybe this was a sign from the Lord to redirect my efforts. Maybe he wanted to turn me back towards my father. Maybe he wanted my eyes focused on Dad. The more I thought about it, the more that conclusion was re-enforced. Perhaps it wasn't God's plan to use us to bring peace to the Middle East as much as it was my own plan. Perhaps it was all a delusion of grandeur. I had to admit I didn't know. I had never heard the voice of the Lord tell me, 'OK, Eric, here's the plan. . . .'

I realised it was actually self-glorifying to think I could fully recognise and comprehend the will of God. Before I fell asleep, I accepted that my duty was foremost to my father's freedom, and if the Lord chose to use me for greater things, he would do so—not out of my insistence, but because it was his plan.

It was difficult to accept, but I had to surrender to the fact that God's plan might never be revealed to me. I should be satisfied simply to know of its existence.

8

7th November–25th December, 1985

I jumped in my bed as if stirred from sleep by an electric shock. Awaking so suddenly, I found myself breathless. My heart raced and then slowed to a hard thumping pattern. The room was black. Familiarity and repetition guided my hand to the phone without my eyes opening.

'Eric?' the female voice said. 'This is Peggy.'

I looked over Cathy's shadowy form at the face of the clock. Two-thirty. 'Hi, Peggy. What's up?'

'Has the press started calling you yet?'

'No.'

'Then you haven't heard?'

'No. Heard what?'

'They just called me. . . . I'm glad I got to you first. A report has just come out of Beirut. An anonymous caller has claimed that all the American hostages are going to be executed. We're supposed to receive another call at 4:00 am, your time, with information as to where to pick up the bodies.'

I did not react. Her words were incomprehensible. To prevent an emotional meltdown, my mind automatically shut itself off. 'I assume this hasn't been confirmed by the State Department.' This wasn't a question but a prediction.

'No.'

'Call me if you hear anything more. I'll do the same.'

Peggy agreed. 'We've got to pray,' were the last words she said before she hung up.

When Cathy heard the news she began to cry. I could only lie on my back, helpless. My thoughts whirred through my head at such a speed that they became a jumble. I couldn't even pray. And then crazy thoughts began to taunt me. Maybe I could somehow reach out to my father. Concentrating, I tried to feel the reassurance go from me stretching, searching, locating, reassuring, calming. ... Nothing.

The phone rang. Was it Peggy with more news?

'Mr Jacobsen?' said a male voice.

'Yes.'

'This is the *Chicago Tribune*. Have you heard the latest report from Beirut?'

'Yes, I have.'

'I was wondering ... how does the possible death of your father make you feel?'

I hung up the receiver.

Sleep. If I could fall asleep, I could escape. I could lose myself in a pleasant, unthreatening place. I could hide in the infinite duration of dreams. I could elude the pain of Dad's possible execution, at least until morning. Then I might be better equipped to deal with things once I had the morning light as an ally.

But sleep was impossible. I put on my dressing-gown, walked downstairs and sat in front of the TV. I left it on the first channel that appeared when the screen lit up. All that I noticed of the black-and-white classic that was playing was the grey-blue light that it threw on the room. Cathy joined me shortly afterwards. Several times, my eyes wandered to the clock on the wall, and I witnessed it trudging along indifferently to the four o'clock deadline.

I wanted to pray, but at the same time, I couldn't. I wanted to believe that God wouldn't allow it to happen. He just wouldn't allow it. And I could not allow myself to question that. But I wasn't strong enough not to doubt and fear; I wasn't at all confident. 'Father, in Jesus' name, please spare my dad.' I only had enough strength for that simple prayer, nothing more. Suddenly, I was at peace. I knew that Dad was all right. Now there was no doubt in my mind. Four o'clock would come, and that phone would not ring. I knew it.

I thought of my family. Should I call them? It could wait until the morning. Until after the deadline had passed. Until the danger had subsided completely. What would it accomplish in calling, anyway?—just the satisfaction that Cathy and I wouldn't be the only ones going without sleep.

Dad's all right, I told myself. The Lord has told me that. But then again. ...

Suddenly I wasn't so sure that I had heard him. I tried to block it, but a thought squeezed through before I could shut the door on it. 'What if he's not all right? Just, what if ...?' How could I handle calling the rest of my family? How would I know what to do for funeral arrangements? Would I have to call my mother for help? How would I get his body home from Beirut? *How could I handle any of it?*

I sank further and further into the sofa cushions under the weight of doubt and depression. By now, I was thinking only in terms of the certainty of my father's death. *I haven't heard the Lord's voice*, I told myself. *It was just wishful thinking.* What reason did I have to think that he would protect Dad in the first place? He allowed him to be kidnapped. If this was a test, I was ready to stand up, walk out of the classroom, and just take an 'F' without argument.

Four o'clock finally came. The hour mark passed, and the rotation of the minute hand on the clock seemed to slow even more as I waited for the call. Five o'clock—still no call. Six o'clock—the phone began to ring, but it was only reporters. 'Stop tying up the line!' I yelled out loud across the empty room at each one as they left their name and number on the tape. How inconsiderate could they get! What do they expect me to say when they ask how I feel after hearing that my father may have been executed? Each call from the news media only notched up the level of my anger.

Some time before 7:00 am, I heard Peggy again. 'Eric? Are you there? Pick up the phone.' She knew I was screening my calls. I forced myself up off the sofa and walked towards her voice, unsure if I wanted to hear the news she had to tell me. 'Please, God ...,' I mumbled.

'They got the call,' she began. I started silently to curse the men who had kidnapped my father. 'They were told to go to an abandoned bombed-out factory, but when some Lebanese policemen got there, they searched the building and didn't find any bodies.'

It took a second to sink in. *No bodies*. Maybe the call had been a hoax after all. I knew that with every minute that passed, the chances of that being the case increased in a geometric progression. 'That's a good sign,' was all I could mutter in relief. 'Let me know if you hear any more.'

I was quick to thank God. 'I'm sorry I didn't trust like I should. I'll never doubt again. Never.' At the time I said that, I was completely sincere in my promise—maybe somewhat premature, but nevertheless sincere.

The remainder of the day passed without further word or threat from Beirut. I did many interviews, in all of which I spoke in guarded optimism that the call had apparently been a cruel hoax. I tried to reassure my family that I was confident Dad was still alive. Privately, I also needed some reassuring, occasionally from myself. Dad's advice of 'wait to worry' kept turning in my head like a malfunctioning tape recorder.

I was exhausted by the end of the day. However, I wasn't going to be able to make up for the sleep I had lost the previous night because I agreed to do NBC's *Today Show* the next morning. With millions of viewers, I knew it was an opportunity to push again for an increased sense of urgency to resolve the hostage issue, especially in the light of this death threat. Although I was now thinking that the call had indeed been false, I knew that the threat of execution was a good emotional 'hook' to increase public support for government action.

Because the *Today Show* was live, and its studios in

New York had a three-hour jump on the West Coast audience, it required that I arrive at the Los Angeles studios before 4:00 am for my 7:15 time segment. It was an hour's drive from my house to Burbank, which meant I had to set the alarm for 2:00 am. My body ached at just the thought of rolling out from under the covers at that hour. I knew I would only get a couple of minutes on the air, and I almost cancelled, preferring to spend the time sleeping.

A limousine was waiting outside my door at 3:00 am to drive me up the deserted freeways. I had gone to bed at about 9:30 but didn't really fall asleep until 11:00. I felt like a car with a failed battery—I had enough juice for a faint glow in the headlights, but not enough to turn over the engine. I tried to rehearse my thoughts sufficiently so that when I got in front of the cameras, they would just spill out without effort.

When we arrived, I followed the driver through the security check, down the empty studio halls, and ended up in a chair facing the camera. I was no longer nervous about being seen live by millions. I knew I was like the crew, also wishing they were in bed. We all just wanted to get it done and go home. I managed to communicate my need for coffee while a make-up man did his best to restore some colour to my sleepy face.

The actual interview happened very quickly. The red light on top of the camera lit up; a couple of questions were asked; I answered them and then tried to make the points I considered more appropriate or essential. The red light went off; I said goodbye to the crew; I was led back out to the waiting limo and driven home—all before the sun rose.

When I walked through the front door, I looked at the clock. *Five-thirty am.* It seemed futile to undress and try to sleep, so I resolved to go directly to the office and see if I could get in a couple hours of uninterrupted work. The press had been on the phone and coming through the office door all the previous day, and I had accomplished very little. This would give me a chance at least to catch up. I had been behind my desk for only a few minutes when Cathy called. One of the guys from the studio at NBC where I had just been was trying to track me down. He had told her that it was vital I return his call as soon as possible.

When I got through to him, he sounded excited. 'We just got a report over the wire that the people holding your father released a package of letters to the Associated Press in Beirut. One of those letters is from your father to you.'

'Who's got the letter?'

'I don't know. But we were wondering, if we sent the limo back, would you be willing to come and do another segment?'

'What could I say about it? I haven't seen the letter. I don't know what it says.' I looked at the pile of work in front of me. 'No, I don't think so. Sorry.'

'My producer wanted me to ask you if you'd be willing to come on tomorrow after you've seen it.'

'I don't know. You'll have to call me later in the day.'

This unexpected news prompted me to call the State Department. Yes, they had heard the report and were in the process of checking it. Apparently, nine letters were tossed from a moving car on to the steps of the Associated Press office in Beirut. Four of the nine were messages from each man to his family, and several joint letters—one to the President, one to Congressmen O'Brien and Dornan, one to the Associated Press, one to the news media, and a confidential message to the Archbishop of Canterbury.

I was promised that as soon as the State Department got the letters they would call and read the one from my father over the phone to me. Long before that phone call came, however, the local television news crews were setting up in my office. They brought with them photo-copies of the joint letters, all signed by the four hostages. I did not recognise the handwriting of the person who wrote them, but I could identify my father's signature on the last page of each.

One letter meant more to me initially than the other. Dated 8th November, 1985, 1:00 pm, it read:

To the AP and all news media,

We have just been told that someone has claimed that Islamic Jihad has killed all of us. Obviously this is not true. Our captors say it was an attempt by the US government to spoil negotiations.

Father Lawrence Martin Jenco, Terry Anderson, David Jacobsen, Thomas Sutherland

It was Dad's signature under his printed name. This confirmed the hoax. I called Cathy immediately and asked her to call the rest of my family. Within a couple of hours, the State Department called and read the contents of my father's letter to me. It was without a doubt composed by him. I told them I had seen the other letters, and that I could identify easily his signature.

'When am I going to get the letter?' I asked impatiently.

'If it's all right with you, we'd like to keep it for forensic studies. We'll send you a xerox copy by express mail.'

Of course I would have preferred to get the original, but I agreed. 'I'll make sure I'm home all day tomorrow.'

The next morning at ten there was a knock on the door. I quickly opened the letter. Although it had been read to me over the phone, I couldn't remember any of it beyond the general tone. To make sure I didn't miss anything, I studied it slowly, concentrating on each word. It too was dated 8th November 1985, and addressed to 'The Jacobsen Family' with my street number and city. It read:

Dear Eric, Cathy, Paul, Lori and Diane;

There is so much to say and so little time to do it. You are constantly in my thoughts and my prayers. I love all of you very much and long for the day that we will be together again.

Trust in the Lord, we will be together soon. My situation is difficult, but you know my strength and determination, and I shall survive. I trust that all is well with you. Love one another, trust one another and support one another.

I hope that you have received my other letter that Ben Weir was to have mailed to you upon his return to the USA. If not, I'll repeat a couple of important points ... [followed by instructions for handling his finances and the purchase of Christmas presents].

Again, I love all of you very much and I want to help in every way even though I am a captive in Lebanon. My situation is not the best, nor is it the worst. I am in a small, windowless room with Tom Sutherland, Father Jenco, and Terry Anderson. We are no longer in chains, which is a relief. The care is minimal, the food marginal and outside information limited to occasional newspapers, magazines and shortwave radio for BBC, Voice of America and Armed Forces Radio.

Exercise is limited by the size of the room. We do some sit-ups, push-ups, and walking in circles. We are provided with medicines when requested. Our captors have not physically abused or tortured us. At times the boredom becomes overwhelming. Father Jenco conducts service twice a day and there is plenty of time to read the Bible.

I hear of your trips to Washington, DC to meet the President and the Vice-President. We are aware of the President's position on not negotiating with terrorists and can understand the rationale for that position, but it doesn't work, nor is he consistent. Negotiations for the hostages in the TWA airplane incident are well known in Lebanon. Israel, El Salvador, Egypt, and even Russia have negotiated for release of hostages.

The conditions for our release are simple. Ben Weir has made them known to the US government and the general public. The release of the *four* of us is within the power of President Reagan and can be accomplished *immediately*. Our captors want to talk, but my government apparently refuses. They, the captors, approve the International Red Cross as intermediaries.

If President Reagan could authorise negotiations for TWA, why not for us? America and Russia exchange spies (criminals) all the time. Why can't we be exchanged? Ask him.

Reagan's quiet diplomacy has *not* resulted in the release of a single hostage in two years. William Buckley is presumed dead. He could and should be alive today if there had been a reasonable effort made on his behalf.

Our captors want a fast resolution to the problem. They are frustrated by the US government's refusal to talk. Negotiations would not be difficult if the US government officials did not become overly concerned with minor details. In fact, if one group were to be released unilaterally, we would be released unconditionally and immediately. Face-to-face negotiations would not even be necessary. Have faith!

Please release the contents of this letter, except parts you might consider too personal, to the *Los Angeles Times* and the *Orange County Register*. Please reassure my dad. God bless everyone. I love you.

Dad

Another sheet of paper included as a postscript accompanied the first. It too was dated 8th November, 1:00 pm.

Dear Eric, Paul, Diane, Cathy and Lori,

We are alive! We were told that yesterday, someone claiming to be Islamic Jihad telephoned the news media and said that all the American hostages had been shot and killed.

Apparently someone wants to disrupt the possibility of talks concerning our release. Our captors believe that the American government is trying to disrupt any and all negotiations for our release.

I cry for the hurt that the false report has given all of you. Please keep the faith. I shall survive!

All my love,

Dad

When I finished reading, I passed the letter to Cathy, and it wasn't long before she was trying to read through her tears. When she had finished, I called the rest of my family and read it over the phone. The press naturally wanted to read it also, and because my father had asked that it be made available to them, I did so. Most of them wanted a picture of me holding the letter, looking forlorn or something, and I agreed, but only under protest. I found it all humiliating and embarrassing, but unfortunately necessary.

The letter sent to President Reagan was similar in content to my father's letter to us. It began, 'We are appealing to you for action ...' and ended, 'It is in your power to have us home for Christmas. Will you not have mercy on us and our families and do so?'

The response from the White House was two fold; they believed that the hostages were forced to write those letters and that they did not reflect their true feelings; and the government would not negotiate with terrorists.

I was furious—more hurt and angry than I had ever been. Here was a letter addressed directly to the President, pleading for his assistance, asking him to save their lives. My father and the others had indicated that they had access to the media and would be waiting along with the captors for his response. And what did they get? Nothing. Not one word of concern. Not one word of commitment. Nothing to give them hope. Just the opposite—discounting the credibility of their message. What did the White House think? That the hostages wanted their captivity to continue indefinitely?

I had to ask God, 'How could they be so cruel? Why couldn't they just say one sentence that Dad might read to let him know they wanted him out of that "small windowless room" where he has been held for over six months? Lord, I don't understand how these people think. Forgive me, but I really hate them for their cold insensitive hearts.'

Thankfully, this utter despair and anger was soon dispersed by a report from England. The Archbishop of Canterbury had responded to his letter in the way that I had hoped President Reagan would have. As a result of the apparent approval by the captors to his involvement, he announced that his special envoy, Terry Waite, would attempt to mediate. Within a couple days, it was announced that contact had been made with the captors, and Terry Waite would be travelling to Beirut to meet them face to face.

For the first time, I saw a real chance of resolution. Here was someone willing to negotiate. The deadlock had been broken. We hoped it was only a matter of days, at the most weeks, before Dad would be a free man again. The other hostage families shared my enthusiasm. We tried not to speak too confidently, but it was impossible. On 14th November, in a news conference from Beirut, Waite announced that contact had been made, and the captors had agreed to meet him. His public comment was one of optimism. But at the same time, he stressed the delicacy of the situation and the danger both to himself and the hostages.

Never before had we had something as tangible as this to bolster our hopes. Finally, we could back out of the public spotlight. In a phone conversation, Peggy Say and I agreed that we would postpone our scheduled monthly meeting in Washington early in December and wait to see what Terry Waite could accomplish. The last thing we wanted to do was disrupt whatever progress he might make.

The world news media had descended on Beirut to follow the story. Over and over, Terry asked that he be given freedom of movement without being tailed by reporters. Without that, contact with the captors was an impossibility and would only increase the danger to himself and the hostages. From my own personal experience, I wasn't the least surprised that they refused to honour his request. My helpless anger gnawed at me until my nerves were raw. 'Those guys are going to screw everything up out of competition for a story! I hate the press!'

I was delighted and relieved when it was reported that Waite had somehow managed to elude the reporters; they were left now to speculate about his whereabouts. He had successfully gone underground, and I knew that meant he was meeting the men who held my father. There was even a chance that he had seen Dad and had talked to him. I could hardly imagine the hope that would give to my father and the others.

Terry surfaced again, speaking more optimistically, but said that several important matters needed to be settled. He travelled back to consult the Archbishop of Canterbury. Another trip to Beirut followed soon after to again meet the captors, resulting in a trip to the US for a meeting with Vice-President Bush and other US officials. It was hard to prevent what was originally a ray of hope from opening up into a floodlight of expectation. Every night when I went to bed, I prayed to be awakened by a phone call. Every day I prepared myself for the time when the word would come.

It seemed everyone addressed in those letters from the hostages, with the exception of the White House, felt an urgent need to act. The families did so for obvious reasons; the Archbishop of Canterbury had sent his special envoy ... and Representative Robert Dornan from a neighbouring southern California congressional district contacted me on 9th November, the next day.

I had met Congressman Bob Dornan at our first 'Hostage Awareness Day' on Capitol Hill, and again a few months later when we appeared together on a television show. With a letter addressed to him and Rep George O'Brien from Illinois, his concern for the hostages was pressed into a desire for immediate action. He contacted me, and we set up a time to meet.

I was a little more than mildly startled when he revealed his plan to me—we were going to Beirut. A boat from Cyprus would land us on a beach in Lebanon, and we would then be spirited into Christian East Beirut. From there, we would try to establish contact with the captors of my father and the others.

I was frightened at the thought of entering Lebanon, but I applied for my passport regardless. Cathy freaked out. 'If I have to, I'm going,' was all I would say in response to her desperate pleas.

In meeting with State Department officials, Dornan was soon convinced to wait until the progress of Terry

Waite could be determined. Our beach landing of Beirut was postponed. Although that plan seems somewhat drastic in retrospect, Bob Dornan was one of a few Congressmen willing to take action, and I will always appreciate that fact.

The remainder of November and early December found my spirits elevated for the first time since my father's abduction. In the midst of Terry Waite's missions to Beirut, my energy turned to finding someone to record the song that Paul and I had written. Were I able to get regular airplay, I hoped to retire from interviews. I personally had no contacts in the music business and had no idea where to begin.

Tony Saavedra, a reporter from the *Daily Pilot*, a local newspaper, seemed interested in approaching his editors about doing a story. I was surprised and embarrassed to find a colour picture of myself singing and playing the guitar on the front page several days later. *I've really sunk to an all-time low*, I thought. *What an act of desperation.*

Tony's article was fine but failed to generate any calls from the large LA-based record companies or recording stars. But in a private conversation, he managed to enlist the help of a local media consultant. She contacted me, offering to help devise a game plan to get copies of my demo out to people who might be interested in recording it. That night, I met Laine Medina, and she provided me with a list of names and phone numbers.

The following day, I began 'hustling' my song on the phone. Unfortunately, my career aptitude does not lie in telemarketing. I would generally begin the conversation by identifying myself as the son of one of the Americans held hostage in Lebanon. The secretaries I talked to must have heard it all. You would think an introduction like that would at least alter the tone of their voices. On the contrary, with the most cheerful inflection, they would thank me for calling, apologise for not being able to help, and then wish me a nice day before they hung up!

After half a dozen identical conversations, I abandoned

that approach. Instead, I called the remaining names on the list and simply got a mailing address. After drafting a cover letter, I sent a copy of the demo to each one. Out of a dozen or so, I received only one response.

Don Henley, an ex-member of the Eagles, actually took the time to respond. 'I have listened to your tape,' he wrote. 'I know that your song is very important to you and that it comes from the heart. However, I'm afraid that it is just not my style. Even though I agree and sympathise with the sentiment you express, I'm afraid I could not record it. . . .'

'I feel for you,' the letter continued. 'I wish there was something I could do. I will try to put some pressure on the Senators that I know—and I know a great many. Also, maybe I can put something in one of my songs about this type of thing. In the meantime, keep me posted on your situation. I do care.'

I wasn't disappointed in his letter; it was more important that at least one person showed enough concern to write back.

Just when I had given up hope of ever seeing 'When the Word Comes' on the label of a 45 single, my friend Ron, who had recorded the demo with me, called. He had played it for a friend of his, Bill Voit, who liked it enough to send a copy off to one of his friends, Mike Curb, the ex-lieutenant governor of California and now president of Curb Records. Curb called Bill back immediately to say he was interested in the producing and distributing of the song. The real shocker to me was that he wanted my voice on the record.

When I talked to Mike on the phone, he insisted that it would be much more powerful as a record for me to sing it. As flattering as that was, I panicked. Once again I found myself getting involved in something in which I was inexperienced, unqualified, and extremely frightened. I was a hack musician. I knew if the record was going to accomplish what it was intended to do, I was going to have to become a professional before I ever set foot in a recording studio.

I had only one place to turn. 'Lord, you've got to help me. ...'

Within a couple of days, Paul and I drove up to meet Mike and our contact person at Curb Records, Nola Leone, at their offices on the Universal Studios lot in Universal City. Much to my surprise, they didn't fit into the stereotypical record executive 'We'll do lunch' image one expects in the entertainment industry. They were nice people, friendly, professional, and quick to make us feel comfortable. Their motives were plain—they simply wanted to help. As usual, I felt I was intruding. *How did I end up here*? kept running through my head.

During our meeting, Mike told a story that helped settle my apprehension. It concerned one of Curb Records' biggest hits, one of the biggest selling singles in the previous decade, Debbie Boone's 'You Light Up My Life'. Apparently it had been a difficult song for her to sing. She had tried repeatedly, but she just couldn't get it right until she decided to sing it to God. It worked. Because I believed that our song was a gift from him, I knew he would be there to coach my vocals as well.

Things began to move fast. Michael Lloyd was lined up to produce the record; studio time was booked; some of the top studio musicians in the business were called in for the session. To combat my nervousness, I tried not to think about all that was taking place. Paul couldn't make it to the first session, so I talked my friend Ron into going for moral support.

'You might get a record contract out of this,' Ron said as we drove to the studio at Michael Lloyd's home in Beverly Hills.

'I'm not going to think about that,' was my reply.

But to be honest, I did think about it. And then I felt guilty. This song had one purpose—to raise public awareness for Dad and the others, not to open the door of a new career for me. Still, I had to make a conscious effort not to daydream about the potential opportunities it might create. The fear that others would view me as trying to capitalise on my father's tragedy embarrassed me no end. It was only through prayer that I finally overcame what I considered unethical, selfish thoughts about stardom dangling in front of my nose.

After the basic rhythm tracks were laid down, it was required that I go back into the studio a week later to sing the vocal. Nervousness and fear filled my voice with vibrato, but I managed to get it done. I drove home happier with the fact that it was over than with my performance.

I expected to find Cathy at home anxiously waiting to hear all the details of my hours of logged studio time, but the house was empty. *Maybe she's out finally starting the Christmas shopping*, I thought as I listened to the messages on the answering machine. A bare Christmas tree sat in the corner of the room waiting for me to pull the box of ornaments from the upstairs cupboard. My thoughts briefly turned to the possibility that, thanks to Terry Waite, Dad might be home in time to enjoy the holidays with us.

The phone rang, and I picked it up without screening the call through the answering machine. It was Cathy.

'Hi, hun,' she said. I noticed her asthma was playing up; her breath wheezed out the words. 'How did the recording go?'

'Fine. I'll tell you all about it when you get home. Where are you?'

Her voice shrank further. 'I'm at the hospital.'

'Are you OK?'

'My asthma's out of control. They're going to admit me.'

I started to get angry, not because she was sick or had to be admitted, but because it meant that she had been having trouble for a couple of days without telling me. As it had happened in the past, instead of going to the doctor immediately, she had waited until it was out of control, and admission was necessary. Two years before she had been in the hospital for seven days under similar circumstances.

'Why didn't you tell me?'

'I knew you had to sing, and I didn't want you to worry.'

'I can't believe you waited until ...,' I stopped myself. 'I'll leave right now.'

I was there in a matter of minutes. As it turned out, she was there for over a week. It took a couple of days, and a couple of bags of medicine dripping through an IV before the asthma finally broke. My free time was spent at the hospital. After visiting hours, I usually sat at home and spent a good deal of time looking at our undecorated tree. Among the Christmas cards we received that year were ones from Vice-President Bush, Secretary of State Schultz, and a nice letter from the President and Mrs Reagan. They did little to make my father's absence any easier.

'What a Christmas,' I would complain to the only person there to listen—myself. 'This tree is pathetic. We haven't bought one gift, and it's only a few days to Christmas. Cathy's in the hospital. Dad's a hostage in Lebanon. And the press is trying to schedule time on Christmas morning to take pictures of me looking sad and helpless. This Christmas is a flop. Things are hopeless. Absolutely hopeless.'

Our State Department contact, John, called to say we might have a way of getting a Christmas message to my dad through Terry Waite. I composed a message that reeked of melancholia and discouragement. *I can't send this*, I thought when I reread it. But then I changed my mind. I brightened it a little for my father's sake; after all, it would be his only present from us that year, if he got it. Still, I left much of it the way it was, hoping the captors might read it first, and that it might touch their hearts.

Two days before Christmas, Cathy was discharged from the hospital. We didn't bother to go to the shopping mall. We didn't feel like decorating the tree. No Christmas records made it on to our turntable. No Christmas cookies were baked in the oven. On the day of Christmas Eve news arrived that Terry Waite had flown out of Beirut earlier in the day having failed to secure the release of any of the hostages. Dad would not be home for

Christmas dinner. It seemed more likely than not that Dad might never come home.

I awoke Christmas morning wondering how my father would be passing the time that day. Was he still keeping track of the days? Did he know it was Christmas? Were he, Father Jenco, Tom Sutherland, and Terry Anderson celebrating in some manner? Would the captors bring them a Christmas cake like they had done for Ben Weir the previous year?

Cathy and I got dressed and went to church to celebrate Mass. We arrived early in order to get a seat because the attendance at Christmas and Easter Masses was always at least twice that of a regular Sunday. We managed to find a place in the first pew, right in front of the lectern.

I found myself at Mass out of a sense of obligation rather than to worship. My mind was thousands of miles away, wandering the streets of Beirut, crawling through the rubble, looking in windows, searching for my father. My heart was empty, yet fierce like a wounded animal. As much as I had fought depression and self-pity in the previous six months, that Christmas morning I welcomed it.

In our liturgy, the gospel reading for Christmas Mass is usually John 1:1-18. The readings had up to that point escaped me, but as the deacon read the gospel scripture, something commanded my attention. 'The light shines on in darkness, a darkness that did not overcome it.'

I listened attentively to the rest of the reading, and a remarkable thing happened. I suddenly realised that the spirit of Christmas was not just 'giving' as our society promotes; the spirit of Christmas was 'hope'. Man's existence was hopeless before Christ. But, on that first Christmas morning, in his perfect love, God gave us true hope through the birth of his Son. A tiny baby would grow up to be the salvation of the world.

As terrible as my problems had seemed, they no longer appeared insurmountable. I had plenty of reason to be hopeful. I tried to imagine the world without Jesus. I tried to imagine how I would be able to deal with my troubles without the support of a loving relationship with God. He had been present since before my father was kidnapped, and he would be there on the day of his release.

The Lord had allowed me to fall into the deepest despair so that I would turn to him and see just that. My life was changed in an instant. Never again in the course of my father's captivity would I find myself without hope! There would still be days of depression, days of despair, but the hope that the Lord gave me that Christmas morning wrapped me like a protective shield. In spite of the prevailing circumstances, it was the best Christmas I ever had.

9
22nd January–30th March, 1986

I stood next to the glass window that formed the entire north wall of the high-rise condominium. From a vantage point of nine stories, I had a spectacular view up the Potomac River. It was mid-January, the dead of winter, brown and grey. The trees were barren. The water looked cold and muddy with the runoff of melting snow. When I had landed in Washington three days before, I still found it hard to believe that I would be staying at the Watergate Complex. But after eight months as a 'hostage son', very little surprised me any more.

Carmella LaSpada, whose organisation, No Greater Love, had been an active support group in the Iranian hostage crisis, had offered her home to several other hostage family members and me for our stay. I was still a little amazed at how people were willing to take in strangers on the spur of the moment. I wondered, if roles were reversed, would I be as generous?

My bags were packed and placed in the entry hall as I waited for a phone call from the lobby. The *Los Angeles Times* had sent a reporter with me to cover the fourth hostage family gathering in DC, and he was due at any minute with a cab to take us to the airport. I looked across the Potomac into Virginia and realised that in my four recent trips to Washington I had yet to do any sightseeing. Then again, I had been in the White House, the old executive office building, the State Department, the Capitol, the Watergate. ... I'd seen enough.

I found myself in Washington this time mainly to satisfy my need to burn off some impatience. When Terry Waite had not succeeded in bringing my father out at Christmas, I found it too difficult to sit on the couch and twiddle my thumbs. The other families were fighting the same uneasiness, and we agreed to resume our monthly meetings in Washington. Robert McFarlane had resigned as National Security Advisor, and it seemed appropriate that we should introduce ourselves to his replacement, Admiral John Poindexter, and meet John Adams, our new State Department contact person, whom I knew only from phone conversations.

The meeting was what I had expected. I had hoped to hear that we were on the brink of resolution, but instead, it followed the course of all the previous meetings—officials expressing sympathy, families struggling against their frustration, some crying, nothing new really said, nothing accomplished.

My impression of Admiral Poindexter was favourable. He seemed to have as good a grasp of the situation as anyone else; he seemed up-to-date on the facts; he was a reserved man who listened more than he spoke. He fiddled with his pipe on occasion, but seemed to offer us his complete attention. I liked him. But I also knew that there was little I could say or do that would alter his course in dealing with my father's plight.

This particular meeting brought another individual into prominence in my mind—Colonel Oliver North. He had been present at every White House appointment; and that morning he seemed to assume a more active role in the discussion around the table. After our meetings with McFarlane and Bush, Paul and I had discussed where he might fit in, but when I walked out of the National Security Council chambers this time, I felt sure he was the man in charge of this operation.

Poindexter, McFarlane, and even Reagan were apprised of all progress, but it seemed to me that it was Ollie North who walked into his office every morning, sat down at his desk, and opened the file on the hostages in Lebanon. I pictured him making the phone calls, drawing up the scenarios, running down the leads, and making most of the daily decisions.

This opinion was reinforced in my mind by the way Mr Poindexter fielded the questions from the hostage family members. Though McFarlane had completely dominated our meetings with him, Poindexter referred several of our questions directly to Colonel North for detailed answers. North sat slightly behind him to the admiral's left; his chair was against the dark, panelled wall, slightly away from the table, separating him from the discussion unless invited to comment by Poindexter.

Poindexter was obviously North's superior, and yet I thought it was obvious where responsibility had been delegated. Although North avoided revealing too many details, the force behind his manner in presenting a few facts about the involvement of third-party nations certainly commanded my attention.

'When you step out to meet the press in a few minutes, you must not reveal what has been discussed in this room,' North insisted just before the meeting ended. 'Confidential information has been discussed, and it would be inappropriate to share this with the news media and the general public.'

Although the facts and issues he was referring to proved to have little bearing or relationship to what would one day be revealed as the government's course of action at that time, I feel I am still bound to honour North's request for confidentiality. What I can say is that even though I left the meeting feeling much the same as I had after the previous White House appointments (as if I had been guided into a room, spun around until I was dizzy, patted on the head, and then pushed out of the door), I walked out with a definite impression: Col Oliver North was the man I wanted to see. He was the individual to whom my questions should be directed. He was the person to whom I should go for progress reports—not the State Department, not President Reagan.

As he ushered us out of the White House, I determined that to contact anyone else in the US government was to rely on intermediaries—just what I had been pressing the government not to do in seeking my father's release. Direct communication with the government was the method, and Ollie North was the man. I was glad to have that resolved in my own mind.

This trip was also beneficial in resolving other aspects of our political lobbying efforts in Washington. As usual, in addition to our State Department/White House meetings, we made the rounds of the foreign embassies. First to the Lebanese embassy, then to the Algerian embassy (they had been chief negotiators in the Iran hostage crisis), and finally to the Syrian embassy.

All these appointments followed basically the same course. We would be greeted by the ambassador or another high-ranking official who would then offer his condolences and sympathy, followed by questions about what he or she wanted us to do. The family members would then take turns expressing their frustration and pain. Many of these complaints had been voiced in previous meetings, and many were voiced several times over in these particular sessions. 'Do something!' was the underlying theme in what we said. 'Tell us what to do,' was the general response. Literally hours would pass without our being able to rise above our paralysing helplessness.

In our final meeting, I sat next to Bushra Kanafani, the Syrian ambassador, disgusted with myself for failing to maintain a business-like approach, embarrassed by how our group presented itself. Members of our group were crying. Others were angry, not at her, but at the knowledge that no end was in sight. I felt we had wasted this woman's time and had accomplished nothing more than probably to leave her an emotional wreck for the remainder of the afternoon. Silently, I promised her that this would be the last time I would put her through this. The purpose in visiting embassies had been played out. That afternoon proved to be my last visit to a foreign embassy for the duration of my father's imprisonment.

In fact I was as guilty as the rest of our group for failing to keep tight reins on my emotions when we asked help from officials. I never shed tears, but often the level of my voice increased, and I found myself spewing forth an often-rehearsed account of our pain and suffering. The futility of it all appeared as an open abyss. I was free to fling myself into it, but it was all-consuming, and no light seemed to shine in the darkness now.

As I flew out of National Airport, I looked down on the streets and familiar buildings of Washington knowing I would never return again as a lobbyist. I had quit. I can't express the relief in my heart when that decision was made. I would return again several times, but always with a different agenda. As the plane climbed through the layer of steel-grey clouds, as the ground faded away and we burst into sunlight, my mind turned to prayer. 'Father, I know now that there's not one person down there, not one government official, not one foreign ambassador, who's going to drop everything to bring my father home. It's up to you and me, I guess.'

It was a long flight home. The plane was full. Much as I liked the reporter who tagged along, I was glad that he wasn't able to get a seat next to me. I had done enough interviews in the past three days. Besides, I was carrying a secret with me, a secret that made me feel isolated from the other hostage families, a secret to which I was still not sure how to react.

Two nights before, I had been alone at Carmella La Spada's when I received a message that I needed to contact Dr Cal Plimpton, the president of the American University of Beirut. I was truly surprised to hear from him because I hadn't talked to anyone from the AUB for over six months, since before the TWA crisis. Maybe he had just seen me on TV, I thought as I dialled his number, and because I was on the East Coast decided to give me a call.

'Has anyone from the AUB contacted you?' he asked.

'No. What about?'

'Have you received a letter from your father recently?'

'Not since the one we got in early November.'

'Well, you should be getting another one shortly. A letter to you and a letter to Kerrie, your dad's friend in Texas, were found shoved under the door of his office at the AUB.'

I didn't know what to make of the news. 'What does it say?'

'I don't know. But it's being mailed to you.'

'How did it get there?' I asked.

'I don't know the details. We have to be very careful to keep this secret. It looks as if your father may have befriended someone who smuggled a letter out for him.'

'When am I going to get it?'

'Probably within a couple of weeks. I think it's vital this remain confidential. Don't even discuss this with the other families until we can find out more.'

'Did they get letters too?'

'No. There were just the two letters from your father.'

My first reaction was to call the other families, but I hesitated long enough to decide otherwise. The fewer people that knew, the better. Maybe Dad had indeed befriended someone, and we might have a channel back in to him if we moved carefully. And besides, Dr Plimpton had been quite adamant about maintaining secrecy. Perhaps he knew more than he was telling me.

The letter arrived in the mail in mid-February. I told no one outside of my immediate family. Dated 23rd December, 1985, it read:

Merry Christmas Everyone,

    May the blessing of this wonderful time be upon each and

every one of you, my dearest loved ones. I pray that this letter finds you healthy and happy.

For a while it appeared that we would be home for Christmas, but that just won't happen. Perhaps next year, if the politicians stop playing their stupid game. Thank God for Terry Waite, the special envoy of the Archbishop of Canterbury. He has developed a realistic, fair, and Arab culturally acceptable means for our release. It is unfortunate that the US State Department with all its experts couldn't have done the same thing months ago. I shouldn't be angry, but I am. I trust that my feelings about the sincerity of our American officials is wrong.

Maybe Santa Claus will bring my present—Freedom—tomorrow night. In this part of the world, his beard is black, and he is powered by a Chevie van, not reindeer.

I am still in good health and normally in good spirits. Life is incredibly boring. Confinement in a room nine-by-twelve foot with three other men leaves no space whatsoever, but thank God for the companionship!

We listen to Voice of America and the British Broadcasting Corporation twice every night from 5 to 7 pm and 10 pm to 12 midnight Beirut time. This with an occasional newspaper and *Time* magazine keeps us current with world events and efforts to gain our release.

It is hard to believe that seven months have gone by so quickly.

All of you—Eric, Cathy, Paul, Lori, Diane, Dad, Dodie, Bob, Carla, Ted, Donald and all of my nephews and nieces are daily in my thoughts and prayers. Be sure to ask Dodie and Carla to save some Christmas cookies for me—especially 'klieners', those delicious fried Danish cookies. Oh yes, give my belated Christmas greetings to the Mohlers, Hultgrens, Wadsworths and the Vallercamps. ...

This Christmas I give you my best wishes for a Merry Christmas and a happy and prosperous New Year. May 1986 be a glorious one for everyone.

I pray that you have received my previous letter of November and have followed my instructions. ...

It is so hard to write under these conditions. You know that I love you and miss you very much. Please be kind to one another, love one another and trust one another. Life is so short and we must make the most of every moment. Keep the faith. Believe in God. Wait to worry and never fear the worst. EGBOK—everything's gonna be OK.

All my love,

Dad

The letter was continued on Friday, 3rd January, 1986:

Dear Eric, Cathy, Paul, Lori, and Diane,

I have not received any letters from you and I want to reassure you that I am well and optimistic for my early release. Heard on radio that UCLA won in the Rose Bowl. God bless Coach Donahue. Please telephone my dear friends the Mohlers. Tell them that I want to sing the UCLA fight song at their front door, but that I am delayed.

Be sure to see that Kerrie is OK. She probably needs money for her tuition and living expenses. Also telephone my dad. Tell him of my love for him and that I will be home soon.

Again, keep the faith, love one another and trust one another. Please don't worry about me. I'm OK, and I'll be home soon.

All my love,

Dad

PS Please tell the families of Tom Sutherland, Father Jenco, and Terry Anderson that they are well and that they hope to write to them soon.

I wanted to tell the other families, especially Peggy; I had just received word that her father, Glen Anderson Sr, had died of cancer. But I still didn't know how this letter had got out. Were the captors aware of it? If not, the possibility that my father had found an ally who was willing to smuggle out letters did not seem entirely implausible. Maybe more letters would follow. Maybe the next letter would have more information as to their whereabouts.

The existence of the letter had to be concealed. I laughed when I thought of the irony considering I had first learned of it while staying at the Watergate. Now I was involved in my own 'cover-up'. But maybe this was the break we were waiting for. I felt as though in a way I was betraying the other families, but if this proved to be the first of many pieces of a map showing the way to our hidden treasure, we could talk about it as we divvied up the loot.

I began to be quite hopeful. My thoughts returned again and again to the message I had received Christmas morning during Mass. This letter arrived when I least expected it. It didn't come through diplomatic channels. It wasn't part of any government initiative. It was just delivered without explanation. Why? Maybe the Lord was telling me that my father would be released, but like the letter, the news of it would come when I least expected it. Maybe this wasn't a test of faith. Maybe he had taken these horrible circumstances and created an opportunity for faith.

Paul and I began to discuss the possibility of changing our tactics and trying to generate a spiritual movement of support. The United States was supposedly a Christian nation; why not unite Americans in prayer for the hostages? The President was not going to alter his public stance on negotiating with terrorists; why not make that rhetoric inapplicable by simply creating a public response of moral support, not political demands? Besides, how much had we really accomplished with the direction we had pursued? Nothing.

As was the case in so many things, the idea seemed appropriate, but the method of accomplishing it was completely foreign. How does one co-ordinate a national ecumenical prayer campaign without the right contacts? I had serious doubts I would receive much support from the secular press. When I recalled the mountain of red tape that the Jencos had encountered in their efforts to motivate the Catholic Church, I wondered if the idea was faced with defeat before it had even begun. Just as we had done with our song, I placed the idea on the back burner, hoping that God would provide the means when the time was right.

At the beginning of March, Peggy Say called to invite me back to Washington, DC to participate in a candlelight vigil marking the captivity of her brother, Terry Anderson, coincidentally the same date as the second anniversary of William Buckley's abduction. I wanted to know what was planned and was told that the Revd Jesse Jackson had agreed to lead a service at the New York Avenue Presbyterian Church in Washington in the morning. That evening, the families would hold a candlelight vigil in Lafayette Park, next to the White House. Peggy wanted Paul and me to sing 'When the Word Comes' during the vigil. (The song was in the end not released until a few months later.)

I felt I was barely over the jet lag from the last trip to Washington, and here I was already expected to go again, but for Peggy's and Terry's sake, I agreed. I would book my reservations and pack my guitar.

Cathy wasn't as excited about the idea. 'Why can't Paul or Diane go?'

'Peggy asked me to sing, and ...'

'Paul can sing the song,' she interrupted. 'It's not fair. You look horrible. You're too tired. You work on this all the time. We have no life for ourselves any more. Why don't you let Paul and Diane do more?'

'We all do what we feel we need to,' I argued.

'They can do more. Paul and Lori can buy a house. They go to their jobs. Everybody gets to go on with their lives but us. We've had to put everything on hold.' Her frustration began to pour out in angry tears. This was the first time Cathy had not just sat quietly by, leaving me to do as I felt proper. 'I want you to tell them that they have to start doing more to help you in this. It's not fair to you, and it's not fair to me.'

'I do talk to them about what's going on ...' I said, trying to defend myself.

'They go on these trips only if you push them. Whose house is always filled with reporters? Who has to handle the press all the time? You. It's always you.'

'I don't mind talking to the press for them. I've done it

so much it's easy for me now. Diane hasn't at all. I know how frightening it can be.'

'Well it's time Diane got over that.'

'OK, I'll talk to them,' I said, trying to put an end to the argument.

She glared at me. 'No you won't. I know you. You'll just go on trying to carry the entire load.'

She was right—on many counts. I *was* tired. Life as a 'hostage son' had become an obsession that dictated every waking second. But something in me didn't want to confront my brother and sister. Maybe it was the protective nature that one inherits as 'head' of the family. I made a final argument by saying, 'I have more flexibility with my job than Paul does.' Cathy gave me a look that let me know I had lost the debate.

When Paul and Diane both objected to joining me in Washington, a faint echo of Cathy's voice in my head made me insistent. In spite of any bad taste that they might still have in their mouths from their last trip, they were going. I began to think I had a right to be selfish on this. They owed it to Dad. And though I never consciously voiced it, I suppose I felt they owed it to me.

I made the travel arrangements for the three of us. John and Marlene Stein, whom I met through the National Organization for Victims Assistance, offered to let us stay at their home—the NOVA 'dorm'. As the date approached, I was relieved to find out that the agenda for the trip had not been expanded to include any visits to foreign embassies or congressional offices. A meeting with Ambassador Oakley from the State Department was the only addition. I could suffer through an hour of that, I thought—as long as I had no intention of uttering one word.

The service that 16th March Sunday at the New York Avenue Presbyterian Church proved to be well worth the air fare. The 1,200-seat church was nearly full. Even State Department officials attended along with former hostages and officials of Associated Press. I felt quite comfortable with the setting, reinforcing my conviction that we needed to turn towards a spiritual effort. Somehow I was persuaded to read from the pulpit the names of the American hostages as well as those men who had been held captive in Lebanon but were now free. Minutes before the service began, a list was handed to me and I scanned over it trying to make sure I was familiar with all the names.

When the time came, I stood in front of the church and said, 'I think the purpose of a roll call is to humanise and put a face to a pretty faceless thing called "hostage". I could probably talk for hours about each of these men and still not show you their faces. The only way to accomplish that is to bring them home.' I then read the names.

After I returned to my place in the pew, Jerry Levin stood up before those in attendance and said, 'In my fifth week of captivity I had a complete and profound spiritual awakening.' He held up a small red Bible that he explained was given to him by his captors. 'Despite the chain on my wrist and the lock on the door, I was free.' As those words settled in me, I realised that I, my father, and all the other hostages and their families had a key to freedom easily in our own grasp.

When Jesse Jackson stepped to the pulpit, I honestly didn't know what to expect. Would he begin a political tirade against the Reagan administration? Was he there as a politician or as a minister? I was grateful to discover it was as the latter.

In his sermon, he referred to Matthew 18:12-14 in the Authorised Version: 'How think ye? if a man have an hundred sheep, and one of them be gone astray, doth he not leave the ninety and nine, and goeth into the mountains, and seeketh that which is gone astray? And if so be that he find it, verily I say unto you, he rejoiceth more of that sheep, than of the ninety and nine which went not astray. Even so, it is not the will of your Father which is in heaven that one of these little ones should perish.'

'We measure our character not by how we care for the ninety-nine, who can take care of themselves,' Jesse Jackson reflected, 'but how we care for the ones who are lost and need our help.' With Easter Sunday only two weeks away, he added, 'Easter reminds us that even good men are held hostage, even good men are crucified ... [but those responsible] cannot stop the stone from being rolled away. They cannot stop the resurrection.'

What I appreciated even more than his words, was how Jesse Jackson responded after the service was over. At a press conference in the church immediately afterwards, he didn't push his way in front of the cameras; instead, he stepped back and allowed us to speak. Although the press hurled questions at him about other unrelated issues, he kept the focus on the immediate purpose of his being present—the hostages.

I walked out on to New York Avenue with my spirits lifted. It felt good to be turning towards a stance of optimism, the optimism that only God can give, and withdrawing from the critical bent that we had often followed. I had felt the presence of the Holy Spirit. A welcome peace engulfed me.

We gathered again that evening in Lafayette Park in front of the White House for our candlelight vigil. The wind was icy cold, and the little late afternoon sun that found its way through the clouds did nothing to warm me. Only a handful of us arrived early—Peggy Say, her husband David, and her brother Glen Anderson Jr, along with Paul, Diane, me and several others.

As six o'clock approached, the crowd remained small. Fearing a tiny turnout, we began to joke among ourselves. We stood facing the lights in the windows of the White House wondering if the President and Mrs Reagan might at least try to sneak a peek at us, but there was no sign of life in the building. A squirrel ran across the lawn in front of us, and someone joked that we should capture it and throw a note over the iron fence of the White House informing the President that we would hold it hostage in that park until our relatives were free. It wasn't a very funny joke, but we laughed quite hard anyway.

Just before we were due to begin, the news camera

crews arrived and began to set up. Then more people. Some I recognised, others I didn't. Paul and I had set our guitars off to the side, out of the way of the people who were to participate behind the news microphones. We put as many people as possible between the cameras and the White House to give the appearance of a large event, and because I wasn't scheduled to sing until towards the end of the hour-long programme, I stood near the back of the crowd.

When the time finally came to sing, my hands were frozen and I could barely play the guitar. Paul and I stood facing the cameras with the majority of people standing behind us. It was the first time I've ever played with my back to the audience. Afterwards, I thought that if the President would have happened to look out at that moment, he would have thought that the whole crowd was giving him the cold shoulder.

The next day we had another typical meeting with the State Department. My code of silence lasted about three seconds. In the room were John Adams, our State Department liaison, Ambassador Robert Oakley, the head of counter-terrorism for the State Department, a gentleman from the Justice Department whose presence we were never to mention (which was easy because I don't remember him saying a word), the hostage family members, and Colonel North, who arrived late and sat quietly as if he was there just to observe a State Department briefing.

I can recall little from the meeting except that I tried to press Mr Oakley to acknowledge the most basic facts. Did they then know who was holding our relatives? He kept speaking in generalities, while I kept pushing for specifics. I don't think either of us took the time to listen to what the other was saying, and the discussion finally expired in mutual frustration and impatience.

After half an hour, Col North took command of the discussion, recapping what had been said in previous meetings, and once again stressing President Reagan's concern for our relatives. I had heard it all before; I wanted proof of action, not just hints of efforts, or sympathy. I hoped to hear that the US was finally negotiating with the captors or that Kuwait had agreed to a prisoner exchange. Instead, nothing was said to make me believe that the US had stepped up its efforts to see my father released.

Late in the meeting, in obvious frustration, North mentioned that he had spent the previous eleven weekends flying overseas in his efforts on behalf of the hostages. There were some statements that seemed so outrageously implausible that one struggles to refrain from laughing out loud—this was one of them. I could sense the other hostage family members reacting in much the same way I was. No one requested a copy of his itinerary. No one said a word in reply.

'He was just telling us what he thinks we want to hear,' Paul complained to me afterwards, and in the months to come we often quoted that line from North when we found ourselves especially discouraged about the apparent lack of effort by the US government. Had North mentioned Tehran and Contras, or cakes and Bibles, maybe we would have taken more interest. On second thoughts, we would have probably felt he was insulting us; or, that the person in charge of rescuing our loved ones was certifiably nuts.

What's really disturbing, in retrospect, is that he was probably being truthful and we missed the very opportunity for which we had come to the State Department that afternoon—to discover what methods were under way to seek our relatives' freedom. Was North opening the door to give us a peek at the government's true plan? Knowing what we know now about the US's dealings with Iran, were we better off having it kept from us? I would think so. It would only have increased the scope of the moral dilemma we already faced.

As Paul, Diane and I flew home, I think we were somewhat elated by some aspects of the trip—specifically the church service, and as always, very discouraged by most others. Paul seemed more mistrustful of North. For some reason, I kind of liked him, and the jury was still out for me. I don't remember what opinion Diane expressed. But by the way my brother and sister spoke, I knew it was probably the last time the three of us would travel on a 'hostage mission' together.

It was understandable. There is no way to express how draining and disheartening those trips were, are, and always would be. Paul could recognise the futility of it all. I couldn't. I would continue. Although in retrospect, I tend to think that I had very little, if any, effect on the outcome of my father's captivity, I imagine if I had to do it over again, I would follow the same course. Like Peggy Say, that's just how we chose to approach the problem.

We arrived home ten days before Easter Sunday—another holiday to struggle through without Dad. In some ways, we seemed farther away than ever from seeing him released. I had no indication, other than the possibility that Ollie North was racking up mileage-plus credit on some airline, that any effort whatsoever was being made.

In conversations with Paul, I discovered something quite disturbing in myself. I hated the men who held my father captive. And I didn't just hate them, I wanted to kill them. I was frightened at being consumed by such a thought. It would be an easy thing to do. But I also sensed that the only one who would really suffer would be myself. I had never before been willing to admit such violent, angry feelings. Now that I had recognised their presence, it was as if the monsters were about to attack, and I stood frozen.

I went to Mass on Easter morning still deluged by those thoughts. I knew I was in trouble. And I knew what the Lord was asking of me. One of my earliest childhood memories is of my father sitting next to my bed and teaching me the Lord's Prayer: 'Forgive us our trespasses, as we forgive those who trespass against us.' How could I ever possibly forgive those men? They didn't deserve it. Their crime against my family was too heinous, too vile, too wicked.

'Lord,' I prayed before the Mass had begun, 'I can't do it. It's too much to ask of me. Don't I have the right to feel this way?'

I was intent on standing firm. I didn't want to put up a roadblock before God, but I wasn't willing to put the effort into moving this obstacle out of the way. I was confident that my anger was justified. I was just like a person in whose lungs cancer is discovered, but he refuses to give up smoking cigarettes. 'I'm just not strong enough. ...'

My eyes drifted to a point above the altar. There, in terribly gruesome detail, hung a reminder of how the Lord had suffered. Nails, the size of those that secure railway tracks to their sleepers, pierced his hands and feet. His crown of thorns. The hole in his side. And more than any of that—all that could not be seen—the rejection, the mockery, the contempt. Had I even come close to suffering like that? If the Lord could forgive what was done to him, if he could use his own suffering as the means of forgiveness, how could I not do likewise? I began to reflect on my own sins; on how I probably offended God many times a day and sinned against him in ways I wasn't even conscious of; yet he was still willing to forgive me, to die for me, to offer me a relationship with him; and it was only through his forgiveness that I did have a relationship with him.

Then it happened. I forgave my father's kidnappers. I finally comprehended that my relationship with God was in jeopardy unless I in turn could forgive. It wasn't that difficult. And once I had truly forgiven them, it was as if a burden had been nullified. The anger was gone for ever.

What a day of healing that Easter Sunday was! What a blessing to have received! Never again was I consumed with the hatred or the need to seek revenge against the men who kidnapped my father. Sure, I'd like to see the guilty parties apprehended, tried, convicted, sentenced, and prevented from ever repeating their crime, but I'm not about to be held hostage for the rest of my life by the anger they implanted in me. Today I am a free man.

PART 3
Old News and No News

. . . Again, part of the seed fell among thorns, which grew up and choked it . . .
Matthew 13:7

10

9th–29th April, 1986

I had spent most of the afternoon just sitting on the couch waiting. Waiting for the phone to ring. Waiting for a brilliant idea to pop into my head. Waiting for my father to be released. If the curtains had been drawn open, the afternoon sunlight would have brightened up the room considerably, but I had kept them closed. Before long, the sun had moved behind the building next door, and it was as if my mood had overtaken the room and left it in a grey haze.

Once again I flipped on the television to divert me from my own unproductivity. The afternoon news was running another story on the recent 5th April bombing of the La Belle discotheque in West Berlin in which a US army sergeant had died. The White House was pointing the finger at Libya and making noises of retaliation. Khadafy was quickly surpassing Khomeini in the eyes of Americans as the counter-nomination for 'The Great Satan'.

It struck me that terrorism had almost become a fad. There was no argument that the acts of violence in themselves were deplorable, but the news media squeezed it for everything it was worth, and the public in ignorance ate it up. The word 'terrorism' was surrounded by mystique. To talk about it was like walking through a graveyard after dark. It was almost as if I could hear a nervous giggle sounding across the nation. As one of the few true victims, it made me sick to watch it broadcast; and ironically, often I was the one talking about it in front of the cameras.

I can't tell you the number of people I spoke with during that period who confused Libya with Lebanon and vice versa. Many expressed the belief that every Arab was a radical Shi'ite fundamentalist, a robot controlled either by Khadafy or Khomeini. Many were still bitter over the Iran hostage ordeal, and that bitterness was evident in their opinions on the war against terrorism.

'You can't deal with them. They're all crazy. They only understand one thing—force.' These were sentiments expressed not just by the beer-bellied truck drivers; I heard them from lawyers, teachers, and other educated people. Because my father's life might have been the third or fourth domino to fall after that initial forceful push, it was a frightening thing to hear from so many.

Only a few days before another report had surfaced in Beirut that all Western hostages had been executed. As always, I tried not to react to the news, but failed. Again, when no bodies turned up, we assumed it was a hoax. However, it had the effect of magnifying that very possibility. If any one of these self-appointed authorities that I heard speak out on the subject had a relative held hostage, they would have certainly been more careful in voicing their opinions, especially about countering violence with violence.

That evening, the President had scheduled a news conference at the White House. I tuned in, wondering if for once a reporter might confront him with a question about my father and the others. I was told at the time that President Reagan purposely avoided the Associated Press reporters because they might bring up the plight of their co-worker, Terry Anderson. Much to my surprise, however, a question did manage to sneak past the defences.

'Mr President, do you have any concerns that the escalation of tensions with Libya, and in that region, may further endanger the American hostages still being held in Lebanon? And also, do you have any news about their well-being that you might share with us?'

Standing behind the podium, President Reagan answered, 'No. Contrary to what some people think, we have constantly been working on that very problem. They've never been out of our mind for a minute, and our efforts have gone in every direction where there seemed an opening. All the information we have indicates that they are well, but again, we do have to deal with this terrorist problem. We cannot allow terrorists to believe that they can do this to the world.'

I listened to the remainder of the press conference before turning off the television. To most of the nation, I assumed the President's remarks, although rambling, probably seemed simple and straightforward. To me, they were filled with contradictions and cause for concern.

The President had just said that all the information they had indicated that the hostages were well. In our last meeting with the State Department, however, they had insisted they still didn't know who held the hostages or where they were imprisoned. They gave the impression that no information was available. Either the President had just lied to the nation to brush off the question, or I had been lied to by the State Department for the very same reason. But what really disturbed me was the apparent willingness and determination to retaliate with force against terrorism. Reagan had made this clear in his answers to the follow-up questions. Sure, he had expressed hope that such action would not affect the hostages in Lebanon, but in the end, the hostages were evidently only of secondary consideration.

The bombs were dropped on Khadafy on 15th April because of US claims of irrefutable evidence that he was behind bombings in Germany and other terrorist acts. Millions of Americans strutted around as if they had personally delivered the knock-out punch to the crazy colonel's nose. Most of them couldn't name a specific act of terrorism linked to him beyond the nightclub bombing in Berlin (if that). An even smaller number could locate Libya on a map.

It may sound as though I'm defending the Libyan leader, which is, of course, not the case. But I did view the bombings as a simplistic answer to a much too complicated problem. In addition, the Libyans claimed that residential areas were hit in the air strike—meaning more innocent casualties in this terrorist war. And there were seven innocent men that I was particularly concerned might also become casualties. I held my breath, waiting to see the affect. The call came the next morning.

John Adams, our State Department contact, was on the line.

'I'm afraid I've got some bad news.' My heart began to feel as if it was strangling itself in a vice-like grip. 'A report has come out of Beirut indicating that three bodies were found this morning in the hills outside of the city.' I felt sudden paralysis was going to send me to the floor. He continued, 'We don't believe that your father was one of them.'

'Was not?' I choked out the words for clarification.

'No. Was not.'

'Who are they?'

'We have yet to receive positive identification, but the report said it was one American and two Englishmen. The American had been shot in the head and so disfigured that identification wasn't immediately possible. It is reported that he is of a smaller physical build than your father. The initial report is that it's Peter Kilburn. The bodies were taken to the morgue at the American University hospital, and staff members from the AUB have been called to make the identification.'

There was nothing I could think of to say.

John continued, 'A note was attached to one indicating that they were executed in retaliation for the bombing of Libya. I'll let you know once a positive ID has been made.' The conversation ended.

Poor Peter Kilburn, I thought. As they put the gun to his

head, did they tell him why he was going to die? Had he felt his country had betrayed him? Did he go to his death feeling abandoned and forgotten by the President and his fellow countrymen? Would—could—his family ever forgive the men who ordered the bombing which cost Peter his life?

These thoughts infuriated and frightened me. Infuriated me because it meant that the US had been willing to sacrifice my father and the others—essentially did sacrifice them. And frightened me because it contradicted the opinions of the experts who claimed that the longer a man is held captive, the harder it is for his captors to kill him. (Supposedly, they begin to know their prisoners as human beings, not just animals in a cage.) But Peter had been held for sixteen months. Obviously his captors still saw him as an animal. How did my father's kidnappers view him after only twelve months?

The next morning, John Adams called again. No, it was not Peter Kilburn after all. It was Alec Collett, the British journalist working for the United Nations. The State Department was going to confirm his identity that evening. The British professors were identified as Leigh Douglas and Philip Padfield. I called Alec's son, David, to offer whatever support I could, which was probably of little substance or comfort.

Believe it or not, the next morning, John called again. A positive ID had been made. It was not Alec Collett's body; it was indeed Peter Kilburn's. *Dear God*, I thought, *am I going to receive another call tomorrow telling me that it was a case of mistaken identity again—finally determined to be my father?*

I called David Collett to see how he was holding up under the constant changing word concerning his father's status. He sounded exhausted, nerves frayed, anxious, but relieved. What an emotional roller-coaster he had been on. At least today, his father was alive.

That reversal, too, proved to be premature. Within a day or two a video was received in Beirut graphically showing the execution of a man by hanging. This was said to be David's father, Alec, hanged also in retaliation for the United States' bombing of Libya. Although positive identification of Alec was impossible from the film, it was indisputable that someone had been hanged while a wild crowd cheered in the background. I decided not to accept Alec's death until David or his wife Elaine had made a positive identification. I saw the video for the first time on that evening's network news in all its gruesome detail. So did Alec's family.

Imagine what it would be like to turn on the television and see actual footage allegedly showing your father being hanged. Shouldn't the Colletts have been allowed to view the film privately before its national broadcast, if they so chose? I found it very hard to excuse the heartless, unsympathetic, disrespectful judgement of the media for their behaviour in this.

These events put me in a state of shock. To discover that things had reached an even higher plateau of insanity, when I already believed I was perched precariously on the summit, left me too weak even to topple off the edge. Why would God allow Alec to die? I kept telling myself that the Lord was in control. He would protect Dad. Then I would remember a still shot from that horrible video of a man, hands bound behind him, a noose around his neck. It may not have been Alec, but *someone* had surely died. How could I continue to feel that God was telling me Dad was going to be all right?

An editor for *USA Today* called early the next week asking if I would be a guest columnist. I agreed, not knowing if I possessed enough rational thoughts between my ears to compose a purposeful commentary. The deadline was the following afternoon, and I wrote this in response to what I now knew was Peter's death:

Peter Kilburn is dead. We had 16 months to prevent his death, and we failed.

The families of the hostages held in Lebanon failed. The people of the USA failed. President Reagan failed. The men responsible for Peter's abduction and execution failed. But only Peter Kilburn pays the ultimate price for our failure.

At this very moment, somewhere in Lebanon, a similar threat of failure literally points a gun to the heads of Father Martin Jenco, Terry Anderson, Thomas Sutherland, David Jacobsen, and Alec Collett. Do we do what is necessary to prevent another tragedy of this magnitude, or do we turn our heads and put our fingers in our ears?

We had 16 months to save Peter's life. Longer than the time needed to bring home the hostages from Iran, TWA, and Achille Lauro combined.

My father wrote Nov. 8: 'Quiet diplomacy has not resulted in the release of a single hostage in two years. William Buckley is presumed dead. He could and should be alive if there had been a reasonable effort made on his behalf.'

Peter Kilburn and William Buckley were not just names on a list of hostages. None of the men still held deserve to be treated as such. It's too easy to sacrifice a list of names. Imagine the roles reversed. It's the only way to get the proper perspective.

If President Reagan was chained to a wall in a small windowless room, he would call for negotiations. If the captors became the captives, they would pray for immediate release. If any of us were seized and held hostage, we would all beg not to be forgotten. These men deserve nothing more than what any of us would expect to be done on our behalf.

All of us fear—justifiably—that we may become the next innocent victim of an act of terrorism. Now is the time to set the precedent that could save our lives should that happen. First save the present hostages, then save the future hostages.

Otherwise, God forbid, should another of us fall victim similar to that of my father and the others, we will receive the same treatment they have received. Some of us will receive the same treatment Peter Kilburn received.

Raise your voice to President Reagan and say, 'These men are our fellow Americans. Don't sacrifice them!'

Raise your voice to the captors and say, 'In the compassionate mercy of God, release these innocent men!'

Raise your voice to God Almighty and say, 'Father, if it be your will, send these innocent men home safely to their families, friends, and country!'

My outrage, especially in front of the media, was initially
tempered by the trauma of the recent events. As the days
passed, however, I became much more critical and angry
towards the President. Not only had I felt betrayed by
the apparent willingness to sacrifice my father and the
others, but in an effort to prevent Dad's death, I wanted
to send a clear message through the press to his captors. I
wanted them to know that I was against the Libyan air
strikes and willing to state that, publicly. It was a twisted
way of begging for mercy.

When I stood in front of the cameras, I still made a
conscious effort to control the image I presented. I
wanted to hint at anger and strong emotion, but at the
same time to present a face of rational indignation.

Looking back, I am always amazed at the timing of
events. I had been scheduled for a month or so to
be a guest speaker at a symposium on 'Terrorism and
International Law' at Whittier College School of Law in
Los Angeles on 18th April. There was of course no way
the organisers could have predicted that three days
before their conference the United States would mount
one of its few military offensives in the war on terrorism,
and there was no way I could back out at such a late date,
even though I was still shell-shocked myself from the
aftermath of the bombing.

I had prepared my speech focusing on what I
considered the only thing I was qualified to comment
on—why the families of hostages react the way they do,
especially to United States policy, and what steps could be
taken to dispel the antagonism and resulting use of the
media to pressure the government. It boiled down to one
factor—the lack of communication between the high
levels of the State Department and individual families.
The fastest way to get me to retire from talking to
the press would be better lines of communication with
government officials.

I tried to outline systematically specific incidents,
reactions to those incidents, and methods to prevent
them in future hostage crises. I wanted to present

an objective speech with constructive suggestions, to avoid simply staging an emotional attack against the bureaucracy. I knew my audience could be influential in promoting these views. I was hoping it would prevent future families from having to suffer unnecessarily as we had.

On the morning of the symposium, I spoke with the gentleman who had invited me to participate. I had been swamped by the press for two days, doing literally three or four dozen separate interviews, and was concerned that the press might disrupt the afternoon's events. Word had got out already that I was scheduled to speak, and as Dr Bazyler seemed quite pleased with the media interest, I didn't feel it appropriate to object to their presence.

As I sat in the lecture hall waiting for the lunch break to end and my introduction to begin, my ears picked up a conversation taking place directly behind me. Two men were looking at the printed agenda and discovered my name was in the next slot.

'Get out your handkerchief for the next speaker,' one voice said, edged in sarcasm.

'Why, who is it?' the other asked.

'It's one of those family members of a Lebanese hostage. ... You know what he's going to say. It'll be an hour of whining, complaining, and tearful emotions.'

The other laughed at his associate's assessment, and I bit my tongue and tried not to reveal myself to them. When I was finally introduced, I stood and took a quick glance over my shoulder. Their embarrassment was obvious, and made it difficult to walk to the podium without breaking into a smile. Once behind the microphone, I stood staring into a dozen or so cyclopean, three-legged cameras, each accompanied by a crew composed of two or three people, all making it virtually impossible to see much of the audience I was addressing.

My forty-five minute speech ran twice what I had planned because I often strayed from my notes. The trauma of the previous days made it impossible for me

to remain clinical or detached from my feelings, and
although the private conversations that followed made
me question whether I had succeeded in conveying my
message, the audience responded warmly to the emotion
expressed through my speech. Ironically, even the two
men who had sat behind me stood and applauded. There
seemed to be no getting around it—people respond
to the humanisation of terrorism much more than to
learned opinion, no matter what kind of intellectual front
they hope to present. If nothing else, I saw the value of
giving a speech fired by emotion.

Another pre-scheduled event to benefit in a distorted
way from the current news was a hostage family gathering in southern California. The people at Hy-Lond
Convalescent Hospital and the city of Westminster had
organised another community awareness day. The Revd
Ben Weir and his wife Carol attended, joined by Fr
Jenco's sisters and brother, Terry Anderson's cousin
Tom and his wife, Thomas Sutherland's daughter Joan,
and members of my family. In spite of Peter Kilburn's
recent death, his niece Patty Little and her husband
Lance also flew down from northern California to
participate.

As I remember, it was a sombre event. Scores of
press members were wandering around Liberty Park in
Westminster with microphones extended and cameras
rolling. Each hostage family member was surrounded by
orbiting reporters who would ask their questions and
then jump to another hostage relative as if they were
electrons being pulled to the nucleus of a more attractive
atom. The public turnout seemed to number about 500
people. I had been asked the night before to sing
'Amazing Grace' at some point during the programme.
In the middle of all these people, I was trying to
remember all the verses to the song.

With all due respect to those who organised the event, I
wished I was at home that day. I just didn't want to be in
front of the public any more as the suffering son of an
American hostage in Lebanon. I cringed at the thought

of more reporters asking the same old questions: 'How do you feel?', 'With the death of Peter Kilburn, do you now fear more for your father's life?' 'Do you think President Reagan was wrong in ordering the bombing of Libya?' 'What does an event like this one today mean to you?' Maybe it was animal instinct, but I just wanted to find a dark place to hide and lick my wounds. I was tired of putting on a show. I was tired of trying to exhibit strength, patience, control, and a sense of responsibility. I didn't want to stand up in front of the community, where I felt like I was being stoned with sympathetic glances; I wanted to suffer privately.

I was angry with the United States government! If they were just willing to negotiate, I wouldn't be here! I would never have to face another reporter! I wouldn't have to expose my pain and suffering to strangers! These thoughts were buried so deeply that they couldn't be seen by the casual onlooker, but they were real to me, anchored to the core of my consciousness.

I was so angry that I was afraid of the bitterness I could feel growing in my heart towards the government. How odd is seems (upon reflection) that I had been able to forgive the men who kidnapped my father immediately and unconditionally that Easter morning, but I could not do the same for the US government. I felt betrayed. They were supposed to protect my father. I still loved the United States, just as I had when I first learned the pledge of allegiance as a child. Nationalistic spirit ran deep within. Yet the government had been willing to sacrifice my father's life!

I didn't even think to pray for God's help in forgiving them. The sense of abandonment was almost too painful to express. I didn't want to admit those feelings. I didn't want to believe that the US had left my father and my family behind like the old and the sick because we were too much of a burden on society. Only my father's freedom would allow for forgiveness.

Because I was torn by that anger and my own denial of it, I now felt the need to disassociate myself from the antagonistic stance I had taken against the President and his staff since the Libyan air strikes. Hence when the families met privately after a luncheon and a tree-planting ceremony, I suggested that we again shift our efforts into a spiritual drive for support. Let's get the churches behind us; let's get people to pray, I urged.

Ben Weir was quick to point out the commitment of the Presbyterian Church and all that it had done. The Jencos added their accounts of having tried to motivate the Catholic Church at the highest levels; but they had only run into spools of red tape. Still, the idea seemed agreeable to everyone, and they all expressed willingness. The catch was that I had to initiate whatever steps were necessary, and I still had no idea where to begin a national inter-denominational prayer campaign. Quickly, our discussion moved to other topics.

In the next few days it became apparent that public reaction to our criticism of the President's strategy in his war against terrorism was generally unfavourable. People were supportive of Reagan's decision. I received a few crank phone calls. We got some nasty threatening mail.

Early the following Tuesday morning (29th April), after the other hostage family members had flown home from southern California, I stood at the boarding gate at John Wayne Airport in Orange County. I had purchased a ticket to San Francisco to attend the funeral of Peter Kilburn. It was a clear, sunny day. The plane was crowded with business travellers.

I rented a car at the San Francisco airport and drove to a hotel near the wharf to pick up Peggy Say. Together, we drove to the US army presidio of San Francisco, where the funeral was to take place.

I was glad to see Peggy since she had been unable to come to California the preceding week. We had begun to talk quite frequently over the phone, and I found that of all the hostage family relatives, I felt the greatest affinity with her. She was intelligent and possessed an enviable amount of energy in her commitment to her brother

Terry, which many times prevented me from just abandoning the whole impossible mess. And more than anything, we had a good time together. We shared the same black sense of humour that helped deflate the immensity of the task which we faced. On that day, however, any attempt at humour would have flopped.

'Did Carmella call you?' she asked as we drove north towards the Golden Gate Bridge. Carmella LaSpada, of No Greater Love, at whose Watergate condominium I had stayed in January, had with little notice or money made the funeral arrangements.

'No. Why?'

'You didn't hear about the bomb threats? ... I guess they've received a couple of phone calls saying that bombs were going to go off at the funeral. Security has really been stepped up on the base.'

'Great.' If Cathy knew about this, I thought, she would have vigorously objected to my attending. 'These phone calls probably didn't come from Lebanese terrorists, did they?'

'No. Fellow Americans.'

I missed the turn-off into the presidio, and we ended up driving around unfamiliar areas of the city, nearly missing the beginning of the service. As usual, the press was present, but thankfully they were kept at bay. As we walked from the chapel to the grave site, my eyes were busy watching for suspicious-looking gardeners and the like.

As the service was ending and I placed a rose on Peter's casket as I passed by, I thought to myself, *I guess the Middle East doesn't have a monopoly on terrorism. We've got terrorists of our own, right here in the good old USA.*

11

27th May–26th July, 1986

The 365th day was quickly approaching. After twelve months, Dad was still a hostage. I just couldn't believe it. In our song, 'When the Word Comes' the line, 'the worries and the fears of the days that have turned to years ...' had been for the other hostage families. Now we found ourselves a part of that group.

I found myself in a constant state of numbness. Driven by the obsession to see my father free, I felt as though I was in the midst of a freezing avalanche, moving without any effort, gaining speed as I tumbled downhill. I was no longer in a state of panic. I was just numb.

My friend Tony, a reporter for the local newspaper, did a story on my father's first anniversary. Days before, another report had come out of Beirut claiming the American hostages had been executed. Another probable hoax. In his interview, Tony made a reference to the 'roller-coaster' ride.

'I'm no longer on it,' I responded. 'I feel like I've fallen off the track. The buffers have all worn away. I'm tired. I'm raw, and I don't have the energy to go up and down any more.'

Only at night as I lay in bed waiting to escape into sleep did that numbness retreat. Then came the depression, the hopelessness, and the fear. I would listen to Cathy breathing softly, and in those dark moments around midnight, the Lord always came to me. I admit I would almost fight his presence so that I could nurse my hurt, but I could not decline his peace. Before I could even offer him thanks, I would be asleep.

It was because of those moments of comfort with which God blessed me that I could never accept the thought that my father would not one day be a free man again. In God's very presence, he told me so. But I still wasn't able to put my complete trust in him. The world was challenging me, and I stood poised as a one-man army. My ego wanted to wear the medals of a hero on its chest. Again I thought back to what Ben Weir had told me upon his release eight months before—my father had put his trust in me to bring him home.

I struggled with the intense guilt at having failed. Twelve months had passed, and I had accomplished absolutely nothing. We were no closer to seeing my father free than on the day he was taken. The State Department was still insisting that it was doing all it could, but after well over two years since William Buckley's abduction on 16th March, 1984, that added up to nothing.

Occasionally, a concerned citizen (or sometimes a certifiable nut) would see me on TV and call the directory for my phone number. One evening, I would have a young woman call to ask whether I was married. A couple of days later, I would receive a call from a stranger who just wanted to let me know that he was praying for my family.

One afternoon in particular, I had left the office early and arrived at home just in time to pick up the ringing phone. It was my boss. A lady had called several times insisting that it was urgent that she talk to me. She even wanted me paged by my beeper. She had told him that she had a means of freeing the hostages. Willing to run down any lead, I called her.

'Your brother's on his way down to your house right now,' she said after I introduced myself. 'He's very excited about what I had to tell him.' She had an unusual accent that I couldn't place.

'What did you have to tell him?' I asked politely.

'He'll tell you when he gets there. I just got off the phone from talking with him about ten minutes ago, and he said he was immediately going to your house to talk about my idea.'

I was intrigued, and yet something seemed a little bit out of kilter. I continued to press her on her 'idea', and she told me in great detail about growing up in France and belonging to the French resistance movement during World War II, only to end up in a Nazi concentration camp. During some period of her life, she had travelled to the Middle East. I began to notice that logic in her words didn't necessarily travel the shortest distance between two points. Often, it failed to connect the points at all. Finally, she revealed her suggestion to end the hostage crisis.

'It's very simple,' she said. 'There is only one language that the men holding your father will understand. I know this from my experience as a teenager in the resistance movement. You must drive to the University of Southern California.' She paused.

'Why?' I asked to fill the pause, knowing more as each second passed that this would not prove to be a fruitful conversation.

'Many Iranian students are there. What you must do, and I want you to consider this before you make your decision, what you must do is—how many American hostages are there?'

'Five,' I answered, thinking of Sutherland, Anderson, Jenco, Buckley ... and my father.

'Fine. Then you must go and kidnap ten Iranian students. Twice as many as there are hostages. Then, you simply let it be known that you will hold them until all the Americans are released. It's the only thing those people will understand.'

'I really don't think I could do that,' I said in as nice a voice as I could muster. 'First of all, those students aren't holding my father. He's held by Lebanese, not Iranians. And besides, I would end up going to jail for kidnapping.'

'No you wouldn't. I have connections in the White

House. I could make sure that you would be pardoned. Mr Jacobsen, just consider the idea. I think it will make more sense once you've had an opportunity to think about it. I know it sounds extreme, but it's the only way.'

The thought of hanging up on this poor lady was quite tempting, but I ended up listening to her for over an hour longer, trying to wait patiently until a break in the conversation would allow me to exit gracefully without adding further misery to her obviously pained existence. I was exhausted when I finally hung up. I immediately called Paul, and we tried to laugh it off.

In retrospect, that wasn't actually the most bizarre call I received during that time. On an otherwise unremarkable afternoon, a rumour was passed on to me via a phone conversation that would have a much greater consequence on the hostage issue. Because it was only a rumour that I had no means of verifying, and because of my numb state, this rumour was like a small, rolling earthquake—inciting a moment of panic, passing quickly, dismissed as insignificant, and soon forgotten.

'You won't believe what I heard today,' said a familiar voice. 'You've got to promise me that you'll never tell anyone where you heard this.'

'I promise.'

The caller was insistent. 'I mean it.'

'I promise,' I repeated emphatically. (Being bound to the promise, I will not reveal the caller's identity now.)

'I heard a rumour that makes me sick. The White House is selling arms to Iran, and they hope that it might influence the release of the hostages.'

'You're kidding! I can't believe they would be so stupid.'

'There's gonna be unbelievable trouble if this ever comes out.'

It was then my turn to say, 'If it ever comes out, I knew nothing about it.'

Of all the stupid, ill-conceived plans, I thought when the conversation had ended. Why would something like that be necessary? Why does the White House continue to deal with Iran, Syria, and other nations when they should deal directly with the captors—just so they can keep their hands clean? As Peggy Say had told me recently, if there was no channel open to the captors, then how did the Archbishop of Canterbury's special envoy Terry Waite manage to meet with them? I reasoned that if the US government had failed at every attempt to identify and establish contact with the men who held my father, then they had overlooked the most obvious means—to call Terry Waite.

Even I had tried that. Soon after his return from Beirut the previous Christmas, I wrote a brief letter of thanks to Lambeth Palace expressing our frustration at the lack of solid facts. I had asked Mr Waite for whatever information he could pass on to us so that our efforts would not be counterproductive to his. I almost begged for a suggestion from him as to where our efforts should be directed.

His response was cordial but non-informative. However, he did reassure us as to his commitment to my father and the others, and that was sufficient for me. He was the only man I knew of who had met directly with the captors, placing his own life at risk, and that knowledge was all I needed. My father had referred to him in his last letter, and as my father's first anniversary approached, I was still confident in his commitment.

To mark that anniversary on 28th May, 1986, we made no plans. Peggy had done an exceptional job in organising Terry Anderson's vigil in Washington several months before, and I was already committed to travelling to Fort Collins, Colorado, in ten days to participate in another community event, this time marking Thomas Sutherland's 365 days of captivity. Enough one-year anniversary vigils were taking place for the public to see. We would mark Dad's by a day of silence.

If I was missing a perfect opportunity to remind Americans that my father was still held hostage, I didn't care. I was depressed and growing more cynical about the possibility that the public would ever respond. I did only a few interviews with the local papers, and otherwise spent that day quietly hiding and in prayer. I was embarrassed to expose the family any more than I had to. It was much easier to travel to Fort Collins where the spotlight was focused on Tom Sutherland and his family. There I could participate, but was safely placed in a secondary position. I felt I was in some way able to hold on to our privacy.

All the same, for someone who was so desperate for privacy, I was not willing to give up my efforts, change my phone number, move to another part of town, or begin sending out resumés to prospective employers. I was locked in. I had lost my peripheral vision. I was a man with a mission: I was a 'hostage son' twenty-four hours a day, seven days a week.

Cathy finally put her foot down. She had to yell to make me hear her. She had to cry to make me want to respond. In my commitment to my father, I had given up every-thing else, including Cathy. In my duty to him, I had relinquished my responsibility to her. She had been so supportive, so unselfish, so willing to trust my judgement, but I discovered I was taking her for granted. Just as I owed the ultimate effort to my father, I also owed it to my wife.

Out of that realisation, we devised 'hostage day off'. We agreed that on one predetermined day per week, we would relax from hostagedom. I would not schedule any hostage-related interviews or meetings. I would stay away from the typewriter and hostage letters. We would not even discuss hostages. It was to be a day completely devoted to enjoying each other's company. Only my father's release or death was to override 'hostage day off'.

Seven days after my father had spent a year in captivity, our record 'When the Word Comes' was released by MCA/Curb Records. Casey Kasem, the famous radio personality we met through Mike Curb, agreed to help us promote the record. Along with his weekly music count-down radio show *The Hits from Coast to Coast*, he enclosed a copy of the single and a cover letter asking the programme directors to consider adding the song to their playlists.

Suddenly I found myself a record promoter. It would take a week for the single to be shipped and delivered. After that, I planned to begin calling the local radio stations trying to promote it myself. If it were warmly received and found regular airplay, I would then have succeeded in putting out a daily reminder before the public, and at the same time, freed myself from some of the usual media work. The song could speak for us.

I had promised an associate producer on the CBS *Morning News* months earlier that I would perform the song on her show first. The competition between the morning news shows is intense, and 'first' is the key word among them. I called Amy to let her know of the release of the record, and she scheduled Cathy and me to fly to New York the following week to appear on Friday. This allowed time for the records to be shipped and received, and it also gave us a couple of days' rest after flying back from the Tom Sutherland vigil in Fort Collins, Colorado.

After the CBS *Morning News* spot was confirmed, I called my contacts for NBC's *Today Show* and ABC's *Good Morning America*. I wasn't able to reach the man at *GMA*, but I did talk to Cheryl from the *Today Show*. She wasn't too happy that I had already agreed to do CBS first, but she spoke to the producers, and they kindly agreed to let me appear anyway on the following Monday morning.

When ABC's *Good Morning America* returned my call a day or two later, the caller was extremely displeased to discover I had already booked the other two shows, but he consulted with his producers and he called me a second time.

'We definitely want you on *Good Morning America*,' he said in a pleasant voice. 'We'd like you to come on next Wednesday.'

'I can't,' I tried to explain patiently. 'I promised them in January, right after I had finished recording the song, that I would do CBS first—on Friday.'

His voice was not so friendly any more. 'If you want to be on our show, you'll have to do it Wednesday. Otherwise,' he said hotly, 'we're not interested.'

'Fine.' I was angry now, too. 'Don't bother to call me again.' As I hung up I made a vow never to appear on *Good Morning America* again. For them it was simply a matter of ratings. I didn't want to be vindictive, but appearing on their show was just no longer an option. In fact, at a much later date, the host David Hartman called personally and left a message on my answering machine, but I erased it.

I was still in a bad mood that evening when I got home and turned on the television to watch the news. I was not prepared for what I saw. As the news anchor introduced the segment, I dropped on to the couch, my tie in a partial knot around my neck, my briefcase left in the middle of the room. Glen Anderson, Terry's brother, was speaking from a hospital bed. Choking back tears, he said, 'This is a message to the people holding my brother Terry. My father died of cancer waiting to see Terry. He did not see him. Now I have cancer, and I made a vow I would not die until I saw Terry. That vow is very close to an end. Please release him. I wish to see him one more time. Please release him. Thank you.'

I cried. It was only the second time that I shed tears during my father's captivity. I knew that Glen was sick; Peggy had told me months before. The doctors had discovered a large tumour on his heart, and further tests showed that the cancer had gone throughout his body. They had given him six months to live.

Glen—or Rich, as the family called him, had asked that the video be broadcast in Lebanon. I prayed that the Hajj would see it and release Terry. I prayed that Rich would not die like his father without having the opportunity to see Terry once more. I prayed for Peggy and the rest of her family. I prayed that the captivity would just end!

Cathy and I flew off to Denver a few days later where we rented a car and drove north to Fort Collins. When we arrived, we received the news that Rich had died the night before. Terry was still a hostage. We found a florist the next morning and sent flowers for his funeral. Rain was falling on Fort Collins. I could think of nothing to write on the card. What could I possibly say to Peggy and her family to express our sorrow, or to be a comfort to theirs?

In spite of the news of Rich's death, the trip to Fort Collins was otherwise uplifting. Tom Sutherland had been on the staff of the Colorado State University before he had accepted the position at the American University of Beirut. He and his wife still owned a house there. I was glad I attended. The people of Tom's hometown organised a simple, dignified ceremony that reflected the community's concern and pledge of continued support. And while we were there in Fort Collins, I actually heard my song played on the radio for the first time.

Two days later we were on yet another plane to New York City where I would sing my song on the CBS *Morning News*. CBS put us up in a good hotel, but we managed to get a room directly over what sounded like a garbage compactor. The noise didn't start until after midnight, and we were too tired to request another room. We hadn't arrived at the hotel until after 10:00 pm, and I was expected to meet the limousine at 6:00 the next morning (3:00 am Pacific Coast Time).

The show seemed to go well, and I surprised myself by not being at all nervous in spite of singing live on television for the first time. We now had an opportunity to spend the weekend in New York, and I think Cathy wanted to, but we were so tired that I vetoed the idea. Nothing seemed more appealing than sleeping in our own bed, and then taking a walk along the beach on Sunday after church.

Before we left New York, we did stop at the headquarters of the American University of Beirut. Not since the 'secret' letter had I talked with my father's employer, and I had more or less given up on their assistance early in my dad's captivity. *Who knows?* I thought as we drove in a taxi through the heavy traffic of downtown Manhattan. *Maybe they'll surprise me.*

But there were no surprises. No new information was offered. I talked with the president of the university, Dr Cal Plimptom, for about half an hour. When I noticed that Cathy had fallen asleep while sitting on the couch in his office, I knew it was time to leave.

On the flight home, I wondered just what good it would really do if the record became successful. Would it only increase my father's value as a hostage? Would it back the State Department into a corner so small that they became restrained and immobile? Would it look like I was just trying to capitalise on my family's suffering? 'It's too late now,' I mumbled to myself.

The same nagging question that always travelled with me again invaded my thoughts. *Am I really accomplishing anything at all? Have I shortened my father's captivity, or in reality have I prolonged it? Was this trip worth it? Has any trip been worth it? Maybe it would be better to do nothing.*

Sunday morning, I found myself in church still wrestling with those thoughts. It was Fathers' Day. That alone was enough to make me depressed. Why couldn't I figure out what to do to get him home? The simple solution seemed just beyond my grasp. It was like a riddle with an easy answer, structured in a way to deceive me into thinking it was much more complicated than it really was. It was driving me crazy. I was ready to throw in the towel.

'Lord, I'm at my wits' end. It's Fathers' Day, and I don't know where my father is. I thought, given enough time, I'd figure out the solution. Well, more than a year's passed, and I'm where I was twelve months ago. It's all been bells and whistles, smoke and lights, but nothing behind them. Why am I failing?'

Suddenly, a question dashed across my mind, 'Have you asked me for direction?' I sat dumbfounded. No, I had never asked God. It was always *What can I do? What idea can I come up with? What brilliant plan can I devise that will free my father?* I had asked the Lord for protection, for opportunities, but I never asked him specifically for guidance. I had been too busy to stop and listen. I had wanted to overcome the challenge by my own means. I still hadn't learned to place my trust completely in him.

'Father in heaven, I want to hear your voice. I want to receive my direction from you. I need your guidance.'

Motivating other Americans spiritually through prayer again dominated my thoughts, but the same stumbling-block tripped me: I didn't know where to begin. I knew that members of our parish were praying for my father, but how could I go about expanding that into an inter-denominational prayer effort?

It had only been eighteen months since I had become a believer. I felt I was still a novice as a Christian. I was afraid I would get blown out of the water by my own ignorance. Sure, I could walk on to a television sound set, play the guitar and sing on live TV without an increase in heart-rate, but I was scared to death to walk into an unfamiliar church, especially of a different denomina-tion, and ask for prayer. It didn't take much to talk myself out of the idea.

'Lord, I need your help. I don't know what to do. And to be honest, I'm really scared to try. I'm numb. I'm tired. I know that my successes would fit on the head of a pin. If you're telling me to put my effort into a spiritual campaign, then I'm going to need your help. I don't know what to do. I'm just going to have to leave it in your hands.'

My emotional state had not changed much as I walked out of St Bonaventure Church. It was still Fathers' Day. I was still depressed. I was still frustrated with myself. Dad was still a hostage. Cathy and I decided escapism was in order and went to a late afternoon matinee and then dinner.

When we returned home around nine o'clock that evening, the answering machine indicated that only one person had called to leave a message. I almost left it for the next day, but the minute chance that it could be important pressed me to listen.

'My name is Lela Gilbert. I'm a freelance writer, and I'm interested in doing an article on the hostages that might motivate people to pray for them. ....'

I couldn't believe it. Was this the beginning of an answer to my prayer at Mass that morning? As much as I wanted to, I chose to wait until the next day to return the call because of the late hour. *Don't get too excited*, I told myself, *it could turn out to be another nutcase calling*. Something in me didn't believe that though. I returned the call the next evening, and we agreed to meet the following Friday.

We met at a restaurant near my house. I was surprised to learn that in addition to being a freelance writer Lela also worked for a non-profit, non-denominational Christian human rights organisation called 'Friends in the West'. I learned from her that the president of Friends in the West, Ray Barnett, had seen Rich Anderson's video plea and was so moved that he felt compelled to do whatever he could to help. Friends in the West was now developing a national prayer campaign. Here was an answer to my prayer!

On 4th July, 1986, Friends in the West announced a massive prayer campaign. It consisted of organising a prayer network as well as distributing prayer bracelets imprinted with the names of each of the hostages and the date of their abduction. There was also a scriptural reference, Hebrews 13:3: 'Be as mindful of prisoners as if you were sharing their imprisonment.' The third part of the campaign consisted of a petition requesting that President Reagan declare Thanksgiving Day 1986 as a national day of prayer for the hostages.

Lela and I began to do some interviews on Christian radio stations and syndicated talk shows. I had no reservations doing these as I had with the secular news media because I felt we were finally moving in the right direction. Another person involved in the early planning stages, Ed Steele, sent copies of my record out to Christian radio stations. Things were really beginning to move.

Providentially, during this period, Cardinal John O'Connor, the Roman Catholic Archbishop of New York, had just returned from a trip to Beirut in search of information about the hostages. He was unsuccessful in uncovering any new information but did hear many times by indirect means that all the hostages were in good health and being humanely treated. Cardinal O'Connor had written me an account of his trip and his continued pledge to help. I was comforted that at least the Catholic Church was still trying.

On the heels of Cardinal O'Connor's trip, Congressman Robert Dornan of California flew to Damascus to meet President Assad. He carried with him a letter signed by 247 members of Congress requesting Assad's assistance in freeing the American hostages. Besides Representative George O'Brien from Illinois, Bob Dornan was the only other US Congressman to take the initiative to travel to the Middle East. Our own representatives, Dan Lungren, Pete Wilson, and Alan Cranston for one reason or another were absent from that trip even though my father was one of their constituents, not Dornan's.

Cardinal O'Connor and Congressman Dornan weren't the only ones with plans to travel to the Middle East. The Washington, DC based Arab-American Anti-discrimination Committee had begun a petition among the Arab-American population and were raising 50,000 signatures calling for the release of the hostages. Their delegation would also soon be travelling in search of my father's kidnappers.

After the death of her brother Rich, Peggy Say began collecting visas to Syria, Lebanon, and anywhere else that might lead her to a reunion with her brother Terry. 'I knew I would have to go to the Middle East eventually,' she told me, 'and now's the time.' I had got my passport six months before for the same purpose and had never used it, so I offered to join her. Once the words had left my mouth, I felt as if I was standing barefoot before a bed of red hot coals, wondering if I really could cross it without melting my feet.

Cathy cried, 'You're going to get kidnapped too. You can't go. Your dad is already held hostage. It's not fair to me, or your family, to put yourself at risk. We've already suffered enough. Who's gonna rescue you if you get kidnapped?'

'I'm not going to get kidnapped,' I insisted. 'There would be so much media around me, kidnappers couldn't even get within twenty yards.'

'I don't want you to go,' she pleaded.

Thankfully, the opportunity didn't in the end arise, not for me, at least. Peggy called a few days later saying everyone thought it would be better for her to go alone. The captors might be more willing to talk and respond to an 'emotional female' than if I was there also. She wanted to give them a way out, and making herself available as the weeping sister begging for mercy might prove to be the way. To say I was disappointed would be a lie. After having thought about my responsibility to Cathy and the family, I was actually hoping it wouldn't come to pass.

I had wished I could use Peggy Say's absence from the States as an excuse to take time off in July, but it seemed a rather flimsy excuse. Peggy would be flying to Damascus. I went to Albuquerque, New Mexico, and met up with Father Jenco's sisters, Sue and Mae, to sing my song at an outdoor festival. At this point, I was beginning to accept that my record was not going to make the charts, in spite of the efforts of Casey Kasem and the people at Curb Records; however, when I sang it live at community functions, it still got a stong response from the audience.

Father Jenco had been a parish priest in Belen, a small city south of Albuquerque, and it proved to be an opportunity to talk with people outside his family who knew and loved him. Just as I had left Fort Collins a month before with a much clearer image of who Tom Sutherland was, so I flew out of Albuquerque with a clearer picture of Father Martin Jenco. If Terry Anderson was anything like his sister, Peggy, it seemed that Dad at least had good company in those three men.

When I arrived home from my weekend in New Mexico, Cathy was obviously upset. I was worn out myself and tried to dodge her, but it was unavoidable. She was upset that I had gone to Albuquerque, and had gone without her.

'When Paul said he didn't want to go, why didn't you ask me?' she asked.

'I didn't think you'd want to. Those are difficult trips. I don't like them. I don't think you'd like them.'

'You should have at least asked me.'

'You went to Denver and New York a few weeks ago,' I reminded her.

'Yeah, that was one of the few times you've ever taken me along. You're busy running around all the time, doing things, keeping busy, working for your dad, and I either sit here at home or go to work so we can pay our bills. I love your dad too, Eric. I want to help, but you won't let me. We've given up everything in our life, and I just can't sit around and be upset any more.'

She was right. In my effort to protect her from further unpleasantness, I was actually causing her further unhappiness by excluding her from my obsessive efforts. I dealt with my frustration and pain by keeping busy, but I had failed to give her the same opportunity. In fact, I had done a disservice to my entire family by carrying the weight alone; I had left them in the same position as my father, in a small, windowless room with only their imaginations and no escape from their fears and suffering.

'You're right,' I conceded. 'Do you want to go to Washington? I think I'll go next week for a few days.'

'Why? I thought you said you were never going back there again.'

I shrugged my shoulders. 'I don't know. It's the same old thing, I guess. I just want to talk to Oliver North and put to rest my fears that nothing is being done. Peggy's been talking to him because of her forthcoming trip, and she seems to be a little more confident. I just think I need to go.'

Cathy shook her head. 'Well, do what you have to do. I can't go. I can't take any more time off work.'

As it happened, the Christian Booksellers' Association

convention was taking place in Washington, DC in a few weeks, and Lela Gilbert from Friends in the West was planning to attend. Thinking it might open some doors for the prayer campaign, I scheduled my trip to coincide with hers. I called John Adams at the State Department to inform him that I was on my way and made an appointment with Colonel North's office.

I was on a 'secret mission'. I wasn't informing the press of my visit, and except for Peggy, I didn't tell any of the other family members. Maybe I would get more information if they knew that as soon as I walked out of the door I wouldn't be stepping in front of a couple of dozen microphones. Besides, the purpose of this trip was to convince myself that I never needed to stand before the press again. It was almost as if I had made up my mind beforehand but was seeking justification for my decision.

Washington was typically hot and humid, both temperature and humidity bordering on 100. John and Marlene Stein once again put me up at their home, the NOVA 'dorm'—much more enjoyable than staying in a stale hotel. Like myself, John and Marlene liked to play music, and we always had a good time together.

Colonel North greeted me warmly when I arrived at his office. I tried to be direct about my purpose of being there, and he seemed to respond. I think it's safe to say that neither of us wanted to see my picture on television any more. He spoke with more candour than on previous occasions, and although he couldn't promise that he had an appointment to pick up my father at the American embassy in Beirut in the near future, I did leave his office feeling my goal was accomplished.

For the first time, he mentioned specifically the name of Imad Mughniyya as the man suspected of kidnapping my father, as had been reported in the newspapers, and as I had heard in countless rumours. Col North appeared brutally honest in saying he believed that the hostages would be released one at a time over a period of months. The government believed at the time that each of the hostages was held by a separate individual group, which made negotiating for their release much more complicated. 'We were that close,' he said, his thumb and index finger nearly touching, 'to getting Peter Kilburn released. A day or two more and we would have had him out.' His controlled voice failed to hide his disappointment. *He's either an accomplished actor or he really does care*, I thought. The more we spoke, the more I felt a personal commitment in him that went beyond mere duty.

When I met with Lela later in the day, I felt somehow freed. 'Secret mission' was accomplished. I had heard what I came to hear. I was confident that never again would a critical remark about the US government escape my lips while the film was rolling or the pen poised to write. Now I could concentrate completely on the prayer campaign. I felt the Lord had truly provided a way out of a catch 22 that would have otherwise been resolved only when Dad was freed.

Ray Barnett, the president of Friends in the West, flew into Washington so that we could meet and talk further about the prayer campaign and any other efforts that might be made. Ray had worked in Lebanon during the Israeli invasion of 1982 providing food and medical relief, and he still had some contacts there. It was suggested that we could perhaps expand the prayer campaign to Lebanon as well—an exciting thought, and he offered to pursue it further.

Although I felt this trip was the first really successful one since my father's abduction, I still had to fight back those familiar feelings of helplessness, frustration, and depression as I flew home. Meanwhile, Peggy flew off to the Middle East that next week, and for several days in a row, I would catch a glimpse of her on the evening news. On the Friday night, her exhausted face yet again appeared from Damascus on the evening news. For some reason, earlier in the day, I had begun to think about how long it had been since the last word from my father. I was trying to fight off the depression but was losing. Her weary face only compounded those feelings.

Where was Dad at that moment? How was his health?

Was he still alive? Seven months without a word! Seven months of his essential non-existence, except in my memory. Seven months of no facts, no new information, no evidence that Dad was still alive. As the evening went on, I became more and more discouraged. The more that Cathy and I talked about it, the more it became apparent that we needed to pray about it.

'Lord, we're trying to be patient and trusting and confident, but it's hard. So much time has passed since Dad's last letter or Terry Waite's last visit to Beirut that we don't even know if he's still alive. If you would, can you just give us a sign that he's OK? We're not even asking for his release. Just a sign. Anything. Some indication that he's alive.'

'Maybe I'm just exhausted,' I told myself as I got ready to go to bed. 'At least tomorrow's Saturday—I can sleep in.' I was asleep as soon as my head hit the pillow.

My plans to stay in bed were foiled when the phone woke us at 7:00 the next morning. I stumbled downstairs angry at being disturbed.

'Eric? John Adams. Have you heard yet?'

'No. Heard what?'

'Father Jenco was released this morning. He's in good health, and he saw your father just yesterday. In fact, there is some word that he has a videotape of your father as well.'

12

26th July–4th October, 1986

'Father Jenco's been released!' I yelled upstairs to Cathy, who was still lying in bed. I kept the receiver in my hand although John Adams had hung up on his end.

She was downstairs almost before I could finish the sentence. 'Where is he? Does he know anything about Dad? Is he all right?' She fired out the questions without waiting for an answer. 'Where is Father Jenco? Why was he released?'

'He's in Damascus. John told me that in a statement the captors said they released him because of poor health, something about his heart, but the initial report is that he looks OK.'

Just as I always tried to keep a cap on my disappointments, I did likewise with good news as well, trying to remain objective, trying not to allow emotion to run away with my mind. Cathy, on the other hand, put no restrictions on her excitement. She demanded to know every detail.

'What about Dad?' she asked as she turned on the television for any news that might give us more information. It was apparently understood that Dad was still being held.

'Father Jenco said they had been kept together, with Terry Anderson and Tom, for the past year. I guess he even brought out a videotape that might have some pictures of Dad and the others. The State Department is working on getting a copy.'

Almost immediately the phone began ringing, and before I even had to hear the first word spilling out of the answering machine, I knew it was the press. What could I say to them? I still knew very little myself, and all they were going to ask was the same old predictable 'How do you feel?' question.

I had to stop and think. Funny, receiving good news seemed almost to create the same physical and emotional reaction as bad news had—the queasy stomach, the momentary confusion, the uncertainty and delay in any kind of reaction. I didn't really know how I felt except that I didn't want to try to explain it for publication and broadcast.

'They're gonna be here at the door any minute,' I said to Cathy. 'I don't want to talk to them. Let's go and hide someplace for the day. I can call the State Department for updates.'

She agreed, and we ran upstairs to get dressed. The phone continued to ring, and I tried to keep an ear open in case the State Department called again. Just before we were to leave, I recognised the voice of Father Jenco's nephew, Andy Mihelich. Standing at the top of the stairs listening, I ran to our bedroom phone as soon as I heard him begin his message. I was quick to apologise for screening my calls.

The tone of his voice was enough for me to confirm his uncle's release. He said they had just talked to him, and he wanted them to call us and assure us that my father was all right. Father Jenco wanted to meet with us personally as soon as he returned to the States, and Andy said he would keep us posted. It was only a short conversation, but I realised he probably had a multitude of calls to make.

The time had come to flee the expectant crowd of reporters. 'They're going to be pulling their hair out when they can't find you,' Cathy said with a laugh.

I laughed too, but at the same time, I felt guilty. *But why do I feel any obligation to them?* I asked myself as I peeked through the curtains to see if the coast was clear.

We opened the door, walked calmly to our car and drove away.

We returned home late in the afternoon, first driving down the street past our house to make sure no one was staked out in the driveway waiting for us. We had spent most of the afternoon driving down the coast with the radio on hoping to pick up more information, but little was said beyond reporting his release.

I planted myself on the couch once inside and turned on the television in time to catch the beginning of the five o'clock news. There, in the lead spot, was footage of Father Jenco, white from head to toe in a white cotton outfit, white hair and white beard, showing a lot of white teeth. Then, more footage, this time Father Jenco was getting out of a car. 'There's Peggy!' Cathy shouted, and I recognised her stepping out from the crowd; the two embraced. How I wished I was there to share in that moment.

'I wonder how Dad is?' I mumbled.

'I'm sure he's fine,' Cathy said reassuringly, more for my comfort than as an indication of her optimism.

I felt disappointment lurking in the shadows behind the couch waiting to spring up and put a damper on the celebration of Father Jenco's release. 'I'm going to be happy,' I commanded myself, 'for Father Jenco, and for his family. I'm going to be happy. ...'

Although my father was still held, I knew I had plenty for which to be grateful. I knew a truly miraculous thing had occurred. The Lord was directly answering my prayers. This was something I had never before experienced. I had prayed often during my father's captivity, but until then I had not seen any of my prayers specifically answered with a 'yes'.

The night before, I had petitioned God for proof that my father was alive, and he had given me that proof. I wondered if, had I prayed for my father's release, that prayer would have been granted also. It didn't matter then, however, because something more important had occurred: I knew beyond a shadow of a doubt that God was listening. He was listening, and he was responding.

I picked up my guitar and absent-mindedly picked at the strings for a minute as I thought about the implications of this turn of events. My eyes drifted to Cathy and then back to the television. The sound from the TV had been blocked out by the volume of my own thoughts, and all I perceived was the picture.

'Who is that?' I said to myself as my thoughts stopped abruptly and my concentration was drawn to the image on the screen. Long, shaggy, ragged hair and beard. Drawn cheeks. A quaver in the voice. Was the hostage coverage over already? Who was this guy, someone just back from an expedition in the Arctic? He was speaking into the camera, and my ears began to tune into his voice, a voice that seemed unfamiliar.

'Please forgive me if I give the impression that I feel I'm one of General Custer's men, or one of the men at the Alamo waiting for help to arrive—' the man was saying.

The voice of the news anchor-man replaced the man on the video, but his picture remained. 'Coming up after this commercial break—another American hostage, David Jacobsen, speaks on video.' Then a commercial overtook the screen.

I couldn't believe it. That was Dad? The commercial dragged on for an eternity as I waited to confirm what I had just heard. How could I not recognise my own father? For over a year, I had tried to work diligently so that I would once again see his face, and yet when I saw it for the first time in fourteen months, it meant nothing to me. It was unrecognisable. It was the face of someone else.

I know why I don't recognise him, I told myself, *it's because I've never seen him with a beard. And those aren't his glasses. And he's lost weight. And his hair is cut and combed differently. His voice is higher too—pushed up in pitch, probably by the stress he's enduring.*

The news broadcast resumed. After a brief introduction, the video was once again playing. 'There's Dad!'

Cathy cried out, her voice trembling into tears. Yes, it was my father. Not the man as I remembered him from our last visit, but someone who had been changed considerably by his circumstances. Changed in physical appearance, altered in posture and presence. The strength and determination that characterised Dad in my mind seemed markedly lessened. He looked exhausted. His shoulders sank as if a burden was laid directly on them. His demeanour was one of a prisoner, a captive, a hostage.

'My captors have told me that Father Jenco, like the good Reverend Benjamin Weir, was released as a sign of good faith, but that the American government did not reciprocate when Ben Weir was released, and I pray that they will do so now,' he said, his voice edged with a deliberate intensity.

'He looks healthy,' I heard Cathy say.

'I think he looks terrible,' I rebuked her.

The video jumped in its edit to the next bite that the news station deemed appropriate to show. 'My captors tell me that this is the very last sign of their good will, and that our release will be by death if the government doesn't negotiate right now. . . .'

Those words put panic in my heart—*William Buckley . . . Peter Kilburn . . . Alec Collett*—and the piece of the video that followed turned the panic into a deep ache. 'There are days,' my father said, looking into the camera, 'when I believe that the government really doesn't care about me and that we've been totally abandoned.' Hearing that, I wanted to leap up off the couch, run out into the street yelling that help was on the way, but I had no idea where I would run. I stayed in my place.

That was all they showed that evening of the video, and the news moved on to other stories. I was left dwelling on that last point: '. . . the government really doesn't care.'

I started to think about what Oliver North had told me just the week before. He'd said that the hostages were all held by separate groups, and as a result, they would be coming out individually over a period of time. He was right on the one count, Father Jenco had come out alone, but he was certainly off the mark on the circumstances of captivity for each of the hostages. Father Jenco had revealed that they were all held together.

How could North have been so mistaken? Was his intelligence information so inaccurate? No wonder our government had failed to secure the release of any of the hostages! I apparently knew more accurately from rumours than they did from gathering intelligence information for two years. The thought was discouraging. Either they were inept, or 'Ollie' hadn't been truthful with me. Whichever the case, it once again planted a seed of doubt in me that would search for any soil, no matter how thin, to sprout roots in.

Sunday morning began early with a phone call. A network news affiliate was willing to exchange a copy of my father's video for a reaction and interview with me. Because I didn't know how long it would take the State Department to forward a copy to me, I agreed. When the camera crew arrived, the producer persisted in asking if they could film my reactions as I watched the video for the first time. I flatly denied the request. 'What do you want more pictures of me for?' I asked. 'Why don't you take that time and show more of the video?'

This time, when Dad's image came on the screen, he was much more recognisable to me—a movement of his head, an inflection in his voice, the phrasing of his ideas— all rang true. The beard, haircut, and glasses were no obstacles to recognition.

'This video has been recorded on the 25th day of July, 1986,' it began. 'I am David Jacobsen, the hospital director of the American University Medical Center. At least I was until Tuesday, May 28, 1985, on which day I was taken a political hostage. . . .'

'. . . To our family and friends: I want you to know that we are alive, that we are reasonably well, that we are provided with the basic necessities of life, that we remain faithful to God, to our moral and ethical principles, and we are determined to be free again. . . .'

That was Dad all right. Most would not see what I saw. He had managed to survive by falling back on determination, stubbornness, and self-confidence. I could sense almost pride in his manner—pride in the fact that he would never allow his captors to control him. I thought back to what Ben Weir had told me upon his release. How he was sometimes shocked at the things Dad would say to the captors. Things that were actually insulting, but because of the cultural differences, only the hostages would understand the insult. 'I don't know how he gets away with it,' Ben had said. Those insults were Dad's way of maintaining a sense of authority over the men who held him. It was his method of 'controlling' the situation—however slightly.

Much of the rest of the video echoed the contents of his previous letters, with several exceptions. Only two lines in the entire eight-minute tape caused me some question. The first referred to William Buckley, taken hostage fourteen months before my father, and claimed by Islamic Jihad to have been executed. In his video, Dad had offered condolences to the wife and four children of Mr Buckley. To our knowledge, Buckley was a bachelor. He had no known family. But I knew my father thought he did by the way his voice cracked as he spoke those words. That was real emotion. As I said when questioned on that in the interview that followed, 'My father's not that good an actor.'

One other line, 'Just remember that one person's terrorist may actually be someone else's freedom fighter . . .' seemed out of character for Dad. That was written by the captors, I told myself as I heard it. That was also a statement that the State Department could point to and thereby argue that the entire video was written by Islamic Jihad, which is exactly what they suggested. I knew better. I knew that most of the words were Dad's.

'I am very tired and I'm frustrated, and to tell you the truth, I'm very angry,' my father said. 'Why won't the government negotiate for our release? They have negotiated for other Americans, why not for us?' (Does that sound like it needed to be written by the captors of a man who had been held already for fourteen months?)

'It is now time that the American Congress perhaps exercised its responsibility to serve as the watchdog of the administration. I am asking that they investigate the handling of this, my hostage crisis.... I ask my family, my friends, the American public and Congressmen to join me in this request. I also ask that the American public contact the White House and ask the President and the State Department to negotiate for our release....' (Would any man held for over a year in a tiny windowless room with three other men make any other request?)

More than any other statement, the one I found the most disturbing, the one that I tried to play up as much as I could in interviews that followed, was when my father said, 'Several golden opportunities have been missed by the American government.' That was obviously a message from the captors. That seemed to be quite a contradiction to the 'We're doing all we can' that had been repeated on infinite occasions by the White House and State Department.

Who was telling the truth? Which side really wanted to see this resolved? Had 'golden opportunities' been presented only to be dismissed by the US government? Or were the captors only trying to increase pressure on the US to submit to their one and only demand—the release of the Dawa prisoners in Kuwait? I reflected on my conversation with Colonel North the week before Father Jenco's release. I studied the video tape of my father. I couldn't reach any conclusion.

Things grew more confused with the release a few days later of a still picture of my father. The message accompanying it, from Islamic Jihad, countered what had been reported by Father Jenco. He carried with him a message for the Archbishop of Canterbury, the Pope, and the President. Or so he thought. In this communique, however, Islamic Jihad claimed that Jenco did not have any word from them.

Almost ten days passed before my first conversation

with Father Jenco. He was obviously still on Beirut time
when he made that initial call—it was 4:30 in the morning
my time. I was getting pretty good at answering the
phone after the first ring, but it still took a while to make
the transition from the dream-state into reality, so I don't
remember much of that first conversation. The tone of
his voice left the greatest impression—quiet, full of
pauses, peaceful. But in spite of his tone, the conversation left me too excited to sleep for the remainder of the
night.

Two weeks after he was released, Cathy, my dad's sister
Doris and I all flew to Chicago to meet him. 'I am a
personal letter from the men to their families,' he had
said on numerous occasions. We were anxious for the
mail.

I'll never forget first spotting him as we exited the gate
at O'Hare. He was several hundred yards down the
terminal walkway, and he must have been stopped a
dozen times before reaching us by people who recognised
him and wanted to welcome him home personally. It
must have taken him a couple of hours to get here from
his car, I thought. The same would happen as we walked
back to the carpark.

Upon our first meeting, I felt an unusual bond with
him. Was it because I considered him the closest I could
get to my father? Was it because I knew and loved his
family? Was it just the excitement of the moment? Was it
because he was a priest and as a Catholic I associated him
with the church? Maybe. But upon reflection, I think I
really saw the Holy Spirit at work.

I saw a man who had obviously suffered a great deal
through his experience. But I also saw a man who, as in
Ben Weir's case, had been ministered to by the Holy
Spirit in his captivity; who had found that his faith was
strengthened; who was not overwhelmed with bitterness
and anger, but who felt the Lord's blessing. 'Isn't God
good?' he said on many occasions, and by the look in his
eyes, and the calm delivery of his speech, I knew he meant
it, and I knew those words were inviting me to agree.

As we drove along the crowded freeways through Chicago, I had an opportunity to ask him questions. They were probably the same questions that had been posed to him by the Anderson and Sutherland families whom he had met with in the past week, but he answered each one patiently.

One thing seemed obvious—he was not happy with the meetings he'd had with US government officials since his release. 'In my meeting at the White House, only Nancy Reagan showed some concern for the human side,' he related to us. I told him some of the things that Ollie North had told me regarding the whereabouts, conditions of captivity and demands for the hostages' release. 'Not true,' he replied to all of them.

Conversations like those only seemed to exhume those haunting words I had tried to ignore since I first heard them from Ben Weir. 'Your father said, "If anyone is going to get me out of here, it will be my sons, Eric and Paul."' How naive I was to believe still that was a possibility.

During our weekend in Chicago, we stayed at Our Lady of Sorrows Basilica, a recently renovated church in a depressed area of downtown. At different times it had been a monastery, a Catholic school, and a church for a large community. Now, except for us and several other priests, it was deserted. The halls were empty. The school had been closed.

Father Jenco celebrated Mass on Sunday morning in the beautiful old church. The neighbourhood was primarily black now, and the size of the congregation had dwindled. The days of flow were over, and the ebb was well in progress. Although there were more empty pews than occupied ones, the Holy Spirit filled the church. The music was joyful. The parishioners were there to 'celebrate' Mass, not just to fulfil their weekly obligation. A spirit of peace and happiness overwhelmed me.

I felt myself splitting into almost two personalities— one that put its trust in God, that knew a true sense of peace, that was marked by patience and trust, that saw resolution and disregarded the time element; and one that was standing up to the challenge of the world, that slept with its armour on, always ready for battle, proud to rise to the challenge, caught up in images of heroism, victory, and competition. 'Come on, you, give me your best shot. I can take whatever you dish out,' seemed to be its voice.

In spite of occasions such as that Mass in Our Lady of Sorrows Church, the part of me that was trusting and confident in God's control became submissive to the impatient, often panic-filled other self. The two had vied for power for some time, especially since the Spirit-reliant one had grown and in a sense threatened the other. It was almost as if the debate in my head concluded when one side said to the other, 'Sure, God will keep your father alive, but don't fool yourself, it's up to you to do the footwork and get him released. If a miraculous release were going to take place, it would have happened by now.' How foolish I was to allow that voice to influence me as it did!

After we had returned from Chicago, another message was delivered from the captors, again accompanied by a picture of my father. This one threatened that if any rescue attempt was made by the United States, they guaranteed that all would die in the process. I was still troubled by the inconsistencies in my last meeting with North, and I thought, *It would be just like the State Department to try something stupid like that.* Sure, I wanted to see my father rescued, but if they were so confused about his location, believing until Father Jenco's release that the hostages were all held separately by different groups, the chances of a military rescue seemed nil.

Father Jenco did not appear to feel that the State Department and the Reagan administration truly had the lives of the hostages foremost in their thoughts, and this influenced me a great deal. I had wondered all along about that possibility, and now the doubts suddenly found new credence. As my father had said in his video, 'My captors tell me that this is the very last sign of their good will, and that our release will be by death if the government doesn't negotiate right now.' I feared time was running out. Two hostages had been released—the next message from the captors might be pinned to the corpse of one of the others.

Then came more heartbreaking news. Joe Cicippio, the comptroller of the AUB, my father's best friend in Lebanon, was kidnapped from the grounds of the university. I knew part of the reason he had remained in Beirut was his sense of responsibility to my father. I had often heard accounts of how hard he was working on every possible lead concerning Dad. Now, he too was a hostage. Within several more days, two more Americans, Frank Reed and Edward Tracy, were kidnapped. Things once again seemed to be deteriorating fast.

There was no excuse for any American to remain in Beirut after that, and I prayed that anyone still there would have the sense to leave. There were more American hostages now than ever before, and as their numbers rose, I saw the difficulty in final resolution increasing as well.

At home, we had further complications. Both my sister, Diane, and my brother's wife, Lori, were pregnant. These would be my father's first grandchildren, and the thought that he wouldn't be home to enjoy their birth only added further pressure. I wondered, when he was finally released and returned to the changes within his own family, how much of his life would seem a blank, as if he was suffering amnesia brought on by his imprisonment?

I half-heartedly considered buying a one-way ticket to Washington, DC and planting myself just outside the White House while I jumped up and down screaming 'Do something!' until my father was released. Or maybe I would symbolically lock myself into my extra bedroom and refuse to come out until my father opened the door and invited me. Anything, *anything* to draw some attention and bring about some sense of urgency. Anything to stir other Americans.

But I didn't need to do either, thanks to a seemingly unrelated event elsewhere in the world. At the end of August 1986, Nicholas Daniloff was arrested in Moscow and charged with spying. As I watched the news report the night of his arrest, I never conceived how important and, in a twisted way, valuable his misfortune would be for our efforts in generating public support.

It may have been the Reagan administration itself that first called Daniloff a 'hostage', I don't remember, but the term was applied, and as a result, a connection was made between him and those held in Lebanon. The press seemed to jump on it more quickly even than I wanted to. And ironically, it was a speech by President Reagan that finally convinced me to act.

When the President stood before the cameras and expressed his outrage by saying he was 'sickened' at the thought of Daniloff being kept in an eight-by-ten foot cell, in the company of an obvious informant, inter-rogated for four hours a day, and then assured prompt and forceful action to secure his release, the restraints that had kept my anger in check came flying off. When had the President ever expressed outrage at my father's captivity in a nine-by-twelve foot room? Never in sixteen months. When was the last time he publicly showed a sense of urgency in a hostage crisis? Not since TWA 847. How could he consider Daniloff's conditions of captivity so inhumane when Daniloff still had contact with US officials and even with his wife, while my father and the others had absolutely no contact with the outside world? The most repeated comment his administration had ever made about the conditions of my father's captivity was 'We don't deal with terrorists.'

If it was true, as they had so often claimed about the men in Lebanon—that they never dealt with terrorists who took hostages—why were they dealing with the Soviets? In the previous year, when the State Department released its list of the five terrorist nations in the world, wasn't the Soviet Union on that list? Hadn't Reagan often referred to the USSR as an 'evil empire'? Wasn't Daniloff referred to as a hostage? How could they justify negotiations for him and not for my father and the others?

The double standard was indisputable. But more than by the double standard about negotiations, I was outraged by the double standard in the President's public remarks. Once again, by showing his personal concern to one hostage, and refusing to do the same for others, he was sending a message to Americans and the world that only certain people were deemed worth saving when they fell victim to terrorism. With my father's name scrawled on the unpreferred list, I was furious.

And I let that fury be known. I still attempted to wear a superficial mask of composure, but I knew that the fire of my rage glowed beneath the surface. For the first time, I felt no remorse over the anger. Thoughts of forgiveness, trust, patience, and even faith, were replaced by bitterness, fury and reckless abandon.

Cathy and I were invited to attend the National Organization for Victims' Assistance annual convention in Denver, which had a slightly sobering effect. I spoke on a panel that consisted of other 'victims' of various violent crimes, and as I had to sit and listen to their stories, it made my own seem less burdensome. In retrospect, I'm sure the Lord was using their stories to drench me with a bucket of iced water.

From Denver, we flew to Washington, DC to join the other families in endorsing a national public awareness campaign conceived and begun by No Greater Love. Because most of the other families were to be represented, we agreed to make use of that opportunity to record a videotape to be shown on television in Beirut. Three of the ex-hostages—Jerry Levin, Ben Weir and Father Jenco—would be together for the first time. We hoped the video would have some effect on the captors, should they view it.

As usual, the timing was tight. Cathy and I needed to race from National Airport to the hotel provided for the filming of the video because Ben and Carol Weir had an engagement that would allow us only forty-five minutes to discuss the contents of our message and to film it. I was drained from two days in Denver when we arrived, wearing an ignited fuse, ready to explode at the slightest inconvenience.

True to form, that inconvenience was waiting as we entered the hotel lobby. Peggy had arranged with a CBS affiliate to film our video message to the captors and see that it expeditiously arrived in Beirut for broadcast. This was never intended to be a news conference. However, a competitive station from Boston also had a camera crew present. Its reporter insisted on remaining in the room as we made our tape.

There was barely enough space for the dozen or so hostage relatives present with one camera crew, let alone two. Although he was assured he would receive a copy of the film, that wasn't sufficient reason for him to leave. In some form of protest, he stood his ground. I looked at my watch. We had already spent ten minutes arguing and now had scarcely half an hour to compose and film our message, and I knew we were wasting valuable time. The man would not listen to reason. I saw Ben and Carol Weir looking at their watches, too.

I stepped up to the reporter. 'Look, we've only got a few minutes to do this. Step outside, and we'll discuss the details when we're done.'

'I am not going to allow these guys to get an exclusive,' he said, pointing to the CBS camera crew.

'Maybe you don't understand.' I felt my voice rising. 'This is not an interview. We're trying to make a tape to send to the people holding our relatives. Exclusivity is not a factor here.'

'I'm not going,' he insisted.

That was it. My patience snapped. 'Either you go, or I'm going to throw you out.'

'Try it.'

As I took another step towards him, I felt someone grabbing my arm and pulling me back. The reporter said something that only infuriated me more, and I lifted my right hand in a gesture of frustration and fury.

Obviously, I was at my worst. I really think it could have deteriorated into a very embarrassing situation, not to mention something of a scandal, had not the reporter been ushered out of the room at that moment. I looked around the room, and my eyes met Father Jenco's. He grinned when he said, 'And you call yourself a Catholic Christian?' I couldn't help but laugh, and my anger dissipated immediately. I had acted badly, and I knew it.

'You're your father's son, all right,' Father Jenco added.

The video was hastily made, and when it was over my feeling of remorse at my loss of temper sent me into the lobby to search out the reporter and apologise. We shook hands and put it to rest. I felt I had enough hostility to endure without adding to it, and I knew that once I had completely calmed down, and then wanted to apologise, I probably wouldn't be able to.

The next morning, as we waited for the press conference to begin announcing No Greater Love's public awareness campaign, we heard the news that a deal had been made for Daniloff's release. We then had a timely precedent to show once again that the government did indeed deal for hostages. Not only did it deal, but it made concessions. In Daniloff's case, it came down to a prisoner exchange— Daniloff for a Soviet agent that was due to go on trial for espionage. One didn't have to look too hard to see parallels, or the double standard.

The press picked up on it, and we received quite favourable coverage. But it wasn't noticed only in the West. The captors seized the opportunity as well. Within days, another letter bearing my father's signature was received. Unlike his video tape, this was inarguably dictated by the men who held him. It was filled with grammatical and spelling mistakes. The phrasing was not of one fluent in American English. However, the signature was identifiable as my father's, as was the accompanying photograph.

Because of the 'mistakes in dictation', it was easily dismissed by the US government as not being a true representation of my father's thoughts, while the press disregarded the message and focused on the misspelling of Daniloff's name. For me, it held even greater significance than Dad's video message because these were obviously the strict words of the captors.

And what did the letter say? '... We fear the possible ending of our story. ...' and 'What are you waiting for? For us to die one by one. ..?'

What was the official White House reaction? 'There is good reason to question whether it was freely written. ...' I was dumbfounded again. It was as if the press could ask the question, 'What is the White House's reaction to the latest letter from the hostage, David Jacobsen?'; the White House could reply with anything: 'Lower inflation', 'Increased defence spending', 'There is good reason to question whether it was freely written.' None of these answers address the question. What really irked me was that the press would let the government get away without a response.

Had the White House ever contacted any of the families for our impressions? No. Had the President even watched the entire video before he made that statement? I doubt it.

Apparently the captors were watching American network news for the reaction, because it wasn't long before another video of my dad was released. This time, at least the script was edited by him. He explained away the mistakes by claiming illness and fatigue. Again, the White House refused to acknowledge the message.

My frustration only intensified. I viewed this increase in communication from Islamic Jihad as a willingness to find a negotiated settlement. Why did our side continue to refuse to go to the bargaining table? They had readily done so for Daniloff, and now he was free. In every other hostage situation—the US embassy in Teheran, TWA 847, the Achille Lauro—negotiations took place. For some unknown reason, this was the exception. It seemed our nation's war on terrorism began and ended right there.

I survived on a constant 'diet' of adrenalin. I spent more of my waking hours being interviewed than not. I existed in a constant state of the unexpected, similar to walking through a dream that moves from one unrelated scene to another, though still retaining some unsubstantiated feeling of logic. Life bordered on complete lunacy.

One Sunday, we received a mysterious message on the answering machine. When I returned the call, the gentleman told me he was an Episcopal priest, and while he was in town wanted to meet me. We arranged a time for him to come to my home, and I called my brother to see if he would come as well.

He arrived shortly before Paul, carrying a small camera and a videotape. After Paul joined us, we turned on the video and watched a press conference by Terry Waite and the Archbishop of Canterbury.

All this time, he appeared to be trying to do the impossible, which was to take our picture without our being aware of it. I watched his movements somewhat amused, and yet concerned. Finally, Cathy came out and asked, 'Would you like me to take a picture of the three of you?' He agreed, and we posed for some 'candid' shots.

'Look natural, as if we are just having a conversation,' he instructed us. We did our best.

'May I use your telephone?' he asked when we were finished. I had no objection. 'I need to call Ollie North,' he informed me. Both Paul and I tried to refrain from showing any reaction.

He made the call, and after the initial greeting, he immediately hung up. 'He has to call me back,' we were told.

As we waited for the phone to ring again, he produced from his pocket an envelope full of pictures. I assumed these were more 'candid' photos. There was one of Vice-President Bush. There were a few foreign dignitaries, some of whom I recognised. *There must be some purpose in all this*, I thought, although I really didn't know what it could be aside from establishing his credibility. Paul, Cathy and I exchanged several glances, showing each other we were all wondering the same thing.

The phone rang, and I answered. Sure enough, it was Colonel North; I immediately recognised his voice. We spoke briefly before I handed the receiver to our guest, and I turned on the TV to give him some sort of privacy for his conversation. Privacy was apparently not what he wanted, for whenever he spoke louder, I would turn the volume up on the set and then he in turn would speak louder. It was obvious that he wanted us to eavesdrop on the conversation.

It all felt like we were being set up for something—as if this man and North had planned their conversation in advance so that they could feed us false information. I wanted to frustrate their scheme and refused to co-operate. The volume on the television was steadily increased; Paul, Cathy and I began talking among ourselves.

Although I wanted to give the appearance of disinterest, I couldn't help but accept the invitation to eavesdrop a little. What I heard only added to my mistrust. I don't know what North was saying, but the priest was talking in a primitive code that went something like, '... Yes, I spoke to the people from "the big country" ...,' and, 'Have you spoken to "our friend" today?' Was this meant to show Paul, Cathy and me that big things were happening? It failed to; instead, it only gave me the impression that these grown men were playing 'spy'.

Finally, much to my relief, he hung up. 'You've got to be very careful when talking on the phone,' he informed us as he sat down. 'These lines are all tapped, and not necessarily by friendly people.'

'What do you mean?' Cathy asked, looking worried.

'The people we are dealing with are not confined to Lebanon,' he explained. 'You must realise you are being monitored at all times. They have extremely sensitive listening devices that record not only your phone calls, but all your conversations. You are probably being tailed at all times without your knowledge.'

'Who's tailing us?' she asked.

'The Iranians.'

I knew that Cathy would panic. This statement by our guest just seemed too far-fetched, and I let the conversation drop. As midnight was approaching, he announced it was time to leave. We stood and he led us in prayer before shaking hands and walking to his car. As he drove away, Paul and I waved from the kerb.

Paul looked at me when the car turned the corner out of sight and said, 'Well, it's been another weird time that we'll never be able to explain.'

'What was his purpose in coming here? I mean, so he knows Ollie North? What did he want with us? What's he going to do with our picture?' I asked as we walked back from the street. Paul just shrugged and turned to head to his car.

'I'll talk to you tomorrow,' I said as we said goodnight.

Cathy was obviously greatly distressed at the thought that we were constantly being tailed by terrorists. 'I'm scared,' she confessed as we got ready for bed.

'There's nothing to be scared of,' I assured her. 'This whole night was too strange to take any of it seriously.'

'I want you to promise me you'll be careful and not take any chances,' she said, and tears filled her eyes. 'I don't know what I'd do if something happened to you.'

'Nothing's going to happen to me,' I said impatiently. 'Look, if I see a blue van parked across the street,' referring to the description of the car involved in my father's abduction, 'I'll run back to the house.'

'Don't make light of this,' she insisted.

For the next two days, her conversation seemed to revolve only around the alleged surveillance. Early Monday morning, I was scheduled to appear on one of the network morning programmes which required leaving my house at 3:00 am. A limousine was to pick me up again. Cathy protested strongly at my decision to go.

'I don't want you to,' she pleaded.

'Nobody is going to kidnap me,' I snapped, irritated with the whole subject.

In spite of her concern, I got up at 2:00 am, showered to help me wake up, and got dressed. She pleaded one final time for me to reconsider. I kissed her, turned off the light, and went out to meet the limo. 'I've got enough real problems without creating more,' I laughed to myself.

The limo was waiting when I got outside. The driver's door was open, and I could see a man's shadowy form stooped over, with his head hidden inside the car. I greeted him, and he stood up when he heard my voice. I couldn't believe it. He was Iranian.

I was embarrassed to find myself considering running back into the house and locking the door. *I can't believe I'm thinking this*, I told myself. *Just get in the car, and don't make a fool of yourself.*

Little was said between us as we got on the freeway and headed towards Los Angeles. The silence of the early hours of the morning began to make all those paranoic suggestions seem all the more feasible. *Cathy would be screaming if she knew who was driving this car*, I thought, trying to calm my own fears.

Finally I submitted myself to my fate. If I was being kidnapped, it was too late then. I looked at the back of the driver's head, and decided to find out one way or the other. I began a conversation.

Within a few words, I realised all those fears were unfounded. I was not being abducted. I had found myself caught up in the lunacy once again. I had a good laugh when I told Cathy about it on my return home, though she failed to see much humour.

Our attention was soon diverted back to the real issue at hand—the threat against the hostages. Another video-tape was released by Islamic Jihad. This time, not only was my father making an appeal, but also Terry Anderson. These were the first pictures of Anderson seen in his eighteen months of captivity. It was my father's third video in just over sixty days. I received news of it when I arrived at work one Friday morning. As always, the timing was unfortunate. I was swamped with

work, and suddenly deluged with requests for interviews. I decided to put off granting any until I had
caught up, especially since no one yet had a copy of the
video.

'We're getting a transmission of the entire video at
11:00 am here at the studio,' a producer from NBC News
informed me over the phone. 'We'd really like to get your
reaction to it.'

It was already 8:30. There was no way I was going to sit
in rush-hour traffic that morning so that they could scoop
the competition. 'I'm really busy here at work, and I can't
possibly drive up there.'

'How about if we send a car?'

I declined. 'Sorry, I've got too much work. I would like
to see the tape if you want to send a crew to my house later
this afternoon with a copy of it.'

'Let me check on something else first,' he said and hung
up.

A few minutes later, he called again. 'How about if we
bring you by helicopter to the Burbank Studios? It could
pick you up at John Wayne Airport and you'd be here in
twenty minutes.'

Before I knew it, I was crawling into the helicopter, and
we were lifting off. I looked down below my feet through
the plexi-glass as we raced across the Los Angeles basin
towards Burbank. 'I can't believe this is really happening,'
I mumbled to myself as we flew a thousand feet over City
Hall in downtown LA.

It only took several frames of the video to shake me
firmly back into reality. I was relieved to see Dad looking
much better than he had in the last one, but his message
was nearly the same as before.

'I am David Jacobsen, one of the three American
hostages in Lebanon, and I am appealing to you for help,'
he began. 'The conditions of our captivity are very bad.
They are far worse now than when Father Jenco was with
us. The pain is real and ever present twenty-four hours a
day. Being ignored is the worst pain. The government
doesn't know when they might hear of our death. They

apparently don't care. For example, when they heard of the murder of Buckley, what did they do? More quiet diplomacy? Silence?

'When Daniloff was arrested by the Russians, his situation was immediately known by the government. Everyone in the government and the press reacted to the situation just like a natural disaster or an earthquake. The American government reacted immediately to free Daniloff because the respect and the honour of the United States would be damaged if the government had not acted quickly.

'President Reagan made his first mistake in the hostage crisis and Buckley died. Mr President, are you going to make another mistake at the cost of our lives? Don't we also deserve the recognition, the respect and the honourable treatment by the United States government? Don't we deserve the same attention and protection that you gave Daniloff?

'How much longer do we have to suffer? How much longer are we to be held captives? Is this captivity only for us? My fellow Americans, family, friends, and free men everywhere: you are witnesses to what is happening and you are now our appellate court and the court of last resort. The time for you individual American citizens to act has come.

'I'm so very proud of my son Eric for the great effort that he and other family members and friends have been making on our behalf. Eric, what you have done until now is good. Keep up your efforts, increase your efforts because you are the light of freedom in a very dark world.

'I ask the American clergy to lend active support to my family, the families of the other hostages and the released hostages, Ben Weir, Father Jenco and Mr Levin. Ask your congregations to pray for us, write letters and send telegrams to the President. Telephone the Congressmen and gather petitions requesting the American government take immediate action for our safe release. A year and a half is far too long to be ignored and be forgotten by your own government.'

The video ended, and I sat at the table in the studio viewing room unaware that a camera was recording my reaction. I never saw the footage of myself, so I can't say how I did react.

The videotape of Terry Anderson followed. His message was just as blunt. '... After two and a half years of empty talk and refusal to act on the part of the Reagan administration, it hurt to see the propaganda and bombast with which that administration solved the problem of Mr Daniloff, a citizen like us who was imprisoned only a short time. How can any official justify the interest and attention and action given in that case and the inattention given ours. ..?'

My reaction to these taped messages held no surprises. They only fuelled my anger and frustration. When my father had mentioned my name and spoke directly to me, I determined to redouble my commitment and resolve. Whatever it required, I would force the US government to act. By negotiating for Daniloff's release, they had backed themselves into a corner. I had no intention of allowing them to slip out quietly when no one was looking.

In the interviews that followed that day, I pulled no punches. When I heard the President's response, I found it easy to respond. 'I have the feeling,' the President had said about making the videotapes, 'they were doing this under the order of their captors.'

'What does he think?' I asked every reporter that would listen. 'That they enjoy being held hostage? That they like being separated for a year and a half from their families, friends, and country? That they really had to be coerced into pleading for help? Is it surprising that they would be hurt at the effort put out for Daniloff and the inaction in their situation? Does he think they would object to checking out of the Hostage Hilton?'

'There is no comparison between the two,' the President said when the parallels between Daniloff and the hostages in Lebanon was drawn.

'He's right,' I agreed. 'There is no comparison. In one

case they act quickly, they negotiate, and they win the freedom of a hostage. In the other, it's apparently at the bottom of the list of priorities. There's no political gain to negotiate for my father and the others. What are they going to get except the lives of these men? They don't have a summit pending.'

I had heard the President's remarks broadcast over the radio earlier in the day. That evening, I watched them on television. What I saw was frightening. He was visibly angry. And that anger was partly directed at me.

The next morning, I appeared on a taping of CBS's *Face the Nation*. I had spent the night tossing and turning, trying to decide whether I should back off a little on my criticism. It was too late. I was too desperate.

'The President says they don't know who is holding the hostages,' the commentator said when the interview began.

'We know who has my father, basically,' I replied. 'We hear rumours all the time, and they all coincide.' I didn't mention that even Colonel North had specifically named Mughniyya as the brains behind the kidnapping. I didn't think the men holding my father would appreciate having their name broadcast worldwide, so I bit my tongue. 'You'd have to have your fingers in your ears not to know who to go and talk to.'

Peggy added, 'I never hear anybody respond to him with, "Excuse me, Mr President, but if you don't know who to talk to, why don't you ask Terry Waite?"'

Before our segment ended, I was asked the question I had been dreading: 'Do you believe the President?' In essence, what the question was really asking was, 'Are you calling the President a liar?'

I paused, hoping for the right words. I settled on the plain truth. 'I'm upset that I've reached this point. I've tried to convince myself otherwise for sixteen months now, but when you see an intense effort put out in every other hostage situation, and you see the neglect of these hostages ... it's really difficult not to become angry and somewhat bitter and to be disbelieving.'

I felt sick for the rest of the day. How had things ever reached this pitch, I wondered. I lay in bed that night unable to sleep. I knew there was a good chance that the President of the United States would watch me question his honesty on national television the following morning. It was frightening that the President thought of me in anger.

'I'm just trying to save my father's life and bring him home,' I repeated to myself over and over again. 'I'm just trying to save his life.'

PART 4

When the Word Comes

. . . Part of it, finally, landed on good soil and yielded grain a hundred—or sixty—or thirtyfold . . .
Matthew 13:8

13
5th–23rd October, 1986

Sunday morning. I woke up buzzing from sheer exhaustion, as if I had spent the night struggling against a fierce current, fighting to prevent myself being swept away, only to see each point of reference on land disappear in the distance. Like a recurring nightmare, too many dreamless hours were passing like that recently.

Without opening my eyes, I could feel the room closing about me—walls of frustration, fear, impatience, and an overwhelming sense of responsibility for my father's life. The floor and ceiling seemed to be crushing me—anger above, bitterness below.

I need to go to church, I told myself. *I need to feel I'm in the midst of the body of Christ as if he was holding me in his arms, speaking softly, comforting me, protecting me.*

Six more days, I reassured myself. *Six busy, hectic days, and then we're out of here—we're taking a break. We're going to pack the car, turn the house over to the answering machine, and disappear for a week.* We hadn't taken off an extended period of time for ourselves since the day of my father's kidnapping. Thanks to the persistence and planning of our close friends, we couldn't put it off any longer. Six of us, three couples, had rented a houseboat on Lake Mead in Arizona for a week. No telephones, no newspapers, no radios, no interviews, no camera crews, no State Department, and no hostage crisis—it was extremely appealing.

That's not to say I didn't have second thoughts about going. In fact as I lay in bed that morning, I had to struggle harder and harder against a desire to cancel. Those little voices of reconsideration inside my head became increasingly louder. 'I'm going. I'm going. *I'm going*,' I would repeat to myself as if trying to settle the debate by simply shouting louder and longer.

I had plenty of things already scheduled. That afternoon, Cathy, Paul, Lori and I were driving up to Lake Arrowhead for the first of what we hoped would be many church programmes sponsored by Friends in the West for the hostages. After that, we would spend two hours driving again before arriving home at midnight, only to get up in two hours for a 4:00 am Monday morning appearance on NBC's *Today Show*.

And then on Tuesday, I had to catch a plane to go to New York to appear on the *Donahue Show* Wednesday morning. From there it was back to the office to try to pull things together for two weeks' absence—two weeks, because on the last day of our 'break', I was going to have to fly to Cincinnati to speak at the Associated Press Managing Editors' Convention. Interwoven through all that would probably be several dozen miscellaneous interviews.

The thought of it all only made my head spin faster. I found myself a seed sown among the briers, and worldly anxiety was choking me. 'If you don't get some rest,' I lectured myself, 'you're not going to last through the month of October.'

On that note, I got out of bed and got ready for church. I made sure we arrived a little early to give me time to kneel in the pew, calm my thoughts, and prepare myself to celebrate Mass.

At one point during the liturgy, prayers of the people are offered to the Lord. On that particular day, my father's name was mentioned. Because we had been travelling, several weeks had passed since we attended church at home, so I didn't know that this had already occurred for several Sundays. That morning, it felt wonderful to know that hundreds of people were joining in prayer every week for my father, but it also made me uncomfortable by touching emotions that were already extremely raw.

I kept my eyes lowered. How many people sitting around me knew that I was the son of David Jacobsen, the hostage in Lebanon? How many had seen me on television or read my comments in the newspaper? How many eyes were sneaking a glance at me at that moment to see my reaction, or to make a sympathetic nod? *Pray for my father*, I wanted to plead, *but give me anonymity*. Even when we went to worship, I was 'on camera'. I could appreciate community prayer, but I also longed for privacy in suffering. In my home parish I felt unusually vulnerable; I wanted to drop the facade of strength and endurance. I wanted to be able to be weak, pained, and helpless.

In the midst of those stretched-out seconds, I realised deep down that only pride was causing that discomfort. It was pride that wanted to present a picture of strength and invincibility. It was pride that threw up the blinds to disguise my vulnerability. It was pride that coached me constantly when I was in public. The thought struck me forcefully, and a seed was planted—*that pride is not the voice I need to listen to*. I prayed to put those feelings away.

But it was no easy task. After sixteen months, pride was deep-rooted. When it came time to stand up in front of a camera on live national TV, I relied on pride. When I stood outside the door of a high-ranking government official, I called on pride. When I was introduced to a stranger as the son of a hostage, pride prompted my words.

How much easier it would have been just to rely on God's guidance! But I wasn't yet quite willing to relinquish control. Although I would never have admitted it, I wanted the glory and praise for my father's release when it came. I wanted the trophy at the finish of the gruelling race I was forced to participate in. I wanted something for my trouble.

Even so, I walked out of the church unaware that the most important seed of that period of my life had just been planted. It would still require some time before it broke through the surface of the soil where it lay hidden at that moment, but it was there. The towering growth, my deep-rooted pride, that shadowed everything in my life was soon to begin withering as its season ended, and this new seed would grow to fill that space.

As soon as we arrived home from church, the gun sounded the beginning of another hectic week. I spent a few minutes on the phone making the final arrangements and pre-interview for the following morning's *Today Show* appearance. I spoke to Joan Sutherland, Tom Sutherland's daughter, who was booked on the same flight to New York for the *Donahue Show*, and made plans to meet at the airport. Then, after a quick phone conversation with Peggy, we changed, tossed my guitar in the car, and started our drive up the side of the mountains to Lake Arrowhead Calvary Chapel.

Since this was to be the first of such programmes, the agenda was still informal. I tried to organise my thoughts a little more during the drive, but soon found myself distracted. I really wanted to focus my mind on bringing people together for my father in prayer, but the events of recent weeks diverted me to politics.

Enough is enough. It'll work out fine, I told myself. I thought back to what Father Jenco's sisters had said at one of our community appearances—'People ask us, "How do you know what to say when you get up in front of a crowd?" and we just tell them, "We don't. We just let the Holy Spirit do the talking."'

We met at Lela Gilbert's house in the mid-afternoon. She had arranged with her pastor to use their church for an ecumenical service that evening. We planned to show some slides of Lebanon, talk a little of the facts about the abduction and captivity of the American hostages and the strife in Lebanon that led to it, and show the last video of my father and Terry Anderson.

Ray Barnett was flying in from Seattle to join us. He

would tell a little of Friends in the West's plans to motivate nationwide prayer; then, prayer bracelets and petitions asking President Reagan to declare Thanksgiving Day, 1986, a national day of prayer for the hostages would be distributed.

Paul and Lori joined us at a coffee shop in Lake Arrowhead village before we went to the church, and Ray soon arrived from the airport. As I sat across the table from Ray and Lela, I couldn't help but think how blessed I was to have them, along with so many others, a part of my life, a part of my struggle to regain my father's freedom. Having dealt with politicians and the media, their humility was fresh and appealing. Their guidance by faith was more than evident. Their effect on me was of stability and hope. They showed obvious enthusiasm for the power and dependability of God, not of people—the opposite of everyone else we had dealt with in the past, just the opposite of myself. Lela was putting in as many hours a day on the hostage situation as I was. Her life had become nearly as disrupted by it as mine, and yet she never complained or even made an issue of it. She was more than just dedicated to the 'cause', and she was to become one of our closest friends. I knew her friendship would be a part of our life long after the hostage situation ended, and it was a direct result of that close and unexpected friendship that I realised afresh that God was continuing to bless us in spite of my father's captivity. Cathy and I began to talk about all the people who had come into our lives as a result of Dad's captivity, and there was suddenly some balance to what I had always perceived as a complete tragedy.

Ray's friendship had an equally profound effect upon my life. In the previous month, unknown to the media and the world, he had taken his prayer campaign to Lebanon. Armed with only prayer bracelets and petitions, he had gone into Beirut. Apart from Terry Waite, he was the only Westerner I knew who had put concern for his own life aside in an effort to free my father and the other hostages. What a lesson I learned from him! Here was a man who had so much faith, trust and confidence in prayer and direction from God, that he was willing to go alone, unprotected, without any real plan into the midst of the most violent and anarchical cities on the earth for the sake of people he had never met—simply because he felt God was telling him to do so. Non-believers, and I suppose even some believers, would consider it at the least unwise and at the worst crazy and irresponsible, but I never questioned his judgement. He did not impress me as a foolish man.

His trip had suddenly added a new dimension to everything. As a result of the days he spent in Lebanon, some key contacts were re-established. These people suggested that they might be able to lead us to the men holding my father and offered to serve as intermediaries. We had decided cautiously to pursue them. Over a few cups of coffee that evening, we agreed that I would travel with Ray the first week of November to Cyprus, which had become the main access into Beirut. Once there, we would meet with his contact people.

Cathy didn't like the idea, afraid that once there I took the next step and entered Beirut, I would only join my father. I assured her over and over that this wouldn't be the case. I would not enter Lebanon. She had no cause for concern. My safety was guaranteed. No one would know I was there, not even the Lebanese we were going to meet. Only after they had arrived would Ray inform them that I was in an adjacent hotel room. It would be their decision whether they met me. I tried to keep my excitement in check. 'If it's God's will, it'll happen,' I told myself. 'If it's a hoax, God will let us know.' The time for me to travel to the Middle East was apparently at hand.

At the church service that night, the people were receptive. I felt the Spirit's power and presence at work. I drove down the mountain once again feeling that I would now concentrate on the prayer campaign. I would also wait to see what would happen with Ray's Lebanese contacts.

Unfortunately, several hours later, as I sat in the back

of a limousine on my way to the NBC studios at 3:30 in the morning, my mind once again flip-flopped back to Daniloff, the State Department and double standard/lack of urgency on the part of the White House. Why couldn't I control it? Why was I so easily drawn back into politics?

The *Today Show* interview was short and predictable. The day that followed had more interviews that were basically retreads of past conversations, and I struggled through them trying to maintain some appearance of energetic commitment in our wrestling match against the giant bureaucratic sloth.

I tried but failed to get to bed early that night. It was late before I got around to packing for the trip to New York. I had learned just that day that Nicholas Daniloff would be appearing on the *Donahue Show* along with the families of the American hostages in Lebanon, and I still was trying to figure out how I felt. Would he help make our points, or would he only distract? In addition, one of the local papers was sending along a reporter for a story in the following Sunday edition. That meant I had to remain in 'hostage son' mode for the entire trip—not very relaxing. I was also becoming exhausted with trying to come up with new and interesting answers for the same repetitive questions. What was left to say that hadn't already been said?

I sat next to Joan Sutherland on the flight East and enjoyed her company immensely. Other hostage family members provided the only opportunity on those kind of trips to talk about things not related to hostages. I was thankful that the reporter was unable to secure a seat next to mine, and aside from a few times when she crouched in the aisle and Joan and I fielded a few questions, the flight was restful.

Once in New York, we had a late dinner with all the other hostage family members. In the end I went to bed long after I had planned to, and an early alarm, plus the time change, made it feel as if I had gone through yet another night without rest.

Before the show, my mind was a blank. Daniloff and

his boss at *US News and World Report*, Mr Zuckerman (who was also to appear with us), were kept apart from us in another room. We tried to talk among the group and determine our strategy when we were before the cameras, and although I was trying to push Friends in the West's prayer campaign, no one else seemed to express much interest. I decided to save for the show what little energy I had.

Although as we filed on to the stage I felt too lethargic to be nervous, the moment we were in front of the audience and Donahue began the introductions, I felt something switch on. Peggy told me afterwards, 'You do "righteous indignation" very well.' Maybe. I just knew I wasn't going to sit there and be an object of pity. I wanted to sound like a football coach at half-time whose team was scoreless, unmotivated, and heading for another humiliating loss—angry, impatient, and aware that the players weren't making a full effort.

As glad as I was that Daniloff was a free man, I would have preferred not to have had our story diluted, and I think confused, by our sharing the programme. What really concerned me was that his boss, Zuckerman, seemed actually to get more air time than Daniloff, and if it weren't for Daniloff sitting to his right, I would have thought that Zuckerman had been sent by the State Department as a spokesperson.

After the show ended and while we were still seated on the stage in front of the studio audience, Zuckerman and I exchanged heated words. He had maintained through the entire show that the US was indeed involved in an exhaustive effort to secure the release of the hostages, basing that argument on information given to him by government officials, although he never revealed details to us.

Why would he have reason to doubt them? Daniloff had been freed in a matter of weeks. My father was still held after sixteen months with no freedom in sight. The government's efforts on behalf of Nicholas Daniloff were well documented in the media. But did any documentation of a single government initiative to seek the release of my father exist? How could Zuckerman really explain the contrast in efforts made in both cases, and how could I ignore them?

On the flight home I began to compose a letter to Zuckerman, because as soon as we were off the stage, he had disappeared, and I didn't have the opportunity to finish our conversation. More than anything, I didn't want to leave it on a sour note and risk creating enmity with such a powerful and influential person in the media as he. I tried to make the tone of my letter conciliatory and positive and mailed it the day after my return. It had no apparent effect on his opinion.

Peggy and I had spent the remainder of my day in New York literally running across Manhattan from one interview to another accompanied by our companion reporter. As was the case when Peggy and I were together, we could do nothing but joke about everything that had and was happening. I was a little concerned that the reporter's story would turn into an account of hostage jokes and black-humour quotes, but we were spared.

Instead the headline would read, 'Eric Jacobsen vows: "No more Mr Nice Guy".' I laughed when I saw it several weeks later, but I was glad I was away on a houseboat when that story ran. Although the piece was complimentary about me, it seemed almost to be referring to someone else, and I reacted to it as though it were.

Although it had been planned for nearly a year, the houseboat holiday couldn't have happened at a more needed time. I was exhausted beyond tiredness, and I walked about almost in a state of delirium caused by adrenalin and elevated blood pressure. But remarkably, once we were floating on the blue waters of Lake Mead, surrounded by the multi-hued hills of the American southwestern desert, it was only a couple of days before I regained my equilibrium. Our friends, Joe and Liz, and Lyn and Diane, were kind enough to avoid all mention of hostages. It was off season, and the lake was deserted although the water and air were still warm. Halfway through the trip I actually suffered some pangs of guilt for having gone an entire day without thinking about hostages. This prompted me to try calling Lela during one of our stops at a marina, but my calling card wouldn't work. I had to accept the fact that I was going to be out of touch with the world for a whole week.

One morning, in the middle of the week, I woke to find Cathy smiling. 'I've just had an interesting dream,' she said when she saw my eyes open. 'I've just dreamt that God told me not to worry, and I wouldn't have to wear Dad's prayer bracelet much longer.'

'How do you know it was God's voice?' I asked.

'I just know,' she assured me. 'He wanted to tell me not to worry—Dad's going to be released soon.' We didn't say much more about it. We would just wait.

As the houseboat motored back towards the marina on the final day, I sat at the small cabin table and wrote my speech for the Associated Press Managing Editors' Convention in Cincinnati, where I would be speaking in two days. I had struggled for several days already trying to compose this vital speech, only to end each effort with a blank piece of paper. At this sitting, I wrote it in one attempt with no second draft or editing. I checked its duration and stuck it in my briefcase.

Cathy reminded me of an abandoned puppy in the car window as she dropped me off at the airport the next morning. As the car drove away, I just hoped that this ending to our holiday wouldn't spoil the positive effects. There was no getting around the fact that we had to return to the hostage situation, no matter how much we wished to remain for ever on that peaceful lake.

It was dark when I arrived in Cincinnati that evening. It would be dark when I drove to the airport two days later, and to this day I have no idea what Cincinnati looks like. It wound up being just another blur in my memory, a photograph taken from a speeding car on a dark highway.

Peggy, Fr Jenco, and I met for dinner along with some

Associated Press executives. My thoughts were focused on what could possibly be the most important speech I would have to give. These were the managing editors of every national newspaper that carried Associated Press stories. These were the people that decided what would make the next edition. These were the people who controlled what Americans read every morning. These people were 'the media'.

The next morning, as I was introduced and approached the podium to address them, I tried to call once again on whatever I had tapped into for *Face the Nation* and *The Donahue Show*. Whatever it was, it had drawn a response from the people attending, and I wanted that same response from this group.

I unfolded the papers of my speech and began by announcing to those present that on that morning my father had awakened to his five hundred and eleventh day of captivity. From there, I began a systematic comparison of the US government's immediate and successful response to Daniloff's imprisonment and the continued, prolonged captivity of my father and the other American hostages.

I began each of the dozen points with a question, 'I want to know why, if in Daniloff's case ... then why not for my father and the others?' In this manner, it was easy to demonstrate the inconsistencies of the Reagan administration policy. 'I want your help in answering these questions,' I told the hundreds of journalists seated in the convention centre auditorium.

My speech ended. 'And finally, I want to know why, if the hostages of the embassy in Iran, TWA, Achille Lauro, and Nicholas Daniloff can be enjoying freedom today, then why not David Jacobsen, Terry Anderson, Thomas Sutherland, Frank Reed, Joe Cicippio, and Alec Collett?'

I knew by the delayed applause that the speech had made an impact. During a question-and-answer period that followed, one member of the convention suggested that transcripts of our speeches be hand delivered to the White House and a formal response be requested to the points made by Peggy, Fr Jenco, and myself. That motion was passed and followed through the same day. All hoped that before the closing of the convention three days later a response would be received.

'The White House won't respond positively,' Peggy and I grumbled. 'But that might be enough to stir up these editors into more aggressive coverage,' we tried to reassure ourselves.

I flew back to California already in need of another week's rest. Peggy called within a couple of days, reporting that the White House had not responded positively, just as we had predicted. Now all we could do was wait to see the reaction of the press. I sat silently at the table and stared at the wall. What more could be said? If the press didn't side with us now, they never would. For the next few days, I expectantly scanned the newspapers each day looking for some evidence of renewed support in the form of an AP wire story, but I never saw a shred of evidence that anything had changed.

Soon after the AP meeting, I appeared on a midnight radio talk show, and after dealing with the call-in audience, I drove home in the black, early hours of morning completely discouraged. It seemed that a majority of the callers felt I was wrong in the way I was handling the hostage issue. Listening to them, one might think I was committing treason by trying to save my father's life.

Then came news from Beirut about the trip Ray and I were intending to make to Cyprus. It was postponed for 'a few weeks' without explanation. Much to Cathy's pleasure, I would spend the first week of November in southern California, not peering across the Mediterranean into Beirut. Much to my disappointment, Ray and I would not succeed in negotiating Dad's release in the near future.

I was beginning to surrender to the facts. I would never influence the US government. I would never ignite the media. I would never have the complete support of other Americans. I would not myself negotiate my father's release.

14
24th October–4th November, 1986

The change in me was inevitable. It was as if I was groaning at the core of my soul. I now know the cause. The seed that was planted in me just weeks before was now establishing its roots. My pride was dying. I had flown out of Cincinnati claiming victory, only to discover that I had in fact failed to accomplish anything more than deliver an interesting speech. It hurt.

On the other hand, I still held on to the hope that through Ray's contacts we could bring Dad out. I thought at the time, 'Wouldn't it be great to succeed at this, and then be able to stand in front of the cameras and say, "As you all know, the Reagan administration has been unsuccessful at freeing my father. Well guess who I have standing behind that closed door?"'

A familiar voice echoed, 'If anyone is going to get me out of here, it'll be my son, Eric.' *Sorry, Dad, it doesn't look that way any more.*

I thought I could do it. For the first time since his abduction seventeen months before, I now knew I couldn't. I had kept myself busy, nothing more. 'That's not true,' a weak little voice would whine in my head. 'You'll do it yet.' But the strength in that voice was now fading and almost inaudible.

'Lord, I've been fighting you,' I said the next morning as I was driving to work. 'I hate to admit it, but I guess I've been trying to ensure that I'd get to steal a little of your

231

glory should Dad be released. I'm sorry, please forgive me.'

I can remember driving across an overpass on the road to the office. The sun was coming directly through the windscreen, having just risen from behind Saddleback Mountain. I suddenly knew just how weak my faith had been. I could see clearly how I had limited God's role. I had as it were subjugated him simply to the staying of my father's execution until I could come to the rescue. It wasn't that I suddenly believed I should have done nothing over the previous seventeen months; but I certainly hadn't tried very hard to listen for any directions. I thought about how Ray went about his efforts; he never took a step without praying and listening for an answer, whereas I made most of my moves with prayer as an afterthought.

I realised finally that I needed to pray first, and then act accordingly. Maybe the cancellation of the trip to Cyprus and the silence of the media was an indication that I should do nothing yet. Maybe God was telling me just to pray and have confidence in him. I thought back over all that had happened in the past year and a half. It seemed that God had been telling me this from the very beginning. It had taken months before I could even acknowledge God's role. It had taken more months after the first realisation of his involvement for me to allow him to influence me and to work in my heart, and I had still spent the last few months trying to regain control.

But now I had reached the point where allowing the Lord to be in control would be a conscious decision. 'I don't know how successful I'll be in surrendering to you, Lord,' I tried to say with all the humility I could muster, 'but I'll try to put it before you and leave it there. You are God. You are in control. I'm not. I just want to listen for your voice. Please, God, help me to recognise you when you speak to me.'

What a burden was lifted from my shoulders with those words! 'If anyone is going to get me out of here, it'll be my son, Eric.' Wrong. Those words would no longer haunt me. I was free from that impossible yoke with a weight nearly heavy enough to choke the life out of me. I could be a factor in his release, but I would never be able to claim responsibility for his freedom. I was powerless, and that was fine.

On Friday afternoon of the following week, a reporter from one of the network news offices called. 'There's a report out that Terry Waite is in the Middle East. Is something up?' she asked.

'Not that I know of,' I told her honestly.

'There's a rumour that a hostage is going to be released. Do you think there's anything to that?'

I had heard the story so many times in the past that I automatically dismissed it. 'I haven't heard,' I told her.

Not long after that conversation, Peggy called. 'There are rumours that Terry Waite is going into Beirut to bring out the hostages,' she said with that familiar excitement in her voice brought on by any possible good news.

'Peggy, we've heard this before.' I was truly sceptical. 'I'm not going to let myself get worked up. If it doesn't happen, I don't want to be disappointed. If it happens, I'd like to be surprised.'

What I said and what I thought were not necessarily in agreement. How could I avoid getting excited at the prospect of the hostages' freedom. Still, I was determined not to allow that excitement get the best of me.

I was again in my car, this time driving home when my thoughts were flooded with the possibility of Terry Waite's success. 'Lord, I'm going to put this in your hands. Yes, I want Dad to be released. Yes, I pray that you would release him this weekend. You know how badly I want that. If you want him out, he'll come out. I'm not going to think about it any more.'

Much to my surprise, I was fairly successful at doing so on this occasion. When a doubt leapt in front of me screaming hysterically, I would tell myself, 'Just trust in God. Have faith.'

The press called all day Saturday, continually checking

to see if I had heard any information. I hadn't. Everyone was very concerned with my whereabouts in case something happened and they needed to get in touch with me. 'Can you let me know where you're going to be at all times,' one of them asked me. I found it ironic that I had been scheduled to spend that weekend in Cyprus with Ray. Imagine the press trying to track me down if I was there!

Friday night and then Saturday passed without a hostage release. At bedtime, I decided to disconnect our upstairs phone. By unplugging the phone, I was hoping to show God that I had complete trust in his decision. If Dad was released, I would know about it soon enough. If Dad was not released, I would not be disappointed.

I fell asleep quickly that night, at peace, but some time in the night, Cathy gently nudged me awake. As I came to my senses, I could hear the muted sound of the phone downstairs.

'The phone's ringing,' she said, 'I think it's rung a couple of other times already since we went to bed.'

My heart started to pound hard, and the rushing adrenalin shook me awake. I walked downstairs in the dark, listening for the caller's voice on the answering machine. Silence. The caller had hung up.

I had almost turned to go back to bed when I noticed the small red light on the answering machine flashing in the darkness. One ... Two ... Three ... Four ... *Four calls. Four messages.* Cathy was right—the phone had indeed rung several times in the night.

As I rewound the tape, I knew what I wanted to hear. I quickly reprimanded myself, *Don't get excited. It's not necessarily going to be what you're hoping to hear. It could be the press just acting on more rumours.*

The tape began to play John Adams' voice from the State Department. 'Eric, I've got some good news.' His voice was almost singing with excitement and happiness. 'We've got word from Beirut that your father has been freed. He's with Terry Waite and the ambassador at the embassy in East Beirut. We're in the process of trying to make telephone contact. Call me when you get in.'

My heart nearly stopped from all the adrenalin. I turned around to find Cathy standing behind me. The moment our eyes met she began to cry uncontrollably. 'Is he free? Is he really free? Oh, thank you, God! Thank you!' she shouted through her joyful tears.

I couldn't react, not until I heard Dad's voice. I couldn't be sure that he was truly free until he told me so himself.

The remaining messages played, all from John Adams, each time becoming a little more impatient about speaking into an answering machine. I called him back as soon as the tape stopped.

When I got him on the line, I said, 'Are you really sure he's free?'

'Yes,' John assured me. 'We even had him on the line and tried to get him through to you, but then we got the answering machine.'

I had to laugh at the thought of it. After Dad spends seventeen months in captivity, he calls home to tell his family he's free and gets an answering machine. It must have driven him crazy! Oh well, nothing else made any sense at any time during the past year and a half—why should things be any different just because he was free?

'What about the others?' I asked.

'Your father's the only one so far. We had heard that Terry Anderson was supposed to be released with him, but there hasn't been any sign of him.'

My happiness was suddenly deflated. 'Have you called Peggy?'

'Yes. She's having a hard time coping.'

Silence fell between us. Terry was the longest held. Everyone expected him to be the next one released, in the same pattern as Jenco and Weir. Always the longest in captivity was the next set free. For some reason, the captors had skipped over him and went to the second man in line—my father.

I thought back to how I felt when I learned that Ben Weir was released and Dad wasn't with him. I relived the moment when I heard the news that Father Jenco was freed, but Dad was still imprisoned. It wasn't that hard to put myself in Peggy's shoes. Or in the shoes of the Sutherland family, or the Cicippios, or.... I found myself feeling guilty that my father was free, and the others weren't.

Why couldn't they all have been released? I thought to myself. I felt the rain falling on my party—the day and all the planning behind it were ruined. I knew I really wouldn't be able to celebrate as I'd like to, knowing that Terry Anderson, Tom, Joe and the other hostages were still imprisoned. Just as disturbing as that thought was, so was the realisation that the hostage crisis was not over for me. Peggy and the others had become my 'family'. Even if it was true that my father was free, still other 'relatives' were held hostage in Lebanon.

Maybe John sensed my pang of guilt because he added, 'There's still a chance that Terry may come out. We're still pushing hard for it. We'd like to ask you not to talk to the press until we give the word.' For the sake of Terry and the others I agreed.

It was time to call my family, and I thanked John for the news. He said they would try again to establish telephone contact with Beirut, and once they did, they would put through the call to us. I thanked him for that too, but those words still seemed unbelievable to me. Was it finally over?

From the same seat at the dining-room table, at nearly the same hour of night, in nearly the same order, I called the same people that I called the night my father was kidnapped. As my hand punched the numbers on the phone, it shook just as much as it had that night a year and a half earlier. Cathy was still breaking into tears every now and then. I noticed my face was getting sore from smiling. I guess I hadn't used those muscles enough.

Everyone was surprised to hear my voice and thrilled at the news I had to tell. For once, it was a real joy for me to make the calls. This time, there was no apprehension in calling my mother. A week later, when Dad returned to southern California, she would be there at the airport to welcome him home. Though his safe return really didn't alter their relationship, we all had a good reason to celebrate.

Paul and Lori arrived at my front door an hour later. By 3:30 am the continuous rapping of reporters began. At 10:00 am we finally got the word from the State Department that they would now publicly confirm Dad's release, so Paul and I stepped out in front of my house and did the first news conference for seventeen months where we were all smiling.

Two concerns dominated my thoughts. 'God gets the glory for my father's release,' I told the reporters. I don't know if that quote was picked up by any of them, but everything I felt was summed up in those few words. The second point was just as simple: 'Remember the remaining hostages.'

Dozens of reporters and camera crews filled the driveway and the street, and to restore some peace to the neighbourhood we arranged to move the news conference down to the Huntington Beach City Hall. Paul, Diane, and I left to meet the press at noon. Cathy, Lori, and Jake stayed at home. Who would have guessed that it was during the time we were gone that the State Department managed to get a call through from Dad!

I was really disappointed on our return home when I discovered that. Cathy and Lori related their conversations with him, but it wasn't the same as hearing his voice. 'Just be patient,' I told myself. 'You're flying to West Germany tomorrow. You'll see him soon enough. If you want to see him sooner, watch the evening news.'

No pictures of Dad showed that night on the news, and it wasn't until the next morning when I was running through the airport terminal that I caught a glimpse of him on a TV monitor. He looked as if he hadn't slept in the entire time he had been held hostage. His hair looked as if it had been cut with a pair of blunt garden shears. Standing next to the six foot six inch Terry Waite, he looked much smaller than I remembered him.

Nearly every local and national news station and news-paper was sending a film crew and reporter with us. Camera lights surrounded us as we walked through the terminal, and reporters shouted questions. I kept my stride, and for the first time in seventeen months didn't mind answering them. It was imperative to remind the nation that although my father was free, others were still held hostage.

When we arrived in Washington we met John Adams and the other people from the State Department. I cannot begin to praise John enough for his work and for his friendship to me and the other hostage families. We were glad to have such an understanding, compassion-ate, and conscientious person as a buffer-zone between us and the impersonal State Department hierarchy.

The number of reporters continued to swell. I was becoming weary of interviews and wanted to take a break. Arrangements were made to separate us from the press and give us some privacy before our flight. We sat in the PSA lounge, drank a beer, and watched every bit of footage of Dad we could find on TV that evening. It was the end of the second day since his release, and I still hadn't spoken to him.

Along with an entourage of State Department officials and newsmen, we soon boarded a commercial flight to Frankfurt, West Germany. I squeezed in a few hours' sleep and awoke just as the sun was rising on Great Britain. I looked at Cathy sitting next to me. She may have been asleep; she may have only had her eyes closed. How blessed I was to have a wife as supportive and unselfish as she had been. *If our marriage can withstand the past year and a half, it can survive anything*, I thought to myself.

Every now and then a news crew would stop in the aisle near our seats and ask a few questions.

'What's the first thing you're going to say to your father when you see him?' they asked.

'I really didn't plan on rehearsing an opening remark,' I replied, weary of questions.

By far the most asked question was 'How long after we get to Wiesbaden do you think we'll be able to get an interview with your father?'

'I don't really know. It depends on his condition.'

Their follow-up question was always 'How will I be able to keep in touch with you?'—along with a gentle reminder of all the help they had given me during my father's captivity.

Once we were on the ground, all but our family and the people from the State Department were ushered from the plane. Not long after the last reporter had gone, Terry Waite came on board, accompanied by several military personnel from the hospital in Wiesbaden. Terry was beaming from ear to ear. *Today is the reason why he risked his life going into Beirut*, I thought as I made my way to him to shake his hand. It seems that in every article I have read about Terry Waite, the first thing mentioned is his height. Most people have heard him referred to as the 'gentle giant'. However, what struck me initially and left the most lasting impression was not his physical size, but his laughter. I had expected him to be a sombre Englishman with a serious nature bent on a mission of saving innocent hostages. Although he did choose moments to exhibit that side of himself during the few days we spent with him in Wiesbaden, I found him to be a jovial man who enjoyed light-hearted conversation and telling a joke.

My father was overwhelmed with him, and I think rightly so. At some point during that afternoon with us, Dad told us of how much hope Terry Waite had given to him and the others as they learned that he had come to Beirut to negotiate for their release. He was the only Westerner they knew of willing to talk directly with the captors. He had risked his life for my father and all the hostages. He had proved to them that they had not been forgotten. And now as we shook hands for the first time, I could think of little more than 'Thank you' to say when the first words passed between us.

We were then quickly led through the terminal between

two parallel walls of cameras, reporters, and curious onlookers to another bus that hustled us from the airport to the gates of the Wiesbaden hospital. A chain of cars filled with reporters followed us as if tied to the bumper of the bus like a string of cans, bouncing around us, trying to get a better camera angle on Dad's family.

Adjacent to the hospital was a residential building for military personnel and their families where we were assigned rooms and had a chance to freshen up before walking inside the compound fence to the hospital for our reunion with my father. I stood on the outside balcony of our room and looked across Wiesbaden. The morning was still grey. The November air was cold by Los Angeles standards. I could see the hospital building below me, a few hundred yards off, and I scanned the windows thinking I might somehow catch a glimpse of Dad enjoying a fresh breath of freedom from his hospital room.

Impatiently, we took the lift down to where we had been instructed to meet before walking to the hospital. We milled about waiting for the rest of our party to join us, and everyone we spoke to said the same thing: 'Your father looks great. He's mentally and physically in great shape.'

I was unusually calm as we passed through a guarded gate that separated the hospital from the building where we were staying. A crowd of reporters lined the fence in the distance, shouting questions and taking pictures.

Inside the hospital lobby, there were more introductions to be made. It felt good finally to smile and enjoy myself with strangers. I was no longer a 'hostage son'— for a brief time I would enjoy the status of being the 'son of an ex-hostage'.

'Your father is waiting upstairs,' we were told as they showed us to the lift. Someone pushed the appropriate button and stepped out, leaving Cathy and me, Paul and Lori, and Diane and Jake alone. I expected someone to meet us on the first floor and show us to Dad's room. The lift began to move, and we exchanged glances, not needing to say a word, all smiles, the lift shaking from our excitement.

When the door opened, Dad was standing alone in the corridor waiting to greet us. We all ran together. I tried to hold back and let the others have their turns, but found it impossible. Some of us cried, some of us just smiled. We all threw our arms around each other at the same time.

As we walked down the corridor together towards Dad's room, I looked hard at him. I examined the side of his face. I listened to the sound of his voice. I studied his gait. He was extremely tired, but I knew he was all right. The ordeal of separation for our family was finally over—we had survived.

In my heart I understood that he was free, not because of a single thing I had done, but solely by the grace of God. Silently I said, 'Thank you, Lord!'

15
4th–5th November, 1986

I pray for Terry Waite, for his safety and for his immediate release.

I pray for Terry Anderson, Tom Sutherland, and all the other Western hostages held. I pray for the thousands of young Lebanese men chained to the walls of hot, dark basements, separated from their families, unsure if they will live to see their homes again. Each of these victims should have your prayers too.

It is impossible for us truly to imagine what it's like to be a hostage in Lebanon. We cannot fully realise the confusion of circumstance, the fear of death, the claustrophobia, or the hopelessness that those who remain still experience. It is nothing like spending time in an American or British prison. It is nothing like being a prisoner of war. In those cases, at least the victim usually understands the reason he is imprisoned.

When we finally sat across from my father in that West German hospital, only then did we begin to understand how those men suffer in captivity. Dad's words finally resolved in my mind some of the mystery regarding his captors. More than anything, they reminded me that others are still imprisoned under horrible conditions and in great despair.

'What was the hardest part of being a hostage?' we

asked as we talked together in a comfortable, private
sitting room in the military hospital in Wiesbaden.

Although free for only a couple of days, my father
answered in a very matter-of-fact manner. 'Well, aside
from being separated from all of you, and the constant
fear of death, I think the hardest part was never seeing
the sun, moon, or stars.'

'You were never taken outside?'

'I saw the sun once, and the moon once,' he answered.

We couldn't believe it, though this news did help
explain some of the overt changes in his physical appearance—the paleness of his skin, the darkness of his normally light brown hair, his sunken eyes.

As if the memory still brought him a certain amount of
pleasure, he proceeded to tell us of the day he saw the
sun. 'They took Terry Anderson and me into the kitchen
of the place where we were held, and they let us sit at the
table and look out of the window. They opened it so we
could enjoy the fresh air. And they fed us hamburgers. It
was a real treat for us. I wouldn't see the sun again until
the morning I was released.'

'What about the moon? When did you see it?'

'One time when one of the guards came to our room,
we asked, "Is the moon still there?" We joked with him,
"Are there still stars in the sky at night?" He went away
and came back a few minutes later and said he had a treat
for us. We were all taken into the living room, and then
one at a time, they led each of us up to the roof for a
couple of minutes.

'I'll never forget it—I lowered my blindfold and looked
up into the heavens and saw the moon, and just then, a
big purple flare shot across the sky and slowly descended
to the ground, lighting up everything with a strange,
iridescent purple glow. It was spectacularly beautiful.
Other than that, we were never allowed outside. We were
kept like rabbits in a cage.'

'How could you cope with the duration of your captivity, without ever seeing daylight?'

'I used a few tricks to combat the pressure of living in a

world of sensory deprivation,' my father explained. 'For instance, I daydreamed a lot. I would pretend I was driving down the San Diego freeway and try to remember the street name of every exit ramp; or I would imagine going south through Huntington Beach, and I'd try to picture every store and building along the way.'

He continued, 'And then on days that were important, like Paul and Lori's wedding day, I would imagine, in detail, all the things that the father of the groom would do on that occasion. And I took as long to go through them in my mind as it actually would take if I was there. I assumed that their wedding was going to take place as planned, so on that day, I woke up and I imagined getting ready, taking a shower, putting on my tuxedo, driving to the church, the marriage ceremony, the reception, everything. .... It took me all day to experience their wedding in my imagination.

'Another trick I used, especially to fight depression, was exercise. I knew I had to keep active, even in the confines of the small room in which we were held. Normally, when we got up in the morning, we'd put our mats up against the wall and walk in circles around the room, about the distance of two or three miles, for a couple of hours. I would sing every song from every Broadway musical I could think of while we walked. In addition to walking, I did a lot of push-ups and sit-ups, about 500 over the course of each day.'

'Five hundred push-ups a day?' we said in unison disbelief.

'Father Jenco used to tease me about doing so many, and he refused to do even one. Terry and Tom did them for a while, but then they stopped.'

'What about Terry and Tom, Ben and Martin? How was it being kept together in a tiny room for over a year?'

'Well, Ben wasn't really with us that long before he got released.' And Dad went on to explain how Ben's release had come about. 'One day, Terry and I were talking to the leader of our kidnappers, the Hajj. He was really discouraged that the US government was ignoring him,

that they wouldn't talk to him. He didn't want to negotiate through the Syrians or the Iranians—he had a
strong sense of independence and pride. He wanted to
talk directly with the United States government. We
suggested that he should release all of us, or at least one
of us. We told him we would be willing to get his message
out to the world.

'The Hajj didn't like the idea at first, but Terry and I
continued to argue with him. Two weeks later he came
back and said he had decided to release one of us. We
were to choose which one. We finally decided on Terry
because he was a journalist, but the Hajj decided to let
Ben Weir go instead, which they did a few days later.
After they had dropped Ben off, Sayid, one of our
guards, came back and said to us, very excited, "Ben was
one happy man."

'We waited, along with our captors, to see what the
reaction would be. But for days after his release there was
nothing in the news about it. The Hajj became extremely
angry because there was no US government announcement about Ben's release. He kept asking us "why?" and
all we could say was that we had no way of knowing. Even
after Ben's release became known, the US refused to talk
directly with the Hajj.

'The four of us who remained just settled into a routine
of waiting. Father Jenco led us in our daily worship
services. We read the Bible. We had our own church that
we called "The Church of the Locked Door". We talked a
lot about everything imaginable. And, because we were
so different in personality and temperaments, we had
some heated arguments at times.'

'I don't know how you could avoid it,' we all agreed.

'Each day, we were taken one by one to the bathroom
for fifteen minutes—in that time we had to shower,
shave, take care of all our bodily functions—and while
each one was gone, the remaining three would use that
opportunity to complain about the one not in the room. I
always knew when I was gone that the other three were
talking about me, but we lived in a world that with the

exception of those fifteen minutes a day, lacked any sense of privacy. We were five men, kept together in a ten-by-twelve-foot room, every minute, twenty-four hours a day, seven days a week, for over a year.'

As though he preferred not to think about it any longer, Dad shifted the conversation. 'I used to play a game where I would say "We're going to be released this coming Sunday." Marty Jenco would play along with me. We would really try to believe it. Then, if we weren't released, we'd just say, "Oh well, we made a mistake. We got the date wrong. It's next Sunday." Terry and Tom would just look at us as if we were crazy, but I knew that hope was the nourishment of survival. We needed a plan. We couldn't just give up. We couldn't just accept that we would be there for ever.'

'When you were released, were you still sharing a cell with Terry and Tom?'

'No, I was in isolation for the last forty-five days. Terry and Tom were still together as far as I know, but my captors were angry with me and had put me by myself. We had been moved to a basement with two rows of tiny cells, too small to stand up straight in. The only light came from a bulb that hung in the passageway. They had taken away everything from me, even the Bible. I kept track of the days by moving an empty medicine vial across the tiles on the floor of the room, and each day, I would put an olive stone in the corner of the cell to keep count of the days. I just lay on my mat in my underwear and tried to pass the time sleeping. . . .'

'Why were your captors angry with you?'

I could see rage erupting in my father as he began the story. 'It was because of speculative reporting by a newsman from an American television network. When I made a video—the one Father Jenco carried with him on his release—I mistakenly referred to William Buckley's wife and children. I didn't know he was a bachelor; I sincerely thought that he had a family. After Father Jenco's release, my captors rolled a TV into our cell so we could watch the American news to see the reaction, and I'll never forget what I saw. We still had a "news blackout" imposed on us, so they wouldn't allow us the audio, only the picture. I watched as they showed that portion of my video on the screen and then in the lower left-hand corner they put a picture of Buckley with the caption "bachelor", and written next to that in script were the words "coded message" with a big question mark.

'When I saw that, I really thought I would be killed. The threat of death was constant anyway. And when my captors saw that news report, they were very, very angry, thinking I had sent out a coded message right under their noses. I had humiliated them in front of all their friends in Lebanon. They took me into another room, beat me and then threw me into isolation.'

We couldn't hide the horror, and when Dad saw our reaction, he suddenly tried to downplay the extent of the beating. 'It wasn't much,' he said. 'They just hit the soles of my feet with a rubber hose a few times. In fact, we often had such bad stomach pains that we would pound on our door and the guards would take for ever to come to us. I'll tell you, those stomach cramps were worse than that beating.' In spite of his words, we knew better, and he later revealed that the extent of his beating went beyond a few blisters on the soles of his feet.

'What about William Buckley? Were you ever kept with him?' we asked, though we dreaded his answer.

Haltingly, he told us how he had been in the room when Buckley died. It was a graphic, painful story, and we listened in silence.

'I have a lot to be grateful to William Buckley for. In a sense, his death saved my life. After he died, our treatment dramatically improved. We were seen by a doctor who said, "If you don't clean this place up and feed them better, they'll all be dead soon." The next day we were allowed to take showers for the first time, and they cleared all the filth and garbage from the floor of the room. Our captors began supplying us with medicine. Our diet improved a little, and our needs weren't as neglected as they had been. Eventually, they began to bring us together for worship time, and on our insistence, they finally allowed us to be kept in one room, all together.'

Dad stopped. For a moment we reflected on the horror of his imprisonment—the death of William Buckley, my father's time in isolation, his beating. The weight of these thoughts, as if the threat was still present, directed our conversation back to safer ground. 'What else did you do to pass the time besides talk?'

'For a while, we were supplied with books—great books, the classics—like Shakespeare, Dickens, Orwell's *1984*, *The Plague* by Albert Camus. Our captors also gave us good books written by academic experts on Middle East terrorism. And of course, we had the Bible. I read through it in its entirety several times. But then, they took them all away from us, and it was only because of our constant nagging that they finally gave us back the Bible.'

'What were your captors really like?'

My father paused. 'I tend to view them as two groups— the leaders as one and the guards as the other. The guards were just uneducated young men—poor Shi'ites— kids really. They didn't understand the atrocity of their act. In fact, they thought they were good to us. I hold no animosity towards them. It was just a job. They were paid twenty-five American dollars a month to watch us and bring us our food. They were just trying to support their families in the midst of a horrible civil war. In fact our diet, the food we were given, was probably the same as they were eating.

'The first squad leader—Michelle—he was crazy. He was violent and mean. But the one who replaced him, Sayid, was a smart kid. He spoke English like an American; he even thought in English. He was kind to me.

'Sayid had been wounded in the abdomen and we didn't see him for a few months while he was convalescing. He was also a widower; he had lost his wife in a mortar fire explosion. He had a little daughter, Fatima, whom he would bring in to see us once in a while. She was just a toddler. Sayid would bring her into our cell and let us look under our blindfold at her. When she first saw us she screamed blue murder—she must have been really frightened. We were big men compared to Lebanese; we had untrimmed beards; our hair was unkept; we were blindfolded. But she got used to us after a while. She was a beautiful little girl, and Sayid really loved her.

'As far as the leaders went—the Hajj and Mughniyya—I have nothing nice to say about them. I want them brought to justice for what they did to me, and to you. They took away seventeen months of our lives. They put us through hell. They killed William Buckley. They've still got Terry and Tom in that dungeon.'

'Do you think that the Hajj and Mughniyya were really the leaders?'

'Yes, no question about it. The Hajj was a very influential Lebanese man.'

'Did you talk to him much?'

'He would drop in every week or two to check on us. He didn't speak English; or at least he always used a translator in our presence. But we spent many hours talking. And sometimes, he would even heed our advice, like when he released Ben Weir. In fact, it was because of us that he agreed to talk with Terry Waite. It was our suggestions that really began any negotiations for our release.

'We had asked for a radio, and one day the Hajj surprised us by giving us one. While listening to the BBC, we heard the Archbishop of Canterbury say that he would like to help the hostages in Lebanon. We suggested to the Hajj that we write a letter to him. Also, I suggested that we write an open letter to President Reagan, and Congressmen O'Brien and Dornan because we had heard on the radio that they were remembering us at each session of Congress. The Hajj agreed, and we wrote the letters.

'After the letter was delivered, and the Archbishop responded by appointing Terry Waite as his special envoy, we then suggested to the Hajj that Terry Waite could come to Beirut and stay at Terry Anderson's apartment, and from there, they could talk by two-way radio. All we needed was a frequency from the Hajj, and we would write another letter to Terry Waite telling him how he could get in touch. As it turned out, the first communication between Terry and the Hajj was just as we suggested, on a two-way radio. Later, they met in person.'

'You know, Dad,' I asked, 'in your letters and videos, were those really your words?'

'With the exception of the letter about Daniloff, which came after the incident of the "coded message" yes, those were my words. My captors never wrote a script for us. They would tell us the general points they wanted us to make, but we were allowed to write our own thoughts and then they would either approve or disapprove them.'

'In your letters, you said that you all felt abandoned by the US government. Did you really feel that way?'

'Yes. What else could we think. We knew that the US had negotiated for TWA 847. We couldn't understand why they wouldn't do the same for us.'

'And when they finally released you fifteen months later, did you believe then that you were really going home?'

'I knew it, but not because of what I was told by my captors.'

'How did you know?'

What we heard from my father next has probably had as great an effect on me as anything that happened during the entire ordeal of his captivity. To this day, it amazes me, encourages me, and strengthens me. He told this story:

'After I had been put in isolation, I was lying on the floor in a dark, tiny cell. One morning in early October, I had this overpowering feeling that I was going to be released on November 1st or 2nd. I knew it was the voice of the Lord. It wasn't a dream, and I wasn't hearing voices at the time, or anything like that—I just knew that God was telling me that I was going home.

'I kept asking the guards to bring me the Bible. Finally they gave it to me for a couple of days, but I was in a cell where the only light came through the transom from a bulb in the passageway. It was like trying to read in the dark. On top of that, the bulb kept flashing on and off every few minutes. I'd have light enough to read for a minute or so, and then it would go out and I'd be sitting in total darkness until it came back on again. I convinced the guards to bring me another light bulb, which they did, and for a few minutes I could study the Scriptures without interruption. But then, they came back and said they needed it elsewhere and replaced it with the old flickering bulb again.

'I was upset, but they assured me they would bring it back again at the same time the next day. So I waited for them to return my reading light. And I waited, and waited, and waited. They didn't come. I started to grow impatient and depressed and finally gave up hope that they would ever bring it. Soon after that, the guard walked down the passage, took out the flickering bulb, and put the good one in its place. Once again I could read the Bible. It dawned on me that the Lord was telling me something. He was showing me that I had to be patient and trust him. I was going to go home soon, but only if I believed him completely.

'I tried to wait patiently and have faith. On 1st November, I told myself, "This is the night." I had so much confidence that I didn't get excited; my blood pressure didn't rise. I just thought, "Tonight, I'm leaving here." A little before midnight I tried to go to sleep. Right when I was drifting off, I heard the guard open the door to my cell, and then he said, "Mr David, I have good news. You're going home in a couple of hours." I calmly got up and dressed. Then all the other guards came in, and you could see how excited they were. Within hours I was a free man again, just as the Lord had told me I would be a month earlier.'

Could there be a more fitting end to my family's ordeal? It was a remarkable affirmation of God's presence, a reason for us to celebrate, an everlasting reminder of the real hope and joy in our lives. This is the very reason why, when people remark on how horrible an experience it must have been for me as a hostage son, I always respond to them by saying that I received much more good from the experience than bad.

Epilogue

My ears were ringing from thirteen hours in the cargo hold of a C-11 air force transport plane that had brought us across the Atlantic into Andrews Air Force Base. Now, standing in the Oval Office, waiting to shake hands with the President and Mrs Reagan, I had not yet decided what to say. I glanced nervously about the room. I looked at my father laughing with the President. I turned my head and caught the gaze of Lt Colonel Oliver North.

He probably hates me, I thought as North began to walk towards me. His expression remained stern until just before he reached me, and then a smile covered his face, and we hugged. I don't believe it was just an act on his part. I knew that he shared equally in the emotion of the hour. How could I not respond? How could I refuse to join him in the celebration?

I looked at President Reagan still speaking warmly to my father. It was becoming more and more apparent to me that these two men, President Reagan and Oliver North, did after all recognise and respond to a facet of the hostage crisis that others in our government, particularly the leadership of the State Department, had failed to see—the hostages in Lebanon were victimised human beings, not just a political problem.

The line of people moving towards the President went forward, and North walked away to talk with someone else. I overheard my sister, Diane, now eight months pregnant, joking with the President and the First Lady, 'If it's a boy,' she laughed, 'maybe we'll name him Ronnie. And if it's a girl, Nancy. ...' Everyone grinned.

'Write and let us know which it is,' the First Lady responded.

I didn't laugh too hard—I was too nervous. It felt like every negative comment I had ever uttered before the cameras was scrawled in bright red ink on my written invitation to the White House. They would all be read aloud along with my introduction. 'Eric Jacobsen, the man who on 30th June, 1986 said. ...'

As Cathy and I stepped up to the President and Mrs Reagan, the flash of the White House cameras recorded our handshakes, smiles, and hugs. Much to my relief, when I finally looked directly into the President's eyes, I didn't see the anger I expected to find. Instead, I thought I detected a hint of embarrassment.

This made me feel embarrassed in turn. I wanted to apologise profusely for the terrible things I had said, but then I stopped myself. I realised that I had done what I felt was appropriate at the time, and I would do the same given another chance. I might have regretted the necessity to voice negative comments about the President, but I could not regret the content of those words.

Mrs Reagan was quite vocal in defending her husband by telling us of the depth of his concern for the hostages in Lebanon. The President seemed uncomfortable with the conversation, but I sensed this time that it stemmed from humility, not from exaggeration on Mrs Reagan's part. I could only express my gratitude for their concern with a simple 'thank you'. Before we were ushered out of the Oval Office, Mrs Reagan stopped me again and impressed upon me the need to tell the remaining hostage families of the President's concern. I agreed to do so.

As we left, I was grateful that God had given me the opportunity to meet the President face to face. It proved to be another time of healing for me, and I hoped that in some way, it was for the President as well.

I know that I care deeply about the people still held. I know I will continue to pray for them. I know I will not sacrifice them. I know I will not ignore my responsibility to them.

I do understand that this is an emotional issue for me. I know that the hostages' story is not finished, and I know that I still feel burdened by it. But I also know that God has blessed us through it. I know he is indeed in control. I am deeply grateful to him that my father is free.

And, I know he has not abandoned the men still imprisoned in Lebanon.

A Prayer for Terry Waite and Others (anonymous)

Lord, in your mercy,
look with compassion on Terry Waite
and all prisoners of injustice.

Strengthen and protect them,
and supply their needs.

May your love enfold them,
your presence cheer them,
your peace sustain them.

Soften the hearts of their captors,
and hasten the time of their release.

AMEN

Kingsway Publications